Ethical and Professional Standards
Study Sessions 1-2

CFA® PROGRAM CURRICULUM • VOLUME 1

LEVEL III
2009

CFA INSTITUTE

PEARSON

Custom Publishing

Cover photograph courtesy of Corbis.

10 9 8 7 6 5 4 3 2 1

ISBN 0-536-53715-1

2007160918

AG/NN

Please visit our web site at *www.pearsoncustom.com*

PEARSON CUSTOM PUBLISHING
501 Boylston Street, Suite 900, Boston, MA 02116
A Pearson Education Company

CONTENTS

◒ indicates an optional segment   www.cfainstitute.org/toolkit—Your online preparation resource

HOW TO USE THE CFA PROGRAM CURRICULUM

Congratulations on passing Level II of the Chartered Financial Analyst (CFA®) Program. This exciting and rewarding program of study reflects your desire to become a serious investment professional. You are participating in a program noted for its high ethical standards and the breadth of knowledge, skills, and abilities it develops. Your commitment to the CFA Program should be educationally and professionally rewarding.

The credential you seek is respected around the world as a mark of accomplishment and dedication. Each level of the program represents a distinct achievement in professional development. Successful completion of the program is rewarded with membership in a prestigious global community of investment professionals. CFA charterholders are dedicated to life-long learning and maintaining currency with the ever-changing dynamics of a challenging profession.

The CFA examination measures your degree of mastery of the assigned CFA Program curriculum. Effective study and preparation based on that curriculum are keys to your success on the examination.

Curriculum Development

The CFA Program curriculum is grounded in the practice of the investment profession. Utilizing a collaborative website, CFA Institute performs a continuous practice analysis with investment professionals around the world to determine the knowledge, skills, and abilities that are relevant to the profession. Regional panels and targeted surveys are also conducted annually to verify and reinforce the continuous feedback. The practice analysis process ultimately defines the Candidate Body of Knowledge (CBOK™) an inventory of knowledge and responsibilities expected of the investment management professional at the level of a new CFA charterholder. The process also determines how much emphasis each of the major topic areas receives on the CFA examinations.

A committee made up of practicing charterholders, in conjunction with CFA Institute staff, designs the CFA Program curriculum to deliver the CBOK to candidates. The examinations, also written by practicing charterholders, are designed to allow you to demonstrate your mastery of the CBOK as set forth in the CFA Program curriculum. As you structure your personal study program, you should emphasize mastery of the CBOK and the practical application of that knowledge. For more information on the practice analysis, CBOK, and development of the CFA Program curriculum, please visit www.cfainstitute.org/toolkit.

Organization

The Level III CFA Program curriculum is organized into two topic areas. Each topic area begins with a brief statement of the material and the depth of knowledge expected.

Each topic area is then divided into one or more study sessions. These study sessions—18 sessions in the Level III curriculum—should form the basic structure of your reading and preparation.

Each study session includes a statement of its structure and objective, and is further divided into specific reading assignments. The outline on the inside front cover of each volume illustrates the organization of these 18 study sessions.

The reading assignments are the basis for all examination questions, and are selected or developed specifically to teach the CBOK. These readings are drawn from CFA Program-commissioned content, textbook chapters, professional journal articles, research analyst reports, and cases. Many readings include problems and solutions as well as appendices to help you learn.

Reading-specific Learning Outcome Statements (LOS) are listed in the pages introducing each study session as well as at the beginning of each reading. These LOS indicate what you should be able to accomplish after studying the reading. We encourage you to review how to properly use LOS, and the descriptions of commonly used LOS "command words," at www.cfainstitute.org/toolkit. The command words signal the depth of learning you are expected to achieve from the reading. You should use the LOS to guide and focus your study, as each examination question is based on an assigned reading and one or more LOS. However, the readings provide context for the LOS and enable you to apply a principle or concept in a variety of scenarios. It is important to study the whole of a required reading.

Features of the Curriculum

▶ **Required vs. Optional Segments** - You should read all of the pages for an assigned reading. In some cases, however, we have reprinted an entire chapter or article and marked those parts of the reading that are not required as "optional." The CFA examination is based only on the required segments, and the optional segments are included only when they might help you to better understand the required segments (by seeing the required material in its full context). When an optional segment begins, you will see an icon and a solid vertical bar in the outside margin that will continue until the optional segment ends, accompanied by another icon. *Unless the material is specifically marked as optional, you should assume it is required.* Keep in mind that the optional material is provided strictly for your convenience and will not be tested. You should rely on the required segments and the reading-specific LOS in preparing for the examination.

▶ **Problems/Solutions** - *All questions and problems in the readings as well as their solutions (which are provided in an appendix at the end of each volume) are required material.* When appropriate, we have included problems within and after the readings to demonstrate practical application and reinforce your understanding of the concepts presented. The questions and problems are designed to help you learn these concepts. Many of the questions are adapted from past CFA examinations.

For your benefit, we have also made available the last three years' LIII essay questions and solutions. Please visit www.cfainstitute.org/toolkit to review these resources.

Beginning with the 2009 exams, the selected response questions on the CFA exam will have three choices (a correct answer and two distracters). This includes both the multiple choice questions at Level I and the item set questions at Levels II and III. In many cases, the questions provided in the curriculum have been modified to match the new three-choice format.

▶ **Margins** - The wide margins in each volume provide space for your note-taking.

▶ **Two-Color Format** - To enrich the visual appeal and clarity of the exhibits, tables, and text, the curriculum is printed in a two-color format.

- **Six-Volume Structure** - For portability of the curriculum, the material is spread over six volumes.

- **Glossary and Index** - For your convenience, we have printed a comprehensive glossary and index in each volume. Throughout the curriculum, a **bolded blue** word in a reading denotes a term defined in the glossary.

- **Source Material** - The authorship, publisher, and copyright owners are given for each reading for your reference. We recommend that you use this CFA Institute curriculum rather than the original source materials because the curriculum may include only selected pages from outside readings, updated sections within the readings, and may have problems and solutions tailored to the CFA Program.

- **LOS Self-Check** - We have inserted checkboxes next to each LOS that you can use to track your progress in mastering the concepts in each reading.

Designing Your Personal Study Program

Create a Schedule - An orderly, systematic approach to examination preparation is critical. You should dedicate a consistent block of time every week to reading and studying. Complete all reading assignments and the associated problems and solutions in each study session. Review the LOS both before and after you study each reading to ensure that you have mastered the applicable content and can demonstrate the knowledge, skill, or ability described by the LOS and the assigned reading. Use the new LOS self-check to track your progress and highlight areas of weakness for later review.

You will receive periodic e-mail communications that contain important study tips and preparation strategies. Be sure to read these carefully.

CFA Institute estimates that you will need to devote a minimum of 10–15 hours per week for 18 weeks to study the assigned readings. Allow a minimum of one week for each study session, and plan to complete them all at least 30–45 days prior to the examination. This schedule will allow you to spend the final four to six weeks before the examination reviewing the assigned material and taking online sample and mock examinations.

At CFA Institute, we believe that candidates need to commit to a *minimum* of 250 hours reading and reviewing the curriculum, and taking online sample examinations, to master the material. This recommendation, however, may substantially underestimate the hours needed for appropriate examination preparation depending on your individual circumstances, relevant experience, and academic background. You will undoubtedly adjust your study time to conform to your own strengths and weaknesses, and your educational and professional background.

You will probably spend more time on some study sessions than on others. You should allow ample time for both in-depth study of all topic areas and additional concentration on those topic areas for which you feel least prepared.

Candidate Preparation Toolkit - We have created the online toolkit to provide a single comprehensive location with resources and guidance for candidate preparation. In addition to in-depth information on study program planning, the CFA Program curriculum, and the online sample and mock examinations, the toolkit also contains curriculum errata, printable study session outlines, sample examination questions, and more. Errata that we have identified in the curriculum are corrected and listed periodically in the errata listing in the toolkit. We encourage you to use the toolkit as your central preparation resource during your tenure as a candidate. Visit the toolkit at www.cfainstitute.org/toolkit.

Online Sample Examinations - As part of your study of the assigned curriculum, use the CFA Institute online sample examinations to assess your exam preparation as you progress toward the end of your study. After each question, you will receive immediate feedback noting the correct response and indicating the relevant assigned reading, so you'll be able to identify areas of weakness for further study. The 120-minute sample examinations reflect the question formats, topics, and level of difficulty of the actual CFA examinations. Aggregate data indicate that the CFA examination pass rate was higher among candidates who took one or more online sample examinations than among candidates who did not take the online sample examinations. For more information on the online sample examinations, please visit www.cfainstitute.org/toolkit.

(NEW!)   **Online Mock Examinations** - In response to candidate requests, CFA Institute has developed mock examinations that mimic the actual CFA examinations not only in question format and level of difficulty, but also in length. The three-hour online mock exams simulate the morning and afternoon sessions of the actual CFA exam, and are intended to be taken after you complete your study of the full curriculum, so you can test your understanding of the CBOK and your readiness for the exam. To further differentiate, feedback is provided at the end of the exam, rather than after each question as with the sample exams. CFA Institute recommends that you take these mock exams at the final stage of your preparation toward the actual CFA examination. For more information on the online mock examinations, please visit www.cfainstitute.org/toolkit.

Tools to Measure Your Comprehension of the Curriculum

With the addition of the online mock exams, CFA Institute now provides three distinct ways you can practice for the actual CFA exam. The full descriptions are above, but below is a brief summary of each:

End-of-Reading Questions - These questions are found at the end of each reading in the printed curriculum, and should be used to test your understanding of the concepts.

Online Sample Exams - Typically available two months before the CFA exam, online sample exams are designed to assess your exam preparation, and can help you target areas of weakness for further study.

Online Mock Exams - In contrast to the sample exams, mock exams are not available until closer to the actual exam date itself. Mock exams are designed to replicate the exam day experience, and should be taken near the end of your study period to prepare for exam day.

Preparatory Providers - After you enroll in the CFA Program, you may receive numerous solicitations for preparatory courses and review materials. Although preparatory courses and notes may be helpful to some candidates, you should view these resources as *supplements* to the assigned CFA Program curriculum. The CFA examinations reference only the CFA Institute assigned curriculum—no preparatory course or review course materials are consulted or referenced.

Before you decide on a supplementary prep course, do some research. Determine the experience and expertise of the instructors, the accuracy and currency of their content, the delivery method for their materials, and the provider's claims of success. Most importantly, make sure the provider is in compliance with the CFA Institute Prep Provider Guidelines Program. Three years of prep course products can be a significant investment, so make sure you're getting a sufficient return. Just remember, there are no shortcuts to success on the CFA examinations. Prep products can enhance your learning experience, but the CFA curriculum is the key to success. For more information on the Prep Provider Guidelines Program, visit www.cfainstitute.org/cfaprog/resources/prepcourse.html.

SUMMARY

Every question on the CFA examination is based on specific pages in the required readings and on one or more LOS. Frequently, an examination question is also tied to a specific example highlighted within a reading or to a specific end-of-reading question/problem and its solution. To make effective use of the curriculum, please remember these key points:

1. All pages printed in the Custom Curriculum are required reading for the examination except for occasional sections marked as optional. You may read optional pages as background, but you will not be tested on them.

2. All questions/problems printed at the end of readings and their solutions in the appendix to each volume are required study material for the examination.

3. Make appropriate use of the CFA Candidate Toolkit, the online sample/mock examinations, and preparatory courses and review materials.

4. Schedule and commit sufficient study time to cover the 18 study sessions, review the materials, and take sample/mock examinations.

5. **Note:** Some of the concepts in the study sessions may be superseded by updated rulings and/or pronouncements issued after a reading was published. Candidates are expected to be familiar with the overall analytical framework contained in the assigned readings. Candidates are not responsible for changes that occur after the material was written.

Feedback

At CFA Institute, we are committed to delivering a comprehensive and rigorous curriculum for the development of competent, ethically grounded investment professionals. We rely on candidate and member feedback as we work to incorporate content, design, and packaging improvements. You can be assured that we will continue to listen to your suggestions. Please send any comments or feedback to curriculum@cfainstitute.org. Ongoing improvements in the curriculum will help you prepare for success on the upcoming examinations, and for a lifetime of learning as a serious investment professional.

ETHICAL AND PROFESSIONAL STANDARDS

STUDY SESSIONS

Study Session 1   Code of Ethics and Standards of Professional Conduct
Study Session 2   Ethical and Professional Standards in Practice

TOPIC LEVEL LEARNING OUTCOME

The candidate should be able to demonstrate a thorough knowledge of the CFA Institute Code of Ethics and Standards of Professional Conduct, including the rules and sanctions relating to disciplinary proceedings.

STUDY SESSION 1
CODE OF ETHICS AND STANDARDS OF PROFESSIONAL CONDUCT

Readings in this study session establish a framework for ethical conduct in the investment profession. The principles and guidance presented in the CFA Institute *Standards of Practice Handbook* (SOPH) form the basis for the CFA Institute self-regulatory program to maintain the highest professional standards among investment practitioners. A clear understanding of the CFA Institute Code of Ethics and Standards of Professional Conduct (both found in the SOPH) should allow practitioners to identify and appropriately resolve ethical conflicts, leading to a reputation for integrity that benefits both the individual and the profession. Material under "Guidance" in the SOPH addresses the practical application of the Code of Ethics and Standards of Professional Conduct. The guidance for each standard reviews its purpose and scope, presents recommended procedures for compliance, and provides examples of the standard in practice.

READING ASSIGNMENTS

Reading 1   Code of Ethics and Standards of Professional Conduct
Standards of Practice Handbook, Ninth Edition

Reading 2   "Guidance" for Standards I–VII
Standards of Practice Handbook, Ninth Edition

3

CODE OF ETHICS AND STANDARDS OF PROFESSIONAL CONDUCT

LEARNING OUTCOMES

The candidate should be able to:	Mastery
a. describe the structure of the CFA Institute Professional Conduct Program and the disciplinary review process for the enforcement of the Code and Standards;	☐
b. state the six components of the Code of Ethics and the seven Standards of Professional Conduct;	☐
c. summarize the ethical responsibilities required by the Code of Ethics and the Standards of Professional Conduct, including the multiple sub-sections of each Standard.	☐

PREFACE

The purpose of the Code and Standards is to provide up-to-date guidance to the people who grapple with real ethical problems in the investment profession, where theory meets practice and ethics gain meaning. The Code and Standards are intended for a diverse and global audience: CFA Institute members navigating ambiguous ethical situations; supervisors and subordinates determining the nature of their responsibilities to one another, to clients and potential clients, and to the securities markets; and candidates preparing for the Chartered Financial Analyst examinations.

Ethics in the Investment Profession

Ethical practices by investment professionals benefit all market participants and stakeholders and lead to increased investor confidence in global capital markets. Clients are reassured that the investment professionals they hire have the clients' best interest in mind and investment professionals benefit from the "reputational capital" such integrity generates. Ethical practices instill a public trust in the fairness of markets, allowing them to function efficiently. In short, good ethics is a fundamental requirement of the investment profession.

5

An important goal of CFA Institute is to ensure that the organization and its members develop, promote, and follow the highest ethical standards in the investment industry. The CFA Institute Code of Ethics and Standards of Professional Conduct (Code and Standards) are the foundation supporting the organization's quest to advance the interests of the global investment community by establishing and maintaining the highest standards of professional excellence and integrity. The Code of Ethics is a set of principles that define the professional conduct CFA Institute expects from its members and candidates in the CFA Program. The Code works in tandem with the Standards of Professional Conduct which outlines conduct that constitutes fair and ethical business practices.

For more than 40 years, CFA Institute members and candidates in the CFA Program have been required to abide by the organization's Code and Standards. Periodically, CFA Institute has revised and updated its Code and Standards to ensure that they remain relevant to the changing nature of the investment profession and representative of the "highest standard" of professional conduct. As the investment profession evolves, the list of ethical issues lengthens, from personal investing and soft commissions to misleading advice and the need to separate objective analysis from company promotion. New challenges are always emerging. As economies become more sophisticated and interconnected, new investment opportunities are constantly being created, along with new financial instruments to make the most of those opportunities for clients. Although the investment world has become a far more complex place since this *Handbook* was first published, distinguishing right from wrong remains the paramount principle of the Code of Ethics and Standards of Professional Conduct.

Evolution of the CFA Institute
Code of Ethics and Standards of Professional Conduct

Generally the changes to the Code and Standards, over the years, have been minor. CFA Institute revised the language of the Standards and occasionally tacked on a new standard addressing prominent issues of the day. For instance, in 1992, CFA Institute added the standard addressing performance presentation to the existing list of standards. The last major changes came in 1996 and were mostly structural in nature. CFA Institute organized them to coincide with the constituencies of investment professionals—clients, employers, investors, the public, and the profession.

After a long review process, several revisions, solicitation and careful consideration of public comment from its members, candidates, and investment professionals, CFA Institute has adopted the new and revised version of the Code and Standards included in this book. The changes include a reorganization of the standards, adoption of new standards, and revisions to existing standards. CFA Institute believes that the revisions clarify the requirements of the Code and Standards and effectively convey to its global membership what constitutes "best practice" in a number of areas relating to the investment profession.

These new standards are effective 1 January 2006. CFA Institute has published the 9th edition of the *Standards of Practice Handbook* to offer guidance, interpretation, applications, and recommended procedures for compliance for the new standards.

Summary of Changes

Reorganization of Standards. The organization of past versions of the Standards was based on the CFA Institute member's or candidate's responsibilities to various constituencies: the public, the client, the employer, and the profession. This led to the repetition of concepts in an attempt to fit broad substantive ideas into specific categories even though those ideas have general application. For example, disclosure of conflicts of interest was addressed in two separate standards, one dealing with disclosure of conflicts to employers, the other dealing with disclosure of conflicts to clients. Also, misrepresentation was addressed in several standards relating to investment recommendations, performance and credentials. Multiple references to similar ideas detracted from clarity and comprehension of the ethical concepts contained in the Code and Standards.

The revised Standards are organized by topic to streamline the structure and improve comprehension. Instead of five standards that discuss member and candidate conduct as it relates to various groups, the new Standards are organized into seven general topics:

    I. Professionalism
   II. Integrity of Capital Markets
  III. Duties to Clients
  IV. Duties to Employers
   V. Investment Analysis, Recommendations, and Actions
  VI. Conflicts of Interest
 VII. Responsibilities as a CFA Institute Member or CFA Candidate

Revising Current Standards. CFA Institute has expanded the Standards (e.g., misrepresentation, duty to employer, suitability, duty of loyalty to clients, disclosure of conflicts, and material nonpublic information) to better address the state of the investment profession and establish clear "best practices" in these areas.

Clarifying Requirements. In some instances, the guidance in prior versions of the Handbook included "requirements" with which all members and candidates had to comply, even though this conduct was not specifically set forth in the Standards themselves. For example, the prior guidance prohibited acceptance of gifts over a specific dollar amount, even though the specific prohibition was not found in the Standards. CFA Institute has eliminated or incorporated these requirements into the new Standards as appropriate so that members and candidates are clearly on notice about what conduct the Code and Standards requires or prohibits. The guidance included in the 9th edition of the Handbook expands on the requirements set forth in the Code and Standards and does not introduce new requirements.

New Standards. CFA Institute added standards relating to market manipulation and record retention to better address the state of the investment profession and establish clear "best practices" in these areas.

Eliminating the Requirement to Inform Employers of the Code and Standards. Previously the Standards of Professional Conduct included a requirement that members and candidates notify their employer of their responsibility to abide by the Code and Standards. Although it is in the member's or candidate's best interest to notify their employer, and thereby potentially avoid being placed in a compromising position, CFA Institute believes that notification should be a recommendation rather than a requirement in the Standards. Such a recommendation is included in the Preamble to the Code of Ethics.

Maintaining Relevance to a Global Membership. In some areas (e.g., use of material nonpublic information and fiduciary duty) the prior versions of the Code and Standards were based on U.S. law and regulation and may not have reflected best practice in the global investment industry. Therefore, CFA Institute has revised the Standards to make them less U.S.-centric to maintain the highest ethical standard on a global basis.

Text Revisions. As the investment industry and, as a result, CFA Institute membership has become more global, it is critical for the Code and Standards to use language that, to the extent possible, can be easily understood and translated into different languages. Therefore, in some instances CFA Institute has eliminated, modified, or added language for clarity, even though it is not the intent to change the meaning of a particular provision.

Changes to the Code and Standards have far-reaching implications for CFA Institute membership, the CFA Program, and the investment industry as a whole. Unlike other voluntary ethical standards promulgated by the organization through the CFA Centre for Financial Market Integrity (e.g., the GIPS® standards, Soft Dollar Standards, Trade Management Guidelines, Research Objectivity Standards, Best Practice Guidelines Governing Analyst and Corporate Issuer Relations, Asset Manager Code of Professional Conduct), members and CFA candidates are required to adhere to the Code and Standards. In addition, the Code and Standards are increasingly being adopted, in whole or in part, by firms and regulatory authorities. Their relevance goes well beyond CFA Institute members and CFA candidates.

It is imperative that the Code and Standards be updated if they are to be effective and represent the highest ethical standards in the global investment industry. CFA Institute strongly believes that the revisions and reorganization of the Code and Standards are not undertaken for cosmetic change but add value by addressing legitimate concerns and improving comprehension.

Standards of Practice Handbook

The periodic revisions to the Code and Standards have come in conjunction with the update of the *Standards of Practice Handbook*. The *Handbook* is the fundamental element of the ethics education effort of CFA Institute and the primary resource for guidance in interpreting and implementing the Code and Standards. The *Handbook* seeks to educate members and candidates on how to apply the Code and Standards to their professional lives and thereby benefit their clients, employers, and the investing public in general. The *Handbook* explains the purpose of the Standards and how they apply in a variety of situations. The guidance discusses and amplifies each standard and suggests procedures to prevent violations.

Examples in the "Application of the Standard" section are meant to illustrate how the standard applies to hypothetical factual situations. The names contained in the examples are fictional and are not meant to refer to any actual person or entity. Unless otherwise stated, individuals in each example are CFA Institute members and/or holders of the Chartered Financial Analyst designation. Because factual circumstances vary so widely and often involve gray areas, the explanatory material and examples are not intended to be all-inclusive. Many examples set forth in the Application of the Standard section involve standards that have legal counterparts; members are strongly urged to discuss with their supervisors and legal and compliance departments the content of the Code and Standards and the members' general obligations under the Code and Standards.

CFA Institute recognizes that the presence of any set of ethical standards can create a false sense of security unless the documents are fully understood, enforced, and made a meaningful part of everyday professional activities. The *Handbook* is intended to provide a useful frame of reference that lends substance to the understanding of professional behavior in the investment decision-making process. This book cannot cover every contingency or circumstance, and it does not attempt to do so. The development and interpretation of the Code and Standards is an evolving process and will be subject to continuing refinement.

CFA Institute Professional Conduct Program

All CFA Institute members and candidates enrolled in the CFA Program are required to comply with the Code and Standards. The CFA Institute Bylaws and Rules of Procedure for Proceedings Related to Professional Conduct (Rules of Procedure) form the basic structure for enforcing the Code and Standards. The Rules of Procedure are based on two primary principles: (1) fair process to the member and candidate and (2) confidentiality of proceedings. The CFA Institute Board of Governors maintains oversight and responsibility for the Professional Conduct Program (PCP) through the Disciplinary Review Committee (DRC), which is responsible for the enforcement of the Code and Standards.

Professional Conduct staff, under the direction of the CFA Institute Designated Officer, conducts professional conduct inquiries. Several circumstances can prompt an inquiry. Members and candidates must self-disclose on the annual Professional Conduct Statement all matters that question their professional conduct, such as involvement in civil litigation, a criminal investigation, or being the subject of a written complaint. Secondly, written complaints received by Professional Conduct staff can bring about an investigation. Third, CFA Institute staff may become aware of questionable conduct by a member or candidate through the media or other public source. Fourth, CFA examination proctors can submit a violation report for any candidate suspected to have compromised his or her professional conduct during the examination.

When an inquiry is initiated, the Professional Conduct staff conducts an investigation that may include requesting a written explanation from the member or candidate; interviewing the member or candidate, complaining parties, and third parties; and collecting documents and records in support of its investigation. The Designated Officer, upon reviewing the material obtained during the investigation, may conclude the inquiry with no disciplinary sanction, issue a cautionary letter, or continue proceedings to discipline the member or candidate. If the Designated Officer finds that a violation of the Code and Standards occurred, the Designated Officer proposes a disciplinary sanction, which may be rejected or accepted by the member or candidate. If the member or candidate rejects the proposed sanction, the matter is referred to a hearing by a panel of CFA Institute members.

Sanctions imposed by CFA Institute may have significant consequences, including condemnation by the sanctioned members' peers and possible ramifications for employment. Candidates enrolled in the CFA Program who have violated the Code and Standards may be suspended from further participation in the CFA program.

Adoption of the Code and Standards

The CFA Institute Code and Standards apply to individual members of CFA Institute and candidates for the CFA designation. However, CFA Institute does encourage firms to adopt the Code of Ethics and Standards of Professional Conduct as part of their firm code of ethics. There are no formal procedures for adopting the Code and Standards but those who claim compliance should fully understand the requirements of the Code and Standards.

Although CFA Institute welcomes public acknowledgement, when appropriate, that firms are using the CFA Institute Code and Standards, no attribution is necessary. For firms that would like to distribute the Code and Standards to clients and potential clients, attractive, one-page copies of the Code and Standards, including translations, are available on the CFA Institute website (www.cfainstitute.org).

CFA Institute, through its CFA Centre for Financial Market Integrity, has also published an Asset Manager Code of Professional Conduct (AMC) that is designed, in part, to help U.S. firms comply with the regulations mandating codes of ethics for investment advisers. The AMC provides specific, practical guidelines for asset managers in six areas: loyalty to clients, the investment process, trading, compliance, performance evaluation, and disclosure. Although the Code and Standards are aimed at individual investment professionals who are members of the CFA Institute or candidates for the CFA designation, the Asset Manager Code of Professional Conduct has been drafted for firms. The AMC is included as an appendix and also can be found on the CFA Institute website.

CFA Institute encourages firms adopting either the Code and Standards or the Asset Manager Code of Conduct to notify CFA Institute that they have adopted or are incorporating these standards as part of their firm codes of ethics.

Acknowledgments

Because CFA Institute is a volunteer organization, its work to promote ethical practice in the investment profession relies to a great degree on the goodwill of its members to devote their time on the organization's behalf. Such goodwill is also in abundance among CFA Institute members acting in an individual capacity to extend ethical integrity.

The CFA Institute Standards of Practice Council (SPC), a group currently consisting of 15 CFA charterholder volunteers from nine different countries, is charged with maintaining and interpreting the Code and Standards and ensuring that they are effective. The SPC draws its membership from a broad spectrum of organizations in the securities field, including brokers, investment advisors, banks, and insurance companies. In most instances, the SPC members also have important supervisory responsibilities within their firms.

The SPC continually evaluates the Code and Standards, as well as the guidance in the Handbook, to ensure that they are:

► Representative of the "highest standard" of professional conduct;

► Relevant to the changing nature of the investment profession;

► Globally applicable;

► Sufficiently comprehensive, practical, and specific;

► Enforceable; and

► Testable for the CFA Program.

Over the last two years, the SPC has spent countless hours reviewing and discussing revisions to the Code and Standards and updates to the Guidance that make up this 9th edition of the *Handbook*. Below is a list of the current members of the SPC who generously donated their time and energy to this effort.

Lee Price, CFA, Chair	Mario Eichenberger, CFA
Ross E. Hallett, CFA	Toshihiko Saito, CFA
Samuel B. Jones, CFA	Richard Wayman, CFA
Lynn S. Mander, CFA	Martha Oberndorfer, CFA
Todd P. Lowe, CFA	Mark Sinsheimer, CFA
Sunil Singhania, CFA	Brian O'Keefe, CFA
Miroslaw Panek, CFA	

Finally, this book is dedicated to the late Jules Huot, CFA, a long-time member of the SPC and volunteer for CFA Institute who tirelessly advocated for ethics in the investment profession and constantly worked to promote ethics and integrity within the industry.

CFA INSTITUTE CODE OF ETHICS AND STANDARDS OF PROFESSIONAL CONDUCT

Preamble to the CFA Institute Code of Ethics and Standards of Professional Conduct

The CFA Institute Code of Ethics and Standards of Professional Conduct (Code and Standards) are fundamental to the values of CFA Institute and essential to achieving its mission to lead the investment profession globally by setting high standards of education, integrity, and professional excellence. High ethical standards are critical to maintaining the public's trust in financial markets and in the investment profession. Since their creation in the 1960s, the Code and Standards have promoted the integrity of CFA Institute members and served as a model for measuring the ethics of investment professionals globally, regardless of job function, cultural differences, or local laws and regulations. All CFA Institute members (including holders of the Chartered Financial Analyst® (CFA®) designation) and CFA candidates must abide by the Code and Standards and are encouraged to notify their employer of this responsibility. Violations may result in disciplinary sanctions by CFA Institute. Sanctions can include revocation of membership, candidacy in the CFA Program, and the right to use the CFA designation.

The Code of Ethics

Members of CFA Institute (including Chartered Financial Analyst® [CFA®] charterholders) and candidates for the CFA designation ("members and candidates") must:

▶ Act with integrity, competence, diligence, respect, and in an ethical manner with the public, clients, prospective clients, employers, employees, colleagues in the investment profession, and other participants in the global capital markets.

▶ Place the integrity of the investment profession and the interests of clients above their own personal interests.

▶ Use reasonable care and exercise independent professional judgment when conducting investment analysis, making investment recommendations, taking investment actions, and engaging in other professional activities.

▶ Practice and encourage others to practice in a professional and ethical manner that will reflect credit on themselves and the profession.

▶ Promote the integrity of, and uphold the rules governing, capital markets.

▶ Maintain and improve their professional competence and strive to maintain and improve the competence of other investment professionals.

Standards of Professional Conduct

I. PROFESSIONALISM

A. Knowledge of the Law. Members and candidates must understand and comply with all applicable laws, rules, and regulations (including the CFA Institute Code of Ethics and Standards of Professional Conduct) of any government, regulatory organization, licensing agency, or professional association governing their professional activities. In the event of conflict, members and candidates must comply with the more strict law, rule, or regulation. Members and candidates must not knowingly participate or assist in and must dissociate from any violation of such laws, rules, or regulations.

B. Independence and Objectivity. Members and candidates must use reasonable care and judgment to achieve and maintain independence and objectivity in their professional activities. Members and candidates must not offer, solicit, or accept any gift, benefit, compensation, or consideration that reasonably could be expected to compromise their own or another's independence and objectivity.

C. Misrepresentation. Members and candidates must not knowingly make any misrepresentations relating to investment analysis, recommendations, actions, or other professional activities.

D. Misconduct. Members and candidates must not engage in any professional conduct involving dishonesty, fraud, or deceit or commit any act that reflects adversely on their professional reputation, integrity, or competence.

II. INTEGRITY OF CAPITAL MARKETS

A. Material Nonpublic Information. Members and candidates who possess material nonpublic information that could affect the value of an investment must not act or cause others to act on the information.

B. Market Manipulation. Members and candidates must not engage in practices that distort prices or artificially inflate trading volume with the intent to mislead market participants.

III. DUTIES TO CLIENTS

A. Loyalty, Prudence, and Care. Members and candidates have a duty of loyalty to their clients and must act with reasonable care and exercise prudent judgment. Members and candidates must act for the benefit of their clients and place their clients' interests before their employer's or their own interests. In relationships with clients, members and candidates must determine applicable fiduciary duty and must comply with such duty to persons and interests to whom it is owed.

B. Fair Dealing. Members and candidates must deal fairly and objectively with all clients when providing investment analysis, making investment recommendations, taking investment action, or engaging in other professional activities.

C. Suitability.

1. When members and candidates are in an advisory relationship with a client, they must:

   a. Make a reasonable inquiry into a client's or prospective client's investment experience, risk and return objectives, and financial constraints prior to making any investment recommendation or taking investment action and must reassess and update this information regularly.

    b. Determine that an investment is suitable to the client's financial situation and consistent with the client's written objectives, mandates, and constraints before making an investment recommendation or taking investment action.

    c. Judge the suitability of investments in the context of the client's total portfolio.

  2. When members and candidates are responsible for managing a portfolio to a specific mandate, strategy, or style, they must only make investment recommendations or take investment actions that are consistent with the stated objectives and constraints of the portfolio.

D. Performance Presentation. When communicating investment performance information, members or candidates must make reasonable efforts to ensure that it is fair, accurate, and complete.

E. Preservation of Confidentiality. Members and candidates must keep information about current, former, and prospective clients confidential unless:

  1. The information concerns illegal activities on the part of the client or prospective client,

  2. Disclosure is required by law, or

  3. The client or prospective client permits disclosure of the information.

IV. DUTIES TO EMPLOYERS

A. Loyalty. In matters related to their employment, members and candidates must act for the benefit of their employer and not deprive their employer of the advantage of their skills and abilities, divulge confidential information, or otherwise cause harm to their employer.

B. Additional Compensation Arrangements. Members and candidates must not accept gifts, benefits, compensation, or consideration that competes with, or might reasonably be expected to create a conflict of interest with, their employer's interest unless they obtain written consent from all parties involved.

C. Responsibilities of Supervisors. Members and candidates must make reasonable efforts to detect and prevent violations of applicable laws, rules, regulations, and the Code and Standards by anyone subject to their supervision or authority.

V. INVESTMENT ANALYSIS, RECOMMENDATIONS, AND ACTIONS

A. Diligence and Reasonable Basis. Members and candidates must:

  1. Exercise diligence, independence, and thoroughness in analyzing investments, making investment recommendations, and taking investment actions.

  2. Have a reasonable and adequate basis, supported by appropriate research and investigation, for any investment analysis, recommendation, or action.

B. Communication with Clients and Prospective Clients. Members and candidates must:

  1. Disclose to clients and prospective clients the basic format and general principles of the investment processes used to analyze investments, select securities, and construct portfolios and must promptly disclose any changes that might materially affect those processes.

  2. Use reasonable judgment in identifying which factors are important to their investment analyses, recommendations, or actions and

include those factors in communications with clients and prospective clients.

3. Distinguish between fact and opinion in the presentation of investment analysis and recommendations.

C. **Record Retention.** Members and candidates must develop and maintain appropriate records to support their investment analysis, recommendations, actions, and other investment-related communications with clients and prospective clients.

VI. CONFLICTS OF INTEREST

A. **Disclosure of Conflicts.** Members and candidates must make full and fair disclosure of all matters that could reasonably be expected to impair their independence and objectivity or interfere with respective duties to their clients, prospective clients, and employer. Members and candidates must ensure that such disclosures are prominent, are delivered in plain language, and communicate the relevant information effectively.

B. **Priority of Transactions.** Investment transactions for clients and employers must have priority over investment transactions in which a member or candidate is the beneficial owner.

C. **Referral Fees.** Members and candidates must disclose to their employer, clients, and prospective clients, as appropriate, any compensation, consideration, or benefit received from, or paid to, others for the recommendation of products or services.

VII. RESPONSIBILITIES AS A CFA INSTITUTE MEMBER OR CFA CANDIDATE

A. **Conduct as Members and Candidates in the CFA Program.** Members and candidates must not engage in any conduct that compromises the reputation or integrity of CFA Institute or the CFA designation or the integrity, validity, or security of the CFA examinations.

B. **Reference to CFA Institute, the CFA Designation, and the CFA Program.** When referring to CFA Institute, CFA Institute membership, the CFA designation, or candidacy in the CFA Program, members and candidates must not misrepresent or exaggerate the meaning or implications of membership in CFA Institute, holding the CFA designation, or candidacy in the CFA program.

"GUIDANCE" FOR STANDARDS I–VII

LEARNING OUTCOMES

The candidate should be able to:	Mastery
a. demonstrate a thorough knowledge of the Code of Ethics and Standards of Professional Conduct by interpreting the Code and Standards in various situations involving issues of professional integrity;	☐
b. recommend practices and procedures designed to prevent violations of the Code of Ethics and Standards of Professional Conduct.	☐

The "Guidance" statements address the application of the Standards of Professional Conduct. For each standard, the Guidance discusses the purpose and scope of the standard, presents recommended procedures for compliance, and gives examples of application of the standard.

STANDARD I—PROFESSIONALISM

A. Knowledge of the Law

Members and candidates must understand and comply with all applicable laws, rules, and regulations (including the CFA Institute Code of Ethics and Standards of Professional Conduct) of any government, regulatory organization, licensing agency, or professional association governing their professional activities. In the event of conflict, members and candidates must comply with the more strict law, rule, or regulation. Members and candidates must not knowingly participate or assist in and must dissociate from any violation of such laws, rules, or regulations.

Members and candidates must have an understanding of applicable laws and regulations of all countries in which they trade securities or provide investment advice or other investment services. This standard does not require members and candidates to become experts in compliance. Investment professionals are not required to have detailed knowledge of or be experts on all laws that could potentially govern the member's or candidate's activities. However, members and candidates must comply with the laws and regulations that directly govern their work.

Relationship between the Code and Standards and Local Law

Some members or candidates may live, work, or provide investment services to clients living in a country that has no law or regulation governing a particular action or that has laws or regulations that differ from the requirements of the Code and Standards. When applicable law and the Code and Standards require different conduct, members and candidates must follow the more strict of the applicable law or the Code and Standards.

"Applicable law" is the law that governs the member's or candidate's conduct. Which law applies will depend on the particular facts and circumstances of each case. The "more strict" law or regulation is the law or regulation that imposes greater restrictions on the action of the member or candidate or calls for the member or candidate to exert a greater degree of action that protects the interests of investors. For example, applicable law or regulation may not require members and candidates to disclose referral fees received from or paid to others for the recommendation of investment products or services. However, because the Code and Standards impose this obligation, members and candidates must disclose the existence of such fees.

Members and candidates must adhere to the following principles:

▶ Members and candidates must comply with applicable law or regulation related to their professional activities.

▶ Members and candidates must not engage in conduct that constitutes a violation of the Code and Standards, even though it may otherwise be legal.

▶ In the absence of any applicable law or regulation or when the Code and Standards impose a higher degree of responsibility than applicable laws and regulations, members and candidates must adhere to the Code and Standards.

Applications of these principles are outlined in Exhibit 1 (on pp. 20–21).

CFA Institute members are obligated to abide by the CFA Institute Articles of Incorporation, Bylaws, Code of Ethics, Standards of Professional Conduct, Rules of Procedure for Proceedings Related to Professional Conduct, Membership Agreement, and other applicable rules promulgated by CFA Institute, all as amended from time to time. CFA candidates who are not members must also abide by these documents (except for the Membership Agreement), as well as rules and regulations related to the administration of the CFA examination, the Candidate Responsibility Statement, and the Candidate Pledge.

Participation or Association with Violations by Others

Members and candidates are responsible for violations in which they *knowingly* participate or assist. Although members and candidates are presumed to have knowledge of all applicable laws, rules, and regulations, CFA Institute acknowledges that members may not recognize violations if they are not aware of all the facts giving rise to the violations. Standard I applies when members and candidates know or should know that their conduct may contribute to a violation of applicable laws, rules, regulations, or the Code and Standards.

If a member or candidate has reasonable grounds to believe that imminent or ongoing client or employee activities are illegal or unethical, the member or candidate must dissociate, or separate, from the activity. In extreme cases, dissociation may require a member or candidate to leave his or her employer. However, there are intermediate steps that members and candidates may take to dissociate from ethical violations of others. The first step should be to attempt to stop the behavior by bringing it to the attention of the employer through a supervisor or the compliance department. Members and candidates may consider directly confronting the person or persons committing the violation. If these attempts are unsuccessful, then members and candidates have a responsibility to step away and dissociate from the activity by taking such steps as removing their name from written reports or recommendations or asking for a different assignment. Inaction combined with continuing association with those involved in illegal or unethical conduct may be construed as participation or assistance in the illegal or unethical conduct.

Although the Code and Standards do not require that members and candidates report violations to the appropriate governmental or regulatory organizations, such disclosure may be prudent in certain circumstances, and mandated if required by applicable law. Similarly, the Code and Standards do not require that members and candidates report to CFA Institute potential violations of the Code and Standards by fellow members and candidates. However, CFA Institute encourages members, nonmembers, clients, and the investing public to report violations of the Code and Standards by CFA Institute members or CFA candidates by submitting a complaint in writing to the CFA Institute Professional Conduct Program: E-mail pconduct@cfainstitute.org or visit the CFA Institute website at www.cfainstitute.org.

Recommended Procedures for Compliance

Members and Candidates

Suggested methods by which members and candidates can acquire and maintain understanding of applicable laws, rules, and regulations include the following:

▶ Stay informed. Members and candidates should establish or encourage their employers to establish a procedure by which employees are regularly informed about changes in applicable laws, rules, regulations, and case law. In many instances, the employer's compliance department or legal counsel can provide such information in the form of memorandums distributed to employees in the organization. Also, participation in an internal or external continuing education program is a practical method of staying current.

▶ Review procedures. Members and candidates should review or encourage their employers to review written compliance procedures on a regular basis in order to ensure that they reflect current law and provide adequate guidance to employees concerning what is permissible conduct under the law and/or the CFA Institute Code and Standards. Recommended compliance procedures for specific items of the CFA Institute Code and Standards are discussed within the guidance associated with each standard.

▶ Maintain current files. Members and candidates should maintain or encourage their employers to maintain readily accessible current reference copies of applicable statutes, rules, regulations, and important cases.

When in doubt, it is recommended that a member or candidate seek the advice of compliance personnel or legal counsel concerning legal requirements. If the potential violation is committed by a fellow employee, it may also be prudent for the member or candidate to seek the advice of the firm's compliance department or legal counsel.

When dissociating from an activity that violates the Code and Standards, members and candidates should document any violations and urge their firms to attempt to persuade the perpetrator(s) to cease such conduct. It may be necessary for a member or candidate to resign his or her employment to dissociate from the conduct.

Firms

The formality and complexity of compliance procedures for firms depend on the nature and size of the organization and the nature of its investment operations. Members and candidates should encourage their firms to consider the following policies and procedures to support the principles of Standard I:

▶ Develop and/or adopt a code of ethics. The ethical culture of an organization starts at the top. Members and candidates should encourage their supervisors or management to adopt a code of ethics. Adhering to a code of ethics facilitates solutions when faced with ethical dilemmas and can prevent the need of employees to resort to a "whistle-blowing" solution.

▶ Make available and/or distribute to employees pertinent information that highlights applicable laws and regulations. Information sources may include primary information developed by the relevant government, governmental agencies, regulatory organizations, licensing agencies, and professional associations (e.g., from their websites); law firm memorandums or newsletters; and association memorandums or publications (e.g., *CFA Magazine*).

▶ Establish written protocols for reporting suspected violations of laws, regulations, and company policies.

Application of the Standard

Example 1: Michael Allen works for a brokerage firm and is responsible for an underwriting of securities. A company official gives Allen information indicating that the financial statements Allen filed with the regulator overstate the issuer's earnings. Allen seeks the advice of the brokerage firm's general counsel, who states that it would be difficult for the regulator to prove that Allen has been involved in any wrongdoing.

> *Comment:* Although it is recommended that members and candidates seek the advice of legal counsel, the reliance on such advice does not absolve a member or candidate from the requirement to comply with the law or regulation. Allen should report this situation to his supervisor, seek an independent legal opinion, and determine whether the regulator should be notified of the error.

Example 2: Lawrence Brown's employer, an investment-banking firm, is the principal underwriter for an issue of convertible debentures by the Courtney Company. Brown discovers that Courtney Company has concealed severe third-quarter losses in its foreign operations. The preliminary prospectus has already been distributed.

Comment: Knowing that the preliminary prospectus is misleading, Brown should report his findings to the appropriate supervisory persons in his firm. If the matter is not remedied and Brown's employer does not dissociate from the underwriting, Brown should sever all his connections with the underwriting. Brown should also seek legal advice to determine whether additional reporting or other action should be taken.

Example 3: Kamisha Washington's firm advertises its past performance record by showing the 10-year return of a composite of its client accounts. However, Washington discovers that the composite omits the performance of accounts that have left the firm during the 10-year period and that this omission has led to an inflated performance figure. Washington is asked to use promotional material that includes the erroneous performance number when soliciting business for the firm.

Comment: Misrepresenting performance is a violation of the Code and Standards. Although she did not calculate the performance herself, Washington would be assisting in violating this standard if she were to use the inflated performance number when soliciting clients. She must dissociate herself from the activity. She can bring the misleading number to the attention of the person responsible for calculating performance, her supervisor, or the compliance department at her firm. If her firm is unwilling to recalculate performance, she must refrain from using the misleading promotional material and should notify the firm of her reasons. If the firm insists that she use the material, she should consider whether her obligation to dissociate from the activity would require her to seek other employment.

Example 4: James Collins is an investment analyst for a major Wall Street brokerage firm. He works in a developing country with a rapidly modernizing economy and a growing capital market. Local securities laws are minimal—in form and content—and include no punitive prohibitions against insider trading.

Comment: Collins should be aware of the risks that a small market and the absence of a fairly regulated flow of information to the market represent to his ability to obtain information and make timely judgments. He should include this factor in formulating his advice to clients. In handling material nonpublic information that accidentally comes into his possession, he must follow Standard II(A).

Example 5: Laura Jameson works for a multinational investment advisor based in the United States. Jameson lives and works as a registered investment advisor in the tiny, but wealthy, island nation of Karramba. Karramba's securities laws state that no investment advisor registered and working in that country can participate in initial public offerings (IPOs) for the advisor's personal account. Jameson, believing that as a U.S. citizen working for a U.S.-based company she need comply only with U.S. law, has ignored this Karrambian law. In addition, Jameson believes that, as a charterholder, as long as she adheres to the Code and Standards requirement that she disclose her participation in any IPO to her employer and clients when such ownership creates a conflict of interest, she is operating on ethical high ground.

Comment: Jameson is in violation of Standard I(A). As a registered investment advisor in Karramba, Jameson is prevented by Karrambian securities law from participating in IPOs regardless of the law of her home country. In addition, because the law of the country where she is working is stricter than the Code and Standards, she must follow the stricter requirements of the local law rather than the requirements of the Code and Standards.

EXHIBIT 1	Global Application of the Code and Standards

Members and candidates who practice in multiple jurisdictions may be subject to varied securities laws and regulations. If applicable law is stricter than the requirements of the Code and Standards, members and candidates must adhere to applicable law; otherwise, they must adhere to the Code and Standards. The following chart provides illustrations involving a member who may be subject to the securities laws and regulations of three different types of countries. Countries with:

NSL = no securities laws or regulations
LS = *less* strict securities laws and regulations than the Code and Standards
MS = *more* strict securities laws and regulations than the Code and Standards

Applicable Law	Duties	Explanation
Member resides in NSL country, does business in LS country; LS law applies.	Member must adhere to the Code and Standards.	Because applicable law is less strict than the Code and Standards, the member must adhere to the Code and Standards.
Member resides in NSL country, does business in MS country; MS law applies.	Member must adhere to the law of MS country.	Because applicable law is stricter than the Code and Standards, member must adhere to the more strict applicable law.
Member resides in LS country, does business in NSL country; LS law applies.	Member must adhere to the Code and Standards.	Because applicable law is less strict than the Code and Standards, the member must adhere to the Code and Standards.
Member resides in LS country, does business in MS country; MS law applies.	Member must adhere to the law of MS country.	Because applicable law is stricter than the Code and Standards, the member must adhere to the more strict applicable law.
Member resides in LS country, does business in NSL country; LS law applies, but it states that law of locality where business is conducted governs.	Member must adhere to the Code and Standards.	Because applicable law states that the law of the locality where the business is conducted governs and there is no local law, the member must adhere to the Code and Standards.
Member resides in LS country, does business in MS country; LS law applies, but it states that law of locality where business is conducted governs.	Member must adhere to the law of MS country.	Because applicable law of the locality where the business is conducted governs and local law is stricter than the Code and Standards, the member must adhere to the more strict applicable law.

(Exhibit continued on next page ...)

EXHIBIT 1	(continued)

Applicable Law	Duties	Explanation
Member resides in MS country, does business in LS country; MS law applies.	Member must adhere to the law of MS country.	Because applicable law is stricter than the Code and Standards, member must adhere to the more strict applicable law.
Member resides in MS country, does business in LS country; MS law applies, but it states that law of locality where business is conducted governs.	Member must adhere to the Code and Standards.	Because applicable law states that the law of the locality where the business is conducted governs and local law is less strict than the Code and Standards, the member must adhere to the Code and Standards.
Member resides in MS country, does business in LS country with a client who is a citizen of LS country; MS law applies, but it states that the law of the client's home country governs.	Member must adhere to the Code and Standards.	Because applicable law states that the law of the client's home country governs (which is less strict than the Code and Standards), the member must adhere to the Code and Standards.
Member resides in MS country, does business in LS country with a client who is a citizen of MS country; MS law applies, but it states that the law of the client's home country governs.	Member must adhere to the law of MS country.	Because applicable law states that the law of the client's home country governs and the law of the client's home country is stricter than the Code and Standards, the member must adhere to the more strict applicable law.

B. Independence and Objectivity

Members and candidates must use reasonable care and judgment to achieve and maintain independence and objectivity in their professional activities. Members and candidates must not offer, solicit, or accept any gift, benefit, compensation, or consideration that reasonably could be expected to compromise their own or another's independence and objectivity.

Standard I(B) states the responsibility of CFA Institute members and candidates in the CFA Program to maintain independence and objectivity so that their clients will have the benefit of their work and opinions unaffected by any potential conflict of interest or other circumstance adversely affecting their judgment. Every member and candidate should endeavor to avoid situations that could cause or be perceived to cause a loss of independence or objectivity in recommending investments or taking investment action.

External sources may try to influence the investment process by offering analysts and portfolio managers a variety of benefits. Corporations may seek expanded research coverage; issuers and underwriters may wish to promote new securities offerings; brokers may want to increase commission business. Benefits may include gifts, invitations to lavish functions, tickets, favors, job referrals, and so on. One type of benefit is the allocation of shares in oversubscribed IPOs to investment managers for their personal accounts. This practice affords managers the opportunity to make quick profits that may not be available to their clients. Such a practice is prohibited under Standard I(B). Modest gifts and entertainment are acceptable, but special care must be taken by members and candidates to resist subtle and not-so-subtle pressures to act in conflict with the interests of their clients. Best practice dictates that members and candidates must reject any offer of gift or entertainment that could be expected to threaten their independence and objectivity.

Receiving a gift, benefit, or consideration from a client can be distinguished from gifts given by entities seeking to influence a member or candidate to the detriment of other clients. In a client relationship, the client has already entered some type of compensation arrangement with the member, candidate, or his or her firm. A gift from a client could be considered supplementary compensation. The potential for obtaining influence to the detriment of other clients, although present, is not as great as in situations where no compensation arrangement exists. Therefore, members and candidates may accept "bonuses" or gifts from clients but must disclose to their employers such benefits from clients. Disclosure allows the employer of a member or candidate to make an independent determination about the extent to which the gift may affect the member's or candidate's independence and objectivity.

Members and candidates may also come under pressure from their own firms to, for example, issue favorable research reports or recommendations for certain companies. The commercial side of a bank may derive substantial revenue from its lending/deposit relationships with a company, and bank managers may be tempted to influence the work of analysts in the investment department. The situation may be aggravated if the head of the company sits on the bank's or investment firm's board and attempts to interfere in investment decision making. Members and candidates acting in a sales or marketing capacity must be especially certain of their objectivity in selecting appropriate investments for their clients.

Left unmanaged, pressures that threaten independence place research analysts in a difficult position and may jeopardize their ability to act independently and objectively. One of the ways that research analysts have coped with these pressures in the past is to use subtle and ambiguous language in their recommendations or to temper the tone of their research reports. Such subtleties are lost on some investors who reasonably expect research reports and recommendations to be straightforward and transparent and to communicate clearly an analyst's views based on unbiased analysis and independent judgment.

Members and candidates are personally responsible for maintaining independence and objectivity when preparing research reports, making investment recommendations, and taking investment action on behalf of clients. Recommendations must convey the member's or candidate's true opinions, free of bias from internal or external pressures, and be stated in clear and unambiguous language.

Members and candidates also should be aware that some of their professional or social activities within CFA Institute or its member societies may subtly threaten their independence or objectivity. When seeking corporate financial support for conventions, seminars, or even weekly society luncheons, the members or candidates responsible for the activities should evaluate both the actual effect of such solicitations on their independence and whether their objectivity might be perceived to be compromised in the eyes of their clients.

Investment-Banking Relationships

Some sell-side firms may exert pressure on their analysts to issue favorable research on current or prospective investment-banking clients. For many of these firms, income from investment banking has become increasingly important to overall firm profitability because brokerage income has declined as a result of price competition. Consequently, firms offering investment-banking services work hard to develop and maintain relationships with investment-banking clients and prospects. These companies are often covered by the firm's research analysts because companies often select their investment bank based on the reputation of its research analysts, the quality of their work, and their standing in the industry.

Research analysts frequently work closely with their investment-banking colleagues to help evaluate prospective investment-banking clients. Although this practice benefits the firm and enhances market efficiency (e.g., by allowing firms to assess risks more accurately and make better pricing assumptions), it requires firms to carefully balance the conflicts of interest inherent in the collaboration of research and investment banking. Having analysts work with investment bankers is appropriate only when the conflicts are adequately and effectively managed and disclosed. Firm management has a responsibility to provide an environment in which analysts are neither coerced nor enticed into issuing research that does not reflect their true opinions. Firms should require public disclosure of actual conflicts of interest to investors.

Given the symbiotic relationship between research and investment banking, the traditional approach to building "firewalls" between these two functions must be managed to minimize resulting conflicts of interest. It is critical that sell-side firms foster and maintain a corporate culture that fully supports independence and objectivity and protects analysts from undue pressure by their investment-banking colleagues. A key element of an enhanced firewall is separate reporting structures for personnel within the research and investment-banking functions. For example, investment-banking personnel should not have any authority to approve, disapprove, or make changes to research reports or recommendations. Another element should be a compensation arrangement that minimizes the pressures and rewards objectivity and accuracy. Compensation arrangements should not link analyst remuneration directly to investment-banking assignments on which the analyst may participate as a team member. Firms should also regularly review their policies and procedures to determine whether analysts are adequately safeguarded and to improve the transparency of disclosures relating to conflicts of interest. The highest level of transparency is achieved when disclosures are prominent and specific, rather than marginalized and generic.

Public Companies

Analysts can also be pressured to issue favorable reports and recommendations by the companies they follow. Company management often believes that the company's stock is undervalued and may find it difficult to accept critical research reports or ratings downgrades. Management compensation may also be dependent on stock performance. Not every stock is a "buy" and not every research report is favorable—for many reasons, including the cyclical nature of many business activities and market fluctuations. For instance, a "good company" does not always translate into a "good stock" rating if the current stock price is fully valued. In making an investment recommendation, the analyst is responsible for anticipating, interpreting, and assessing a company's prospects and stock-price performance in a factual manner.

Due diligence in financial research and analysis involves gathering information from a wide variety of sources, including company management and investor-relations personnel, suppliers, customers, competitors, and other relevant sources in addition to public disclosure documents, such as proxy statements, annual reports, and other regulatory filings. Research analysts may justifiably fear that companies will limit their ability to conduct thorough research by denying "negative" analysts direct access to company management and/or barring them from conference calls and other communication venues. Retaliatory practices include companies bringing legal action against analysts personally and/or their firms to seek monetary damages for the economic effects of negative reports and recommendations. Although few companies engage in such behavior, the perception that a reprisal is possible is a reasonable concern for analysts. This concern may make it difficult for them to conduct the comprehensive research needed to make objective recommendations. For further information and guidance, members and candidates should refer to the CFA Institute *Best Practice Guidelines Covering Analyst/Corporate Issuer Relations* (www.cfainstitute.org).

Buy-Side Clients

A third source of pressure on sell-side analysts may come from buy-side clients. Institutional clients are traditionally the primary users of sell-side research, either directly or with soft dollar brokerage. Portfolio managers may have significant positions in the security of a company under review. A rating downgrade may adversely affect the portfolio's performance, particularly in the short term, because the sensitivity of stock prices to ratings changes has increased in recent years. A downgrade may also impact the manager's compensation, which is usually tied to portfolio performance. Moreover, portfolio performance is subject to media and public scrutiny, which may affect the manager's professional reputation. Consequently, some portfolio managers may implicitly or explicitly support sell-side ratings inflation.

Portfolio managers have a responsibility to respect and foster the intellectual honesty of sell-side research. Therefore, it is improper for portfolio managers to threaten or engage in retaliatory practices, such as reporting sell-side analysts to the covered company to instigate negative corporate reactions. Although most portfolio managers do not engage in such practices, the perception by the research analyst that a reprisal is possible may cause concern, making it difficult to maintain independence and objectivity.

Issuer-Paid Research

In light of the recent reduction of sell-side research coverage, many companies, seeking to increase visibility both in the financial markets and with potential investors, hire analysts to produce research reports analyzing their companies. These reports bridge the gap created by the lack of coverage and can be an effective method of communicating with investors.

Issuer-paid research, however, is fraught with potential conflicts. Depending on how the research is written and distributed, investors can be misled into believing that research appears to be from an independent source when, in reality, it has been paid for by the subject company.

It is critical that research analysts adhere to strict standards of conduct that govern how the research is to be conducted and what disclosures must be made in the report. Analysts must engage in thorough, independent, and unbiased analysis and must fully disclose potential conflicts, including the nature of their compensation. Otherwise, analysts risk misleading investors by becoming an extension of an issuer's public relations department while appearing to produce "independent" analysis.

Investors need clear, credible, and thorough information about companies and research based on independent thought. At a minimum, research should include a thorough analysis of the company's financial statements based on publicly disclosed information, benchmarking within a peer group, and industry analysis. Analysts must exercise diligence, independence, and thoroughness in conducting their research in an objective manner. Analysts must distinguish between fact and opinion in their reports. Conclusions must have a reasonable and adequate basis, and must be supported by appropriate research.

Analysts must also strictly limit the type of compensation that they accept for conducting research. Otherwise, the content and conclusions of the reports could reasonably be expected to be determined or affected by compensation from the sponsoring companies. This compensation can be direct, such as payment based on the conclusions of the report or more indirect, such as stock warrants or other equity instruments that could increase in value based on positive coverage in the report. In those instances, analysts would have an incentive to avoid negative information or conclusions that would diminish their potential compensation. Best practice is for analysts to accept only a flat fee for their work prior to writing the report, without regard to their conclusions or the report's recommendations.

Recommended Procedures for Compliance

Members and candidates should follow certain practices and should encourage their firms to establish certain procedures to avoid violations of Standard I(B):

▶ Protect integrity of opinions. Members, candidates, and their firms should establish policies stating that every research report on issues by a corporate client reflects the unbiased opinion of the analyst. Firms should also design compensation systems that protect the integrity of the investment decision process by maintaining the independence and objectivity of analysts.

▶ Create a restricted list. If the firm is unwilling to permit dissemination of adverse opinions about a corporate client, members and candidates should encourage the firm to remove the controversial company from the research universe and put it on a restricted list so that the firm disseminates only factual information about the company.

▶ Restrict special cost arrangements. When attending meetings at an issuer's headquarters, members or candidates should pay for commercial transportation and hotel charges. No corporate issuer should reimburse members or candidates for air transportation. Members and candidates should encourage issuers to limit the use of corporate aircraft to situations in which commercial transportation is not available or in which efficient movement could not otherwise be arranged. Members and candidates should take particular care that when frequent meetings are held between an individual issuer and an individual member or candidate, the issuer should not always host the member or candidate.

▶ Limit gifts. Members and candidates must limit the acceptance of gratuities and/or gifts to token items. Standard I(B) does not preclude customary, ordinary, business-related entertainment so long as its purpose is not to influence or reward members or candidates.

► **Restrict investments.** Members and candidates should restrict (or encourage their investment firms to restrict) employee purchases of equity or equity-related IPOs. Strict limits should be imposed on investment personnel acquiring securities in private placements.

► **Review procedures.** Members and candidates should implement (or encourage their firms to implement) effective supervisory and review procedures to ensure that analysts and portfolio managers comply with policies relating to their personal investment activities.

► Firms should establish a formal written policy on the independence and objectivity of research and implement reporting structures and review procedures to ensure that research analysts do not report to and are not supervised or controlled by any department of the firm that could compromise the independence of the analyst. More detailed recommendations related to a firm's policies regarding research objectivity are set forth in the CFA Institute Research Objectivity Standards (www.cfainstitute.org).

Application of the Standard

Example 1: Steven Taylor, a mining analyst with Bronson Brokers, is invited by Precision Metals to join a group of his peers in a tour of mining facilities in several western U.S. states. The company arranges for chartered group flights from site to site and for accommodations in Spartan Motels, the only chain with accommodations near the mines, for three nights. Taylor allows Precision Metals to pick up his tab, as do the other analysts, with one exception—John Adams, an employee of a large trust company who insists on following his company's policy and paying for his hotel room himself.

> *Comment:* The policy of Adams's company complies closely with Standard I(B) by avoiding even the appearance of a conflict of interest, but Taylor and the other analysts were not necessarily violating Standard I(B). In general, when allowing companies to pay for travel and/or accommodations under these circumstances, members and candidates must use their judgment—keeping in mind that such arrangements must not impinge on a member's or candidate's independence and objectivity. In this example, the trip was strictly for business and Taylor was not accepting irrelevant or lavish hospitality. The itinerary required chartered flights, for which analysts were not expected to pay. The accommodations were modest. These arrangements are not unusual and did not violate Standard I(B) so long as Taylor's independence and objectivity were not compromised. In the final analysis, members and candidates should consider both whether they can remain objective and whether their integrity might be perceived by their clients to have been compromised.

Example 2: Susan Dillon, an analyst in the corporate finance department of an investment services firm, is making a presentation to a potential new business client that includes the promise that her firm will provide full research coverage of the potential client.

> *Comment:* Dillon may agree to provide research coverage, but she must not commit her firm's research department to providing a favorable recommendation. The firm's recommendation (favorable, neutral, or unfavorable) must be based on an independent and objective investigation and analysis of the company and its securities.

Example 3: Walter Fritz is an equity analyst with Hilton Brokerage who covers the mining industry. He has concluded that the stock of Metals & Mining is over-priced at its current level, but he is concerned that a negative research report will hurt the good relationship between Metals & Mining and the investment-banking division of his firm. In fact, a senior manager of Hilton Brokerage has just sent him a copy of a proposal his firm has made to Metals & Mining to under-write a debt offering. Fritz needs to produce a report right away and is concerned about issuing a less-than-favorable rating.

> *Comment:* Fritz's analysis of Metals & Mining must be objective and based solely on consideration of company fundamentals. Any pressure from other divisions of his firm is inappropriate. This conflict could have been eliminated if, in anticipation of the offering, Hilton Brokerage had placed Metals & Min-ing on a restricted list for its sales force.

Example 4: As support for the sales effort of her corporate bond department, Lindsey Warner offers credit guidance to purchasers of fixed-income securities. Her compensation is closely linked to the performance of the corporate bond department. Near the quarter's end, Warner's firm has a large inventory position in the bonds of Milton, Ltd., and has been unable to sell the bonds because of Milton's recent announcement of an operating problem. Salespeople have asked her to contact large clients to push the bonds.

> *Comment:* Unethical sales practices create significant potential violations of the Code and Standards. Warner's opinion of the Milton bonds must not be affected by internal pressure or compensation. In this case, Warner must refuse to push the Milton bonds unless she is able to justify that the market price has already adjusted for the operating problem.

Example 5: Jill Jorund is a securities analyst following airline stocks and a rising star at her firm. Her boss has been carrying a "buy" recommendation on International Airlines and asks Jorund to take over coverage of that airline. He tells Jorund that under no circumstances should the prevailing "buy" recom-mendation be changed.

> *Comment:* Jorund must be independent and objective in her analysis of International Airlines. If she believes that her boss's instructions have com-promised her, she has two options: Tell her boss that she cannot cover the company under these constraints, or pick up coverage of the company, reach her own independent conclusions, and if they conflict with her boss's opinion, share the conclusions with her boss or other supervisors in the firm so that they can make appropriate recommendations. Jorund must only issue recommendations that reflect only her independent and objective opinion.

Example 6: Edward Grant directs a large amount of his commission business to a New York-based brokerage house. In appreciation for all the business, the bro-kerage house gives Grant two tickets to the World Cup in South Africa, two nights at a nearby resort, several meals, and transportation via limousine to the game. Grant fails to disclose receiving this package to his supervisor.

> *Comment:* Grant has violated Standard I(B) because accepting these substan-tial gifts may impede his independence and objectivity. Every member and candidate should endeavor to avoid situations that might cause or be per-ceived to cause a loss of independence or objectivity in recommending investments or taking investment action. By accepting the trip, Grant has opened himself up to the accusation that he may give the broker favored treatment in return.

Example 7: Theresa Green manages the portfolio of Ian Knowlden, a client of Tisbury Investments. Green achieves an annual return for Knowlden that is consistently better than that of the benchmark she and the client previously agreed to. As a reward, Knowlden offers Green two tickets to Wimbledon and the use of Knowlden's flat in London for a week. Green discloses this gift to her supervisor at Tisbury.

> *Comment:* Green is in compliance with Standard I(B) because she disclosed the gift from one of her clients. Members and candidates may accept bonuses or gifts from clients so long as they disclose them to their employers, because gifts in a client relationship are deemed less likely to affect a member's or candidate's objectivity and independence than gifts in other situations. Disclosure is required, however, so that supervisors can monitor such situations to guard against employees favoring a gift-giving client to the detriment of other fee-paying clients (such as by allocating a greater proportion of IPO stock to the gift-giving client's portfolio).

Example 8: Tom Wayne is the investment manager of the Franklin City Employees Pension Plan. He recently completed a successful search for a firm to manage the foreign equity allocation of the plan's diversified portfolio. He followed the plan's standard procedure of seeking presentations from a number of qualified firms and recommended that his board select Penguin Advisors because of its experience, well-defined investment strategy, and performance record, which was compiled and verified in accordance with the CFA Institute Global Investment Performance Standards. Following the plan selection of Penguin, a reporter from the Franklin City Record called to ask if there was any connection between this action and the fact that Penguin was one of the sponsors of an "investment fact-finding trip to Asia" that Wayne made earlier in the year. The trip was one of several conducted by the Pension Investment Academy, which had arranged the itinerary of meetings with economic, government, and corporate officials in major cities in several Asian countries. The Pension Investment Academy obtains support for the cost of these trips from a number of investment managers, including Penguin Advisors; the Academy then pays the travel expenses of the various pension plan managers on the trip and provides all meals and accommodations. The president of Penguin Advisors was one of the travelers on the trip.

> *Comment:* Although Wayne can probably put to good use the knowledge he gained from the trip in selecting portfolio managers and in other areas of managing the pension plan, his recommendation of Penguin Advisors may be tainted by the possible conflict incurred when he participated in a trip paid in part by Penguin Advisors and when he was in the daily company of the president of Penguin Advisors. To avoid violating Standard I(B), Wayne's basic expenses for travel and accommodations should have been paid by his employer or the pension plan; contact with the president of Penguin Advisors should have been limited to informational or educational events only; and the trip, the organizer, and the sponsor should have been made a matter of public record. Even if his actions were not in violation of Standard I(B), Wayne should have been sensitive to the public perception of the trip when reported in the newspaper and the extent to which the subjective elements of his decision might have been affected by the familiarity that the daily contact of such a trip would encourage. This advantage would probably not be shared by competing firms.

Example 9: Javier Herrero recently left his job as a research analyst for a large investment advisor. While looking for a new position, he is hired by an investor-relations firm to write a research report on one of its clients, a small educational software company. The investor-relations firm hopes to generate investor interest in the technology company. The firm will pay Herrero a flat fee plus a bonus if any new investors buy stock in the company as a result of Herrero's report.

>   *Comment:* If Herrero accepts this payment arrangement, he will be in violation of Standard I(B) because the compensation can reasonably be expected to compromise his independence and objectivity. Herrero will receive a bonus for attracting investors, which is an overwhelming incentive to draft a positive report regardless of the facts and to ignore or play down any negative information about the company. Herrero should accept for his work only a flat fee that is not tied to the conclusions or recommendations of the report. Issuer-paid research that is objective and unbiased can be done under the right circumstances so long as the analyst takes steps to maintain his or her objectivity and includes in the report proper disclosures regarding potential conflicts of interest.

C. Misrepresentation

Members and candidates must not knowingly make any misrepresentations relating to investment analysis, recommendations, actions, or other professional activities.

Trust is the foundation of the investment profession. Investors must be able to rely on the statements and information provided to them by those with whom investors trust their financial well being. Investment professionals who make false or misleading statements not only harm investors but also reduce the level of investor confidence in the investment profession and threaten the integrity of capital markets as a whole.

A misrepresentation is any untrue statement or omission of a fact or any statement that is otherwise false or misleading. A member or candidate must not knowingly misrepresent or give a false impression in oral representations, advertising (whether in the press or through brochures), electronic communications, or written materials (whether publicly disseminated or not). In this context, "knowingly" means that a member or candidate either knows or should have known that the misrepresentation was being made.

Written materials for a general audience include, but are not limited to, research reports, market letters, newspaper columns, and books. Electronic communications include, but are not limited to, Internet communications, web pages, chat rooms, and e-mail.

Members and candidates must not misrepresent any aspect of their practice, including (but not limited to) their qualifications or credentials, the qualifications or services provided by their firm, their performance record or the record of their firm, or the characteristics of an investment. Any misrepresentation made by the member or candidate relating to the member or candidate's professional activities is a breach of this standard.

Standard I(C) prohibits members and candidates from guaranteeing clients specific return on investments that are inherently volatile ("I can guarantee that you will earn 8 percent on equities this year," or "I can guarantee that you will not lose money on this investment"). For the most part, the majority of investments contain some element of risk that makes their return inherently unpredictable. In those situations, guaranteeing either a particular rate of return or a guaranteed preservation of investment capital is misleading to investors. Standard I(C) does not prohibit members and candidates from providing clients with information on investment products that have guarantees built into the structure of the product itself or for which an institution has agreed to cover any losses.

Standard I(C) also prohibits plagiarism in the preparation of material for distribution to employers, associates, clients, prospects, or the general public. Plagiarism is defined as copying or using in substantially the same form materials prepared by others without acknowledging the source of the material or identifying the author and publisher of such material. Members and candidates must not copy, or represent as their own, original ideas or material without permission and must acknowledge and identify the source of ideas or material that is not their own.

The investment profession uses a myriad of financial, economic, and statistical data in the investment decision-making process. Through various publications and presentations, the investment professional is constantly exposed to the work of others and to the temptation to use that work without proper acknowledgment.

Misrepresentation through plagiarism in investment management can take various forms. The simplest and most flagrant example is to take a research report or study done by another firm or person, change the names, and release the material as one's own original analysis. This action is a clear violation of Standard I(C). Other practices include (1) using excerpts from articles or reports prepared by others either verbatim or with only slight changes in wording without acknowledgment, (2) citing specific quotations supposedly attributable to "leading analysts" and "investment experts" without specific reference, (3) presenting statistical estimates of forecasts prepared by others with the source identified but without qualifying statements or caveats that may have been used, (4) using charts and graphs without stating their sources, and (5) copying proprietary computerized spreadsheets or algorithms without seeking the cooperation or authorization of their creators.

In the case of distributing third-party, outsourced research, members and candidates can use and distribute these reports so long as they do not represent themselves as the author of the report. The member or candidate may add value to the client by sifting through research and repackaging it for clients. The client should fully understand that he or she is paying for the ability of the member or candidate to find the best research from a wide variety of sources. However, members and candidates must not misrepresent their abilities, the extent of their expertise, or the extent of their work in a way that would mislead their clients or prospective clients. Members and candidates should consider disclosing whether the research being presented to clients comes from an outside source, from either within or outside the member's or candidate's firm. Clients should know who has the expertise behind the report or if the work is being done by the analyst, other members of the firm, or an outside party.

The standard also applies to plagiarism in oral communications, such as through group meetings; visits with associates, clients, and customers; use of audio/video media (which is rapidly increasing); and telecommunications, such as through electronic data transfer and the outright copying of electronic media.

One of the most egregious practices in violation of this standard is the preparation of research reports based on multiple sources of information without acknowledging the sources. Such information would include, for example, ideas, statistical compilations, and forecasts combined to give the appearance of original work. Although there is no monopoly on ideas, members and candidates must give credit when it is clearly due. Analysts should not use undocumented forecasts, earnings projections, asset values, and so on. Sources must be revealed to bring the responsibility directly back to the author of the report or the firm involved.

Recommended Procedures for Compliance

Members and candidates can prevent unintentional misrepresentations of the qualifications or services they or their firms provide if each member and candidate understands the limit of the firms's or individual's capabilities and the need to be accurate and complete in presentations. Firms can provide guidance for employees who make written or oral presentations to clients or potential clients by providing a written list of the firm's available services and a description of the firm's qualifications. This list should suggest ways of describing the firm's services, qualifications, and compensation that are both accurate and suitable for client or customer presentations. Firms can also help prevent misrepresentation by specifically designating which employees are authorized to speak on behalf of the firm. Whether or not the firm provides guidance, members and candidates should make certain they understand the services the firm can perform and its qualifications.

In addition, in order to ensure accurate presentations to clients, each member and candidate should prepare a summary of his or her own qualifications and experience as well as a list of the services the member or candidate is capable of performing. Firms can assist member and candidate compliance by periodically reviewing employee correspondence and documents that contain representations of individual or firm qualifications.

Members and candidates who publish web pages should regularly monitor materials posted to the site to ensure the site maintains current information. Members and candidates should also ensure that all reasonable precautions have been taken to protect the site's integrity, confidentiality, and security, and that the site does not misrepresent any information and provides full disclosure.

To avoid plagiarism in preparing research reports or conclusions of analysis, members and candidates should take the following steps:

► Maintain copies. Keep copies of all research reports, articles containing research ideas, material with new statistical methodology, and other materials that were relied on in preparing the research report.

► Attribute quotations. Attribute to their sources any direct quotations, including projections, tables, statistics, model/product ideas, and new methodologies prepared by persons other than recognized financial and statistical reporting services or similar sources.

► Attribute summaries. Attribute to their sources paraphrases or summaries of material prepared by others. For example, to support his analysis of Brown's competitive position, the author of a research report on Brown Company may summarize another analyst's report of Brown's chief competitor, but the author of the Brown report must acknowledge in his own report his reliance on the other analyst's report.

Application of the Standard

Example 1: Allison Rogers is a partner in the firm of Rogers and Black, a small firm offering investment advisory services. She assures a prospective client who has just inherited $1 million that "we can perform all the financial and investment services you need." Rogers and Black is well equipped to provide investment advice but, in fact, cannot provide asset allocation assistance or a full array of financial and investment services.

> *Comment:* Rogers has violated Standard I(C) by orally misrepresenting the services her firm can perform for the prospective client. She must limit herself to describing the range of investment advisory services Rogers and Black can provide and offer to help the client obtain elsewhere the financial and investment services that her firm cannot provide.

Example 2: Anthony McGuire is an issuer-paid analyst hired by publicly traded companies to electronically promote their stocks. McGuire creates a website that promotes his research efforts as a seemingly independent analyst. McGuire posts a profile and a strong buy recommendation for each company on the website indicating that the stock is expected to increase in value. He does not disclose the contractual relationships with the companies he covers on his website, in the research reports he issues, or in the statements he makes about the companies on Internet chat rooms.

> *Comment:* McGuire has violated Standard I(C) because the Internet site and e-mails are misleading to potential investors. Even if the recommendations are valid and supported with thorough research, his omissions regarding the true relationship between himself and the companies he covers constitute a misrepresentation. McGuire has also violated Standard VI(A) by not disclosing the existence of an arrangement with the companies through which he receives compensation in exchange for his services.

Example 3: Hijan Yao is responsible for the creation and distribution of the marketing material for his firm. Yao creates and distributes a performance presentation for the firm's Asian equity composite that complies with GIPS® and states that the composite has 350 billion yen in assets. In fact, the composite has only 35 billion yen in assets, and the higher figure on the presentation is a result of a typographical error. Nevertheless, the erroneous material is distributed to a number of clients before Yao catches the mistake.

> *Comment:* Once the error is discovered, Yao must take steps to cease distribution of the incorrect material and correct the error by informing those who have received the erroneous information. However, because Yao did not knowingly make the misrepresentation, he did not violate the Code and Standards.

Example 4: Syed Muhammad is the president of an investment management firm. The promotional material for the firm, created by the firm's marketing department, incorrectly claims that Muhammad has an advanced degree in finance from a prestigious business school in addition to the CFA designation. Although Muhammad attended the school for a short period of time, he did not receive a degree. Over the years, Muhammad and others in the firm have distributed this material to numerous prospective clients and consultants.

> *Comment:* Even though Muhammad may not have been directly responsible for the misrepresentation about his credentials contained in the firm's promotional material, he used this material numerous times over an extended period and should have known of the misrepresentation. Thus, Muhammad has violated Standard I(C).

Example 5: Cindy Grant, a research analyst for a Canadian brokerage firm, has specialized in the Canadian mining industry for the past 10 years. She recently read an extensive research report on Jefferson Mining, Ltd., by Jeremy Barton, another analyst. Barton provided extensive statistics on the mineral reserves, production capacity, selling rates, and marketing factors affecting Jefferson's operations. He also noted that initial drilling results on a new ore body, which had not been made public, might show the existence of mineral zones that could increase the life of Jefferson's main mines, but Barton cited no specific data as to the initial drilling results. Grant called an officer of Jefferson, who gave her the initial drilling results over the telephone. The data indicated that the expected life of the main mines would be tripled. Grant added these statistics to Barton's report and circulated it as her own report within her firm.

Comment: Grant plagiarized Barton's report by reproducing large parts of it in her own report without acknowledgment.

Example 6: When Ricki Marks sells mortgage-backed derivatives called interest-only strips (IOs) to her public pension plan clients, she describes them as "guaranteed by the U.S. government." Purchasers of the IOs, however, are entitled only to the interest stream generated by the mortgages not the notional principal itself. The municipality's investment policies and local law require that securities purchased by the public pension plans be guaranteed by the U.S. government. Although the underlying mortgages are guaranteed, neither the investor's investment nor the interest stream on the IOs is guaranteed. When interest rates decline, causing an increase in prepayment of mortgages, the interest payments to the clients decline, and the clients lose a portion of their investment.

Comment: Marks violated Standard I(C) by misrepresenting the terms and character of the investment.

Example 7: Khalouck Abdrabbo manages the investments of several high-net-worth individuals in the United States who are approaching retirement. Abdrabbo advises that a portion of their investments be moved from equity to certificates of deposit and money-market accounts so the principal will be "guaranteed" up to a certain amount. The interest is not guaranteed.

Comment: While there is risk that the institution offering the certificates of deposits and money-market accounts could go bankrupt, in the U.S., these accounts are insured by the United States government through the Federal Deposit Insurance Corporation. Therefore, using the term "guaranteed" in this context is not inappropriate as long as the amount is within the government-insured limit. Abdrabbo should explain these facts to the clients.

Example 8: Steve Swanson is a senior analyst in the investment research department of Ballard and Company. Apex Corporation has asked Ballard to assist in acquiring the majority ownership in stock of Campbell Company, a financial consulting firm, and to prepare a report recommending that stockholders of Campbell agree to the acquisition. Another investment firm, Davis and Company, had already prepared a report for Apex analyzing both Apex and Campbell and recommending an exchange ratio. Apex has given the Davis report to Ballard officers, who have passed it on to Swanson, who then reviewed the Davis report along with other available material on Apex and Campbell companies. From his analysis, he concludes that the common stocks of Campbell and Apex represent good value at their current prices; he believes, however, that the Davis report does not consider all the factors a Campbell stockholder would need to know to make a decision. Swanson reports his conclusions to the partner in charge, who tells him to "use the Davis report, change a few words, sign your name, and get it out."

Comment: If Swanson does as requested, he will violate Standard I(C). He could refer to those portions of the Davis report that he agrees with if he identifies Davis as the source; he could then add his own analysis and conclusions to the report before signing and distributing it.

Example 9: Claude Browning, a quantitative analyst for Double Alpha, Inc., returns in great excitement from a seminar. In that seminar, Jack Jorrely, a well-publicized quantitative analyst at a national brokerage firm, discussed one of his new models in great detail, and Browning is intrigued by the new concepts. He proceeds to test this model, making some minor mechanical changes but retaining the concept, until he produces some very positive results. Browning quickly announces to his supervisors at Double Alpha that he has discovered a new model and that clients and prospective clients alike should be informed of this positive finding as ongoing proof of Double Alpha's continuing innovation and ability to add value.

> *Comment:* Although Browning tested Jorrely's model on his own and even slightly modified it, he must still acknowledge the original source of the idea. Browning can certainly take credit for the final, practical results; he can also support his conclusions with his own test. The credit for the innovative thinking, however, must be awarded to Jorrely.

Example 10: Fernando Zubia would like to include in his firm's marketing materials plain-language descriptions of various concepts, such as the price-to-earnings multiple and why standard deviation is used as a measure of risk, that are taken from other sources without reference to the original author. Is this a violation of Standard I(C)?

> *Comment:* Copying verbatim any material without acknowledgement, including plain-language descriptions of the price-to-earnings multiple and standard deviation, violates Standard I(C). Even though these are general concepts, best practice would be for Zubia to describe them in his own words or cite the source from which the descriptions are quoted. Members and candidates responsible for creating marketing materials and those who knowingly use plagiarized materials could potentially be sanctioned if the matter was brought to the attention of the CFA Institute Professional Conduct Program.

Example 11: Through a mainstream media outlet, Erika Schneider learns about a study that she would like to cite in her research. Should she cite both the mainstream intermediary source as well as the author of the study itself when using that information?

> *Comment:* In all instances, it is necessary to cite the actual source of the information. Best practice would be to obtain the information directly from the author and review it before citing it in a report. In that instance, Schneider would not need to report how she found out about the information. For example, suppose Schneider reads in the *Financial Times* about a study issued by CFA Institute; best practice for Schneider would be to obtain a copy of the study from CFA Institute, review it, and then cite it in her report. If she does not use any interpretation from the *Financial Times* and it is not adding value to the report itself, the newspaper is merely a conduit to the original information she wants to use in the report and it need not be cited. If she does not obtain the report and review the information, Schneider runs the risk of relying on second-hand information that may misstate the source. If, for example, the *Financial Times* erroneously reported the information from the original CFA Institute study and Schneider copied that erroneous information without acknowledging CFA Institute, she would open herself to complaint. Best practice would be either to obtain the complete study from its original author and cite only that author or to use the information provided by the intermediary and cite both sources.

Example 12: Gary Ostrowski runs a small, two-person investment management firm. Ostrowski's firm subscribes to a service from a large investment research firm that provides research reports that can be repackaged as in-house research from smaller firms. Ostrowski's firm distributes these reports to clients as its own work.

> *Comment:* Ostrowski can rely on third-party research that has a reasonable and adequate basis, but he cannot imply that he is the author of the report. Otherwise, Ostrowski would misrepresent the extent of his work in a way that would mislead the firm's clients or prospective clients.

D. Misconduct

Members and candidates must not engage in any professional conduct involving dishonesty, fraud, or deceit or commit any act that reflects adversely on their professional reputation, integrity, or competence.

Whereas Standard I(A) addresses the obligation of members and candidates to comply with applicable law that governs their professional activities, Standard I(D) addresses conduct that reflects poorly on the professional integrity, good reputation, or competence of members and candidates. Although CFA Institute discourages any sort of unethical behavior by members and candidates, the Code and Standards are aimed at conduct related to a member's or candidate's professional life. Any act that involves lying, cheating, stealing, or other dishonest conduct that reflects adversely on a member's or candidate's professional activities, would violate this standard.

Conduct that damages trustworthiness or competence can include behavior that may not be illegal but could negatively affect a member's or candidate's ability to perform his or her responsibilities. For example, abusing alcohol during business hours could constitute a violation of this standard because it could have a detrimental effect on the member or candidate's ability to fulfill his or her professional responsibilities. Personal bankruptcy may not reflect on the integrity or trustworthiness of the person declaring bankruptcy, but if the circumstances of the bankruptcy involve fraudulent or deceitful business conduct, it may be a violation of this standard.

Individuals may attempt to abuse the CFA Institute Professional Conduct Program by actively seeking CFA Institute enforcement of the Code and Standards, and Standard I(D) in particular, as a method to settle personal, political, or other disputes unrelated to professional ethics. CFA Institute is aware of this issue, and appropriate disciplinary policies, procedures, and enforcement mechanisms are in place to address misuse of the Code and Standards and the Professional Conduct Program in this way.

Recommended Procedures for Compliance

To prevent general misconduct, members and candidates should encourage their firms to adopt the following policies and procedures to support the principles of Standard I(D):

▶ Develop and/or adopt a code of ethics to which every employee must subscribe and make clear that any personal behavior that reflects poorly on the individual involved, the institution as a whole, or the investment industry will not be tolerated.

▶ Disseminate to all employees a list of potential violations and associated disciplinary sanctions, up to and including dismissal from the firm.

▶ Check references of potential employees to ensure that they are of good character and not ineligible to work in the investment industry because of past infractions of the law.

Application of the Standard

Example 1: Simon Sasserman is a trust investment officer at a bank in a small affluent town. He enjoys lunching every day with friends at the country club, where his clients have observed him having numerous drinks. Back at work after lunch, he clearly is intoxicated while making investment decisions. His colleagues make a point of handling any business with Sasserman in the morning because they distrust his judgment after lunch.

> *Comment:* Sasserman's excessive drinking at lunch and subsequent intoxication at work constitute a violation of Standard I(D) because this conduct has raised questions about his professionalism and competence. His behavior thus reflects poorly on him, his employer, and the investment industry.

Example 2: Howard Hoffman, a security analyst at ATZ Brothers, Inc., a large brokerage house, submits reimbursement forms over a two-year period to ATZ's self-funded health insurance program for more than two dozen bills, most of which have been altered to increase the amount due. An investigation by the firm's director of employee benefits uncovers the conduct. ATZ subsequently terminates Hoffman's employment and notifies CFA Institute.

> *Comment:* Hoffman violated Standard I(D) because he engaged in intentional conduct involving fraud and deceit in the workplace that adversely reflected on his honesty.

Example 3: Jody Brink, an analyst covering the automotive industry, volunteers much of her spare time to local charities. The board of one of the charitable institutions decides to buy five new vans to deliver hot lunches to low-income elderly people. Brink offers to donate her time to handle purchasing agreements. To pay a long-standing debt to a friend who operates an automobile dealership—and to compensate herself for her trouble—she agrees to a price 20 percent higher than normal and splits the surcharge with her friend. The director of the charity ultimately discovers the scheme and tells Brink that her services, donated or otherwise, are no longer required.

> *Comment:* Brink engaged in conduct involving dishonesty, fraud, and misrepresentation and has violated Standard I(D).

Example 4: Carmen Garcia manages a mutual fund dedicated to socially responsible investing. She is also an environmental activist. As the result of her participation at nonviolent protests, Garcia has been arrested on numerous occasions for trespassing on the property of a large petrochemical plant that is accused of damaging the environment.

> *Comment:* Generally, Standard I(D) is not meant to cover legal transgressions resulting from acts of civil disobedience in support of personal beliefs because such conduct does not reflect poorly on the member's or candidate's professional reputation, integrity, or competence.

STANDARD II—INTEGRITY OF CAPITAL MARKETS

A. Material Nonpublic Information

Members and candidates who possess material nonpublic information that could affect the value of an investment must not act or cause others to act on the information.

Trading on material nonpublic information erodes confidence in capital markets, institutions, and investment professionals by supporting the idea that those with inside information and special access can take unfair advantage of the general investing public. Although trading on inside information may lead to short-term profits, in the long run, individuals and the profession as a whole will suffer as investors avoid capital markets perceived to be "rigged" in favor of the knowledgeable insider. Standard II(A) promotes and maintains a high level of confidence in market integrity, which is one of the foundations of the investment profession.

Information is "material" if its disclosure would likely have an impact on the price of a security or if reasonable investors would want to know the information before making an investment decision. In other words, information is material if it would significantly alter the total mix of information currently available regarding a security such that the price of the security would be affected.

The specificity of the information, the extent of its difference from public information, its nature, and its reliability are key factors in determining whether a particular piece of information fits the definition of material. For example, material information may include, but is not limited to, information on the following:

- ▶ earnings;
- ▶ mergers, acquisitions, tender offers, or joint ventures;
- ▶ changes in assets;
- ▶ innovative products, processes, or discoveries;
- ▶ new licenses, patents, registered trademarks, or regulatory approval/rejection of a product;
- ▶ developments regarding customers or suppliers (e.g., the acquisition or loss of a contract);
- ▶ changes in management;
- ▶ change in auditor notification or the fact that the issuer may no longer rely on an auditor's report or qualified opinion;
- ▶ events regarding the issuer's securities (e.g., defaults on senior securities, calls of securities for redemption, repurchase plans, stock splits, changes in dividends, changes to the rights of security holders, public or private sales of additional securities, and changes in credit ratings);
- ▶ bankruptcies;
- ▶ significant legal disputes;
- ▶ government reports of economic trends (employment, housing starts, currency information, etc.);
- ▶ orders for large trades before they are executed.

In addition to the substance and specificity of the information, the source or relative reliability of the information also determines materiality. The less reliable a source, the less likely the information provided would be considered material. For example, factual information from a corporate insider regarding a significant new contract for a company would likely be material, while an assumption based on speculation by a competitor about the same contract might be less reliable and, therefore, not material.

Also, the more ambiguous the effect on price, the less material the information becomes. If it is unclear whether the information will affect the price of a security and to what extent, information may not be considered material. The passage of time may also render information that was once important immaterial.

Information is "nonpublic" until it has been disseminated or is available to the marketplace in general (as opposed to a select group of investors). Dissemination can be defined as "made known to." For example, a company report of profits that is posted on the Internet and distributed widely through a press release or accompanied by a filing has been effectively disseminated to the marketplace. Members and candidates must have a reasonable expectation that people have received the information before it can be considered public. It is not necessary, however, to wait for the slowest method of delivery. Once the information is disseminated to the market, it is public information that is no longer covered by this standard.

Members and candidates must be particularly aware of information that is selectively disclosed by corporations to a small group of investors, analysts, or other market participants. Information that is made available to analysts remains nonpublic until it is made available to investors in general. Corporations that disclose information on a limited basis create the potential for insider-trading violations.

Issues of selective disclosure often arise when a corporate insider provides material information to analysts in a briefing or conference call before that information is released to the public. Analysts must be aware that a disclosure made to a room full of analysts does not necessarily make the disclosed information "public." Analysts should also be alert to the possibility that they are selectively receiving material nonpublic information when a company provides them with guidance or interpretation of such publicly available information as financial statements or regulatory filings.

Mosaic Theory

A financial analyst gathers and interprets large quantities of information from many sources. The analyst may use significant conclusions derived from the analysis of public and nonmaterial nonpublic information as the basis for investment recommendations and decisions even if those conclusions would have been material inside information had they been communicated directly to the analyst by a company. Under the "mosaic theory," financial analysts are free to act on this collection, or mosaic, of information without risking violation.

The practice of financial analysis depends on the free flow of information. For the fair and efficient operation of the capital markets, analysts and investors must have the greatest amount of information possible to facilitate well-informed investment decisions about how and where to invest capital. Accurate, timely, and intelligible communication are essential if analysts and investors are to obtain the data needed to make informed decisions about how and where to invest capital. These disclosures must go beyond the information mandated by the reporting requirements of the securities laws and should include specific business information about items used to guide a company's future growth, such as new products, capital projects, and the competitive environment. Analysts seek and use such information to compare and contrast investment alternatives.

Much of the information used by analysts comes directly from companies. Analysts often receive such information through contacts with corporate insiders, especially investor relations and finance officers. Information may be disseminated in the form of press releases, through oral presentations by company executives in analysts' meetings or conference calls, or during analysts' visits to company premises. In seeking to develop the most accurate and complete picture of a company, analysts should also reach beyond contacts with companies themselves and collect information from other sources, such as customers, contractors, suppliers, and companies' competitors.

Analysts are in the business of formulating opinions and insights—not obvious to the general investing public—concerning the attractiveness of particular securities. In the course of their work, analysts actively seek out corporate information not generally known to the market for the express purpose of analyzing that information, forming an opinion on its significance, and informing their clients who can be expected to trade on the basis of the recommendation. Analysts' initiatives to discover and analyze information and communicate their findings to their clients significantly enhance market efficiency, thus benefiting all investors (see U.S. Supreme Court case *Dirks v. Securities and Exchange Commission* [463 US 646]).

Accordingly, violations of Standard II(A) will not result when a perceptive analyst reaches a conclusion about a corporate action or event through an analysis of public information and items of nonmaterial nonpublic information. Investment professionals should note, however, that although analysts are free to use mosaic information in their research reports, they should save and document all their research [see Standard V(C)]. Evidence of the analyst's knowledge of public and nonmaterial nonpublic information about a corporation strengthens the assertion that the analyst reached his or her conclusions solely through appropriate methods rather than through the use of material nonpublic information.

When a particularly well-known or respected analyst issues a report or makes changes to his or her recommendation, that information alone could have an effect on the market and, thus, could be considered material. Theoretically, under this standard, such a report would have to be made public before it was distributed to clients. However, the analyst is not a company insider and does not have access to inside information. Presumably, the analyst created the report with information available to the public (mosaic theory) using his or her expertise to interpret the information. The analyst's hard work, paid for by the client, generated the conclusions. Simply because the public in general would find the conclusions material does not require that the analyst make his or her work public. Investors who are not clients of the analyst can either do the work themselves or become a client of the analyst if they want access to the analyst's expertise.

Recommended Procedures for Compliance

If a member or candidate determines that information is material, the member or candidate should make reasonable efforts to achieve public dissemination of the information. This effort usually entails encouraging the issuer company to make the information public. If public dissemination is not possible, the member or candidate must communicate the information only to the designated supervisory and compliance personnel within the member's or candidate's firm and must not take investment action on the basis of the information. Moreover, members and candidates must not knowingly engage in any conduct that may induce company insiders to privately disclose material nonpublic information.

Members and candidates should encourage their firms to adopt compliance procedures to prevent the misuse of material nonpublic information. Particularly important is improving compliance in such areas as the review of employee and proprietary trading, documentation of firm procedures, and the supervision of interdepartmental communications in multiservice firms. Compliance procedures should suit the particular characteristics of a firm, including its size and the nature of its business.

Members and candidates should encourage their firms to develop and follow disclosure policies designed to ensure that information is disseminated to the marketplace in an equitable manner. For example, analysts from small firms should receive the same information and attention from a company as analysts from large firms receive. Similarly, companies should not provide certain information to buy-side analysts but not to sell-side analysts, or vice versa. Furthermore, a company should not discriminate among analysts in the provision of information or blackball particular analysts who have given negative reports on the company in the past.

Companies should consider issuing press releases prior to analyst meetings and conference calls and scripting those meetings and calls to decrease the chance that further information will be disclosed. If material nonpublic information is disclosed for the first time in an analyst meeting or call, the company should promptly issue a press release or otherwise make the information publicly available.

An information barrier commonly referred to as a "firewall" is the most widely used approach to preventing the communication of material nonpublic information within firms. It restricts the flow of confidential information to those who need to know the information to perform their jobs effectively. The minimum elements of such a system include, but are not limited to, the following:

▶ substantial control of relevant interdepartmental communications, preferably through a clearance area within the firm in either the compliance or legal department;

▶ review of employee trading through the maintenance of "watch," "restricted," and "rumor" lists;

▶ documentation of the procedures designed to limit the flow of information between departments and of the enforcement actions taken pursuant to those procedures;

▶ heightened review or restriction of proprietary trading while a firm is in possession of material nonpublic information.

Although documentation requirements must, for practical reasons, take into account the differences between the activities of small firms and those of large, multiservice firms, firms of all sizes and types benefit by improving the documentation of their internal enforcement of firewall procedures. Therefore, even at small firms, procedures concerning interdepartmental communication, the review of trading activity, and the investigation of possible violations should be compiled and formalized.

As a practical matter, to the extent possible, firms should consider the physical separation of departments and files to prevent the communication of sensitive information. For example, the investment-banking and corporate finance areas of a brokerage firm should be separated from the sales and research departments, and a bank's commercial lending department should be segregated from its trust and research departments.

There should be no overlap of personnel between such departments. A single supervisor or compliance officer should have the specific authority and responsibility to decide whether or not information is material and whether it is sufficiently public to be used as the basis for investment decisions. Ideally, the supervisor or compliance officer responsible for communicating information to a firm's research or brokerage area would not be a member of that area.

For a firewall to be effective in a multiservice firm, an employee can be allowed to be on only one side of the wall at any given time. Inside knowledge may not be limited to information about a specific offering or a current financial condition of the company. Analysts may be exposed to a host of information about the company, including new product developments or future budget projections that clearly constitute inside knowledge and thus preclude the analyst from returning to his or her research function. For example, an analyst who follows a particular company may provide limited assistance to the investment bankers under carefully controlled circumstances when the firm's investment-banking department is involved in a deal with the company. That analyst must then be treated as though he or she were an investment banker; the analyst must remain on the investment-banking side of the wall until any information he or she learns is publicly disclosed. In short, the analyst cannot use any information learned in the course of the project for research purposes and cannot share that information with colleagues in the research department.

A primary objective of an effective firewall procedure is to establish a reporting system in which authorized people review and approve communications between departments. If an employee behind a firewall believes that he or she needs to share confidential information with someone on the other side of the wall, the employee should consult a designated compliance officer to determine whether sharing the information is necessary and how much information should be shared. If the sharing is necessary, the compliance officer should coordinate the process of "looking over the wall" so that the necessary information will be shared and the integrity of the procedure will be maintained.

An information barrier is the minimum procedure a firm should have in place to protect itself from liability. Firms should also consider restrictions or prohibitions on personal trading by employees and should carefully monitor both proprietary trading and personal trading by employees. Firms should require employees to make periodic reports (to the extent that such reporting is not already required by securities laws) of their own transactions and transactions made for the benefit of family members. Securities should be placed on a restricted list when a firm has or may have material nonpublic information. The broad distribution of a restricted list often triggers the sort of trading the list was developed to avoid. Therefore, a watch list shown to only the few people responsible for compliance should be used to monitor transactions in specified securities. The use of a watch list in combination with a restricted list is an increasingly common means of ensuring an effective procedure.

Multiservice firms should maintain written records of the communications between various departments. Firms should place a high priority on training and should consider instituting comprehensive training programs, particularly for employees in sensitive areas.

Procedures concerning the restriction or review of a firm's proprietary trading while it is in the possession of material nonpublic information will necessarily vary depending on the types of proprietary trading in which a firm may engage. A prohibition on all types of proprietary activity when a firm comes into possession of material nonpublic information is *not* appropriate. For example, when a firm acts as a market maker, a proprietary trading prohibition may be counterproductive to the goals of maintaining the confidentiality of information and market liquidity. This concern is particularly keen in the relationships between small, regional broker/dealers and small issuers. In many situations, a firm will take a small issuer public with the understanding that the firm will continue to be a market maker in the stock. In such instances, a withdrawal by the firm from market-making acts would be a clear tip to outsiders. However, firms that continue market-making activity while in the possession of material nonpublic information should instruct their market makers to remain passive to the market—that is, take only the contra side of unsolicited customer trades.

In risk-arbitrage trading, the case for a trading prohibition is more compelling. In contrast to market making, the impetus for arbitrage trading is neither passive nor reactive and the potential for illegal profits is greater. The most prudent course for firms is to suspend arbitrage activity when a security is placed on the watch list. Those firms that do continue arbitrage activity face a high hurdle in proving the adequacy of their internal procedures and must demonstrate stringent review and documentation of firm trades.

Written compliance policies and guidelines should be circulated to all employees of a firm. Policies and guidelines should be used in conjunction with training programs aimed at enabling employees to recognize material nonpublic information. As noted, material nonpublic information is not always clearly identifiable as such. Employees must be given sufficient training to either make an informed decision or consult a supervisor or compliance officer before engaging in questionable transactions.

Application of the Standard

Example 1: Frank Barnes, the president and controlling shareholder of the SmartTown clothing chain, decides to accept a proposed tender offer and sell the family business at a price almost double the market price of its shares. He describes this decision to his sister (SmartTown's treasurer), who conveys it to her daughter (who owns no stock in the family company at present), who tells her husband, Staple. Staple, however, tells his stockbroker, Alex Halsey, who immediately buys SmartTown stock for himself.

> *Comment:* The information regarding the pending sale is both material and nonpublic. Staple has violated Standard II(A) by communicating the inside information to his broker. Also, Halsey has violated the standard by initiating the transaction to buy the shares based on material nonpublic information.

Example 2: Josephine Walsh is riding an elevator up to her office when she overhears the chief financial officer (CFO) for the Swan Furniture Company tell the president of Swan that he has just calculated the company's earnings for the past quarter and they have unexpectedly and significantly dropped. The CFO adds that this drop will not be released to the public until next week. Walsh immediately calls her broker and tells him to sell her Swan stock.

> *Comment:* Walsh has sufficient information to determine that the information is both material and nonpublic. By trading the inside information, she has violated Standard II(A).

Example 3: Samuel Peter, an analyst with Scotland and Pierce Incorporated, is assisting his firm with a secondary offering for Bright Ideas Lamp Company. Peter participates, via telephone conference call, in a meeting with Scotland and Pierce investment-banking employees and Bright Ideas' CEO. Peter is advised that the company's earnings projections for the next year have significantly dropped. Throughout the telephone conference call, several Scotland and Pierce salespeople and portfolio managers walk in and out of Peter's office, where the telephone call is taking place. As a result, they are aware of the drop in projected earnings for Bright Ideas. Before the conference call is concluded, the salespeople trade the stock of the company on behalf of the firm's clients and other firm personnel trade the stock in a firm proprietary account and in employee personal accounts.

> *Comment:* Peter violated Standard II(A) because he failed to prevent the transfer and misuse of material nonpublic information to others in his firm. Peter's firm should have adopted information barriers to prevent the communication of nonpublic information between departments of the firm. The salespeople and portfolio managers who traded on the information have also violated Standard II(A) by trading on inside information.

Example 4: Madison & Lambeau, a well-respected broker/dealer, submits a weekly column to *Securities Weekly* magazine. Once published, the column usually affects the value of the stocks discussed. Ron George, an employee of Madison & Lambeau, knows that *Securities Weekly* is published by Ziegler Publishing, for which his nephew is the night foreman. George's nephew faxes him an advance copy of the weekly column before it is printed. George regularly trades in the securities mentioned in the Madison & Lambeau column prior to its distribution, and to date, he has realized a personal profit of $42,000 as well as significant profits for his clients.

> *Comment:* George has violated Standard II(A) by trading on material nonpublic information. George's nephew has also violated the standard by communicating the information that causes George to trade.

Example 5: Greg Newman and his wife volunteer at a local charitable organization that delivers meals to the elderly. One morning, Newman's wife receives a telephone call from Betsy Sterling, another volunteer, who asks if Newman and his wife can fill in for her and her husband that afternoon. Mrs. Sterling indicates that her husband is busy at work because his company has just fired its chief financial officer for misappropriation of funds. Mrs. Newman agrees to perform the volunteer work for the Sterlings and advises her husband of the situation. Newman knows that Mr. Sterling is the CEO at O'Hara Brothers Incorporated. Newman determines that this information is not public and then sells his entire holding of 3,000 shares of O'Hara Brothers. Three days later, the firing is announced and O'Hara Brothers stock drops in value.

> *Comment:* Because the information is material and nonpublic, Newman has violated Standard II(A) by trading on this information.

Example 6: Elizabeth Levenson is based in Taipei and covers the Taiwanese market for her firm, which is based in Singapore. She is invited to meet the finance director of a manufacturing company along with the other 10 largest shareholders of the company. During the meeting, the finance director states that the company expects its workforce to strike next Friday, which will cripple productivity and distribution. Can Levenson use this information as a basis to change her rating on the company from "buy" to "sell"?

> *Comment:* Levenson must first determine whether the material information is public. If the company has not made this information public (a small-group forum does not qualify as a method of public dissemination), she cannot use the information according to Standard II(A).

Example 7: Leah Fechtman is trying to decide whether to hold or sell shares of an oil and gas exploration company that she owns in several of the funds she manages. Although the company has underperformed the index for some time already, the trends in the industry sector signal that companies of this type might become takeover targets. In the midst of the decision, her doctor, who casually follows the markets, mentions that she thinks that the company in question will soon be bought out by a large multinational conglomerate and that it would be a good idea to buy the stock right now. After talking to various investment professionals and checking their opinions on the company as well as industry trends, Fechtman decides the next day to accumulate more company stock.

> *Comment:* Although information on an expected takeover bid may be of the type that is generally material and nonpublic, in this case, the source of information is unreliable and could not be considered material. Therefore, Fechtman is not prohibited from trading the stock based on this information.

Example 8: Jagdish Teja is a buy-side analyst covering the furniture industry. Looking for an attractive company to recommend as a buy, he analyzed several furniture makers by studying their financial reports and visiting their operations. He also talked to some designers and retailers to find out which furniture styles are trendy and popular. Although none of the companies that he analyzed turned out to be a clear buy, he discovered that one of them, Swan Furniture

Company (SFC), might be in trouble. Swan's extravagant new designs were introduced at substantial costs. Even though these designs initially attracted attention, in the long run, the public is buying more conservative furniture from other makers. Based on that and on P&L analysis, Teja believes that Swan's next-quarter earnings will drop substantially. He then issues a sell recommendation for SFC. Immediately after receiving that recommendation, investment managers start reducing the stock in their portfolios.

> *Comment:* Information on quarterly earnings figures is material and nonpublic. However, Teja arrived at his conclusion about the earnings drop based on public information and on pieces of nonmaterial nonpublic information (such as opinions of designers and retailers). Therefore, trading based on Teja's correct conclusion is not prohibited by Standard II(A).

Example 9: Roger Clement is a senior financial analyst who specializes in the European automobile sector at Rivoli Capital. Because he has been repeatedly nominated by many leading industry magazines and newsletters as "best analyst" for the automobile industry, he is widely regarded as an authority on the sector. After speaking with representatives of Turgot Chariots, a European auto manufacturer with sales primarily in Korea, as well as salespeople, labor leaders, his firm's Korean currency analysts, and banking officials, Clement reviewed his analysis of Turgot Chariots and concluded that (1) its newly introduced model will probably not meet sales anticipation, (2) its corporate restructuring strategy might well face serious opposition from the unions, (3) the depreciation of the Korean won should lead to pressure on margins for the industry in general and Turgot's market segment in particular, and (4) banks could take a tougher-than-expected stance in the soon-to-come round of credit renegotiations. For these reasons, he changed his recommendation from market overperform to underperform.

> *Comment:* To reach a conclusion about the value of the company, Clement has pieced together a number of nonmaterial or public bits of information that affect Turgot Chariots. Therefore, under the "mosaic theory," Clement has not violated Standard II(A) in drafting the report.

Example 10: The next day, Clement is preparing to be interviewed on a global financial news television program where he will discuss his changed recommendation on Turgot Chariots for the first time in public. While preparing for the program, he mentions to the show's producers and Mary Zito, the journalist who will be interviewing him, the information he will be discussing. Just prior to going on the air, Zito sells her holdings in Turgot Chariots.

> *Comment:* Zito knows that Clement's opinions will have a strong influence on the stock's behavior, so when she receives advanced notice of Clement's change of opinion, she knows it will have a material impact on the stock price, even if she is not totally aware of Clement's underlying reasoning. She is not a client of Clement but obtains early access to the material nonpublic information prior to publication. Her actions are thus trades based on material nonpublic information and violate Standard II(A).

Example 11: Timothy Holt is a portfolio manager for the Toro Aggressive Growth Fund, a large mutual fund with an aggressive growth mandate. As a result, the fund is heavily invested in small-cap companies with strong growth potential. Based on an unfavorable analysis of McCardell Industries by his research department, Holt decides to liquidate the fund's holdings in the company. Holt knows that this action will be widely viewed as negative by the market and that the company's stock is likely to plunge. He contacts several family members to tell them to liquidate any of their holdings before Toro's holdings are sold.

Comment: Holt knows that Toro's trades have a strong influence on the market. Therefore, when he tells his family to sell stock in advance of Toro's trade, he has violated Standard II(A) by causing others to trade on material nonpublic information.

Example 12: Holt executes his sell order of McCardell Industries with Toro's broker, Karim Ahmed. Ahmed immediately recognizes the likely effect this order will have on the stock price of McCardell and sells his own holdings in the company prior to placing the order.

Comment: Ahmed has violated Standard II(A) by trading on material nonpublic information.

B. Market Manipulation

Members and candidates must not engage in practices that distort prices or artificially inflate trading volume with the intent to mislead market participants.

Standard II(B) requires that members and candidates uphold market integrity by prohibiting market manipulation. Market manipulation includes practices that distort security prices or trading volume with the intent to deceive people or entities that rely on information in the market. Market manipulation damages the interests of all investors by disrupting the smooth functioning of financial markets and damaging investor confidence. Although it may be less likely to occur in more mature financial markets, cross-border investing increasingly exposes all global investors to the potential for such practices.

Market manipulation can be related to (1) transactions that deceive market participants by distorting the price-setting mechanism of financial instruments or (2) the dissemination of false or misleading information. The development of new products and technologies enhances the incentives, means, and opportunities for market manipulation.

Transaction-based manipulation includes, but is not limited to:

▶ transactions that artificially distort prices or volume to give the impression of activity or price movement in a financial instrument and

▶ securing a controlling, dominant position in a financial instrument to exploit and manipulate the price of a related derivative and/or the underlying asset.

By requiring that violations include the intent to mislead by creating artificial price or volume levels, this standard is not meant to prohibit legitimate trading strategies that exploit a difference in market power, information, or other market inefficiencies. Legitimate orders in a thinly traded security could overwhelm the liquidity for that security, which would be different from efforts to artificially affect the price of the security at the close of trading. In addition, this standard is not meant to prohibit transactions done for tax purposes, such as selling and immediately buying back a particular stock. The intent of the action is critical to determining whether it is a violation of this standard.

Information-based manipulation includes, but is not limited to, spreading false rumors to induce trading by others. For example, members and candidates must refrain from "pumping up" the price of an investment by issuing misleading positive information or overly optimistic projections of a security's worth only to later "dump" ownership in the investment once the price of the stock, fueled by the misleading information's effect on other market participants, reaches an artificially high level.

Application of the Standard

Example 1: The principal owner of Financial Information Services (FIS) entered into an agreement with two microcap companies to promote the companies' stock in exchange for stock and cash compensation. The principal owner caused FIS to disseminate e-mails, design and maintain several Internet websites, and distribute an online investment newsletter—all of which recommended investment in the two companies. The systematic publication of purportedly independent analysis and recommendations containing inaccurate and highly promotional and speculative statements increased public investment in the companies and led to dramatically higher stock prices.

> *Comment:* The principal owner of FIS violated Standard II(B) by using inaccurate reporting and misleading information under the guise of independent analysis to artificially increase the stock price of the companies. Furthermore, the principal owner violated Standard V(A) by not having a reasonable and adequate basis for recommending the two companies and violated Standard VI(A) by not disclosing to investors the compensation agreements (which constituted a conflict of interest).

Example 2: An employee of a broker/dealer acquired a significant ownership interest in several publicly traded microcap stocks and held that stock in various brokerage accounts in which the broker/dealer had a controlling interest. The employee orchestrated the manipulation of the stock price by artificially increasing the bid price for the stock through transactions among the various accounts.

> *Comment:* The employee of the broker/dealer violated Standard II(B) by distorting the price of the stock through false trading and manipulative sales practices.

Example 3: Matthew Murphy is an analyst at Divisadero Securities & Co., which has a significant number of hedge funds among its most important brokerage clients. Two trading days before the publication of the quarter-end report, Murphy alerts his sales force that he is about to issue a research report on Wirewolf Semiconductor, which will include his opinion that:

▶ quarterly revenues are likely to fall short of management's guidance;

▶ earnings will be as much as 5 cents per share (or more than 10 percent) below consensus; and

▶ Wirewolf's highly respected chief financial officer may be about to join another company.

Knowing that Wirewolf had already entered its declared quarter-end "quiet period" before reporting earnings (and thus would be reluctant to respond to rumors, etc.), Murphy times the release of his research report specifically to sensationalize the negative aspects of the message to create significant downward pressure on Wirewolf's stock to the distinct advantage of Divisadero's hedge fund clients. The report's conclusions are based on speculation, not on fact. The next day, the research report is broadcast to all of Divisadero's clients and to the usual newswire services.

Before Wirewolf's investor-relations department can assess its damage on the final trading day of the quarter and refute Murphy's report, its stock opens trading sharply lower, allowing Divisadero's clients to cover their short positions at substantial gains.

> *Comment:* Murphy violated Standard II(B) by trying to create artificial price volatility designed to have material impact on the price of an issuer's stock.

Moreover, by lacking an adequate basis for the recommendation, Murphy also violated Standard V(A).

Example 4: Rajesh Sekar manages two funds—an equity fund and a balanced fund—whose equity components are supposed to be managed following the same model. According to that model, the funds' holdings in stock CD are excessive. Reduction of CD holdings would not be easy because the stock has low liquidity in the stock market. Sekar decides to start trading larger portions of CD stock back and forth between his two funds to slowly increase the price, believing that market participants would see growing volume and increasing price and become interested in the stock. If other investors are willing to buy the CD stock because of such interest, then Sekar would be able to get rid of at least some part of his overweight position without inducing price decreases, so the whole transaction would be for the benefit of fund participants, even if additional brokers' commissions are accounted for.

> *Comment:* Sekar's plan would be beneficial for his funds' participants but is based on artificial distortion of both trading volume and price of CD stock and therefore constitutes a violation of Standard II(B).

Example 5: Sergei Gonchar is the chairman of the ACME Futures Exchange, which seeks to launch a new bond futures contract. In order to convince investors, traders, arbitragers, hedgers, and so on to use its contract, the exchange attempts to demonstrate that it has the best liquidity. To do so, it enters into agreements with members so that they commit to a substantial minimum trading volume on the new contract over a specific period in exchange for substantial reductions on their regular commissions.

> *Comment:* Formal liquidity on a market is determined by the obligations set on market makers, but the actual liquidity of a market is better estimated by the actual trading volume and bid-ask spreads. Attempts to mislead participants on the actual liquidity of the market constitute a violation of Standard II(B). In this example, investors have been intentionally misled to believe they chose the most liquid instrument for some specific purpose and could eventually see the actual liquidity of the contract dry up suddenly after the term of the agreement if the "pump-priming" strategy fails. If ACME fully discloses its agreement with members to boost transactions over some initial launch period, it does not violate Standard II(B). ACME's intent is not to harm investors but on the contrary to give them a better service. For that purpose, it may engage in a liquidity-pumping strategy, but it must be disclosed.

Example 6: Emily Gordon is a household products analyst employed by a research boutique, Picador & Co. Based on information that she has picked up during a trip through Latin America, she believes that Hygene, Inc., a major marketer of personal care products, has generated better-than-expected sales from its new product initiatives in South America. After modestly boosting her revenue and gross profit margin projections in her worksheet models for Hygene, Gordon estimates that her earnings projection of $2.00 per diluted share for the current year may be as much as 5 percent too low. She contacts the CFO of Hygene to try to gain confirmation of her findings from her trip and to get some feedback regarding her revised models. The CFO declines to comment and reiterates management's most recent guidance of $1.95 to $2.05 for the year.

Gordon decides to try to force a comment from the company by telling Picador & Co. clients who follow a momentum investment style that consensus earnings projections for Hygene are much too low, and that she's considering raising her published estimate by an ambitious $0.15 to $2.15 per share. She believes that, when word of an unrealistically high earnings projection filters back to Hygene's investor relations department, the company will feel compelled to update its earnings guidance. Meanwhile, Gordon hopes that she is at least correct with respect to the earnings direction and that she will help clients that act on her insights to profit from a quick gain trading on her advice.

Comment: By exaggerating her earnings projections in order to try to fuel a quick gain in Hygene's stock price, Gordon is in violation of Standard II(B). Furthermore, by virtue of previewing to only a select group of clients her intentions of revising upward her earnings projections, she is in violation of Standard III(B). It would have been acceptable for Gordon to have instead written a report that:

▶ framed her earnings projection in a range of possible outcomes;

▶ outlined clearly her assumptions used in her Hygene models that took into consideration the findings from her trip through Latin America; and

▶ distributed the report to all Picador & Co. clients in an equitable manner.

Example 7: In an effort to pump up the price of his holdings in Moosehead & Belfast Railroad Company, Steve Weinberg logs on to several investor chat rooms on the Internet to start rumors that the company is about to expand its rail network in anticipation of receiving a large contract for shipping lumber.

Comment: Weinberg has violated Standard II(B) by disseminating false information about Moosehead & Belfast with the intent to mislead market participants.

STANDARD III—DUTIES TO CLIENTS

A. Loyalty, Prudence, and Care

Members and candidates have a duty of loyalty to their clients and must act with reasonable care and exercise prudent judgment. Members and candidates must act for the benefit of their clients and place their clients' interests before their employer's or their own interests. In relationships with clients, members and candidates must determine applicable fiduciary duty and must comply with such duty to persons and interests to whom it is owed.

Standard III(A) clarifies that client interests are paramount. A member's or candidate's responsibility to a client includes a duty of loyalty and a duty to exercise reasonable care. Investment actions must be carried out for the sole benefit of the client and in a manner the manager believes to be in the best interest of the client, given the known facts and circumstances. Members and candidates must exercise the same level of prudence, judgment, and care that they would apply in the management and disposition of their own interests under similar circumstances.

Prudence requires caution and discretion. The exercise of prudence by an investment professional requires that they must act with the care, skill, and diligence under the circumstances that a reasonable person acting in a like capacity and familiar with such matters would use. In the context of managing a client's portfolio, prudence requires following the investment parameters set forth by the client and balancing risk and return. Acting with care requires members and candidates to act in a prudent and judicious manner in avoiding harm to clients.

Standard III(A) also requires members and candidates to understand and adhere to any legally imposed fiduciary responsibility they assume with each client. Fiduciary duties are often imposed by law or regulation when an individual or institution is charged with the duty of acting for the benefit of another party, such as managing of investment assets. The duty required in fiduciary relationships exceeds what is acceptable in many other business relationships because the fiduciary is in an enhanced position of trust. Members and candidates must abide by any fiduciary duty legally imposed on them.

The first step for members and candidates in fulfilling their duty of loyalty to clients is to determine the identity of the "client" to whom the duty of loyalty is owed. In the context of an investment manager managing the personal assets of an individual, the client is easily identified. When the manager is responsible for the portfolios of pension plans or trusts, however, the client is not the person or entity who hires the manager but, rather, the beneficiaries of the plan or trust. The duty of loyalty is owed to the ultimate beneficiaries and not just the client.

Members and candidates must also be aware of whether they have "custody" or effective control of client assets. If so, a heightened level of responsibility arises. Members and candidates are considered to have custody if they have any direct or indirect access to client funds. Members and candidates must manage any pool of assets in their control in accordance with the terms of the governing documents (such as trust documents and investment management agreements), which are the primary determinant of the manager's powers and duties. Whenever their actions are contrary to provisions of those instruments or applicable law, members and candidates are exposed to potential violations of the standard.

Situations involving potential conflicts of interest with respect to responsibilities to clients can be extremely complex because they can involve a number of competing interests. The duty of loyalty, prudence, and care applies to a large number of persons in varying capacities, but the exact duties may differ in many respects, depending on the nature of the relationship with the client or the type of account under which the assets are managed. Members and candidates must put their obligation to clients first in all dealings. In addition, members and candidates should endeavor to avoid all real or potential conflicts of interest and forgo using opportunities for their own benefit at the expense of those to whom their duty of loyalty is owed.

The duty of loyalty, prudence, and care owed to the individual client is especially important because the professional investment manager typically possesses greater knowledge than the client. This disparity places the individual client in a vulnerable position of trust. The manager in these situations should ensure that the client's objectives and expectations for the performance of the account are realistic and suitable to the client's circumstances and that the risks involved are appropriate. In most circumstances, recommended investment strategies should relate to the long-term objectives and circumstances of the client. Particular care must be taken to ensure that the goals of the investment manager or the firm in placing business, selling products, or executing security transactions do not conflict with the best interests and objectives of the client.

Members and candidates must follow any guidelines set out by their clients for the management of their assets. Some clients, such as charitable organizations and pension plans, have strict investment policies that limit investment options to certain types or classes of investments or prohibit investments in certain securities. Other organizations have aggressive policies that do not prohibit investments by type but instead set criteria on the basis of the portfolio's total risk and return.

Investment decisions may be judged in the context of the total portfolio rather than by individual investments within the portfolio. The member's or candidate's duty is satisfied with respect to a particular investment if they have thoroughly considered the investment's place in the overall portfolio, the risk of loss and opportunity for gains, tax implications, and the diversification, liquidity, cash flow, and overall return requirements of the assets or the portion of the assets for which the manager is responsible.

The duty of loyalty, prudence, and care can apply in a number of other situations faced by the investment professional other than with issues related directly to investing assets.

Part of a member's or candidate's duty of loyalty includes voting proxies in an informed and responsible manner. Proxies have economic value to a client, and members and candidates must ensure that they properly safeguard and maximize this value. A fiduciary who fails to vote, casts a vote without considering the impact of the question, or votes blindly with management on nonroutine governance issues (e.g., a change in firm capitalization) may violate this standard. Voting of proxies is an integral part of the management of investments. A cost-benefit analysis may show that voting all proxies may not benefit the client, so voting proxies may not be necessary in all instances. Members and candidates should disclose to clients their proxy-voting policies.

An investment manager often has discretion over the selection of brokers executing transactions. Conflicts arise when an investment manager uses client brokerage to purchase research services that benefit the investment manager, a practice commonly called "soft dollars" or "soft commissions." Whenever a manager uses client brokerage to purchase goods or services that do not benefit the client, the manager should disclose to clients the method or policies followed by the manager in addressing the potential conflict. A manager who pays a higher commission than he or she would normally pay to purchase goods or services, without corresponding benefit to the client, violates the duty of loyalty to the client.

From time to time, a manager's client will direct the manager to use the client's brokerage to purchase goods or services for the client, a practice that is commonly called "directed brokerage." Because brokerage is an asset of the client and is used to benefit that client, not the manager, such practice does not violate any duty of loyalty. In such situations, the manager is obligated to seek best price and execution and be assured by the client that the goods or services purchased with brokerage will benefit the account beneficiaries, and the manager should disclose to client that they may not be getting best execution.

Recommended Procedures for Compliance

Members and candidates with control of client assets should submit to each client, at least quarterly, an itemized statement showing the funds and securities in the custody or possession of the member or candidate, plus all debits, credits, and transactions that occurred during the period; disclose to the client where the assets are to be maintained, as well as where or when they are moved; and separate the client's assets from any other party's assets, including the member's or candidate's own assets.

Members and candidates should review investments periodically to ensure compliance with the terms of the governing documents.

Members and candidates should establish policies and procedures with respect to proxy voting and the use of client brokerage, including soft dollars.

If a member or candidate is uncertain about the appropriate course of action with respect to a client, the member or candidate should ask what he or she would expect or demand if the member or candidate were the client. If in doubt, a member or candidate should disclose the questionable matter in writing and obtain client approval.

Members and candidates should address and encourage their firms to address the following topics when drafting their policies and procedures statements or manuals regarding responsibilities to clients:

▶ Follow all applicable rules and laws. Members and candidates must follow all legal requirements and applicable provisions of the CFA Institute Code of Ethics and Standards of Professional Conduct.

▶ Establish the investment objectives of the client. When taking investment actions, members and candidates must consider the appropriateness and suitability of the portfolio relative to (1) the client's needs and circumstances or (2) the investment's basic characteristics or (3) the basic characteristics of the total portfolio.

▶ Diversify. Members and candidates should diversify investments to reduce the risk of loss, unless diversification is not consistent with plan guidelines or is contrary to the account objectives.

▶ Deal fairly with all clients with respect to investment actions. Members and candidates must not favor some clients over others and should establish policies for allocating trades and disseminating investment recommendations.

▶ Disclose conflicts of interest. Members and candidates must disclose all actual and potential conflicts of interest so that clients can evaluate those conflicts.

▶ Disclose compensation arrangements. Members and candidates should make their clients aware of all forms of manager compensation.

▶ Vote proxies. Members and candidates should determine who is authorized to vote shares and vote proxies in the best interest of the clients and ultimate beneficiaries.

▶ Maintain confidentiality. Members and candidates must preserve the confidentiality of client information.

▶ Seek best execution. Members and candidates must seek best execution for their clients. Best execution refers to the trading process firms apply that seeks to maximize the value of a client's portfolio within the client's stated investment objectives and constraints.

▶ Place client interests first. Members and candidates must serve the best interest of the clients.

Application of the Standard

Example 1: First Country Bank serves as trustee for the Miller Company's pension plan. Miller is the target of a hostile takeover attempt by Newton, Inc. In attempting to ward off Newton, Miller's managers persuade Julian Wiley, an investment manager at First Country Bank, to purchase Miller common stock in the open market for the employee pension plan. Miller's officials indicate that such action would be favorably received and would probably result in other accounts being placed with the bank. Although Wiley believes the stock to be overvalued and would not ordinarily buy it, he purchases the stock to support Miller's managers, to maintain the company's good favor, and to realize additional new business. The heavy stock purchases cause Miller's market price to rise to such a level that Newton retracts its takeover bid.

Comment: Standard III(A) requires that a member or candidate, in evaluating a takeover bid, act prudently and solely in the interests of plan participants and beneficiaries. To meet this requirement, a member or candidate must carefully evaluate the long-term prospects of the company against the short-term prospects presented by the takeover offer and by the ability to invest elsewhere. In this instance, Wiley, acting on behalf of his employer, the trustee, clearly violated Standard III(A) by using the profit-sharing plan to perpetuate existing management, perhaps to the detriment of plan participants and the company's shareholders, and to benefit himself. Wiley's responsibilities to the plan participants and beneficiaries should take precedence over any ties to corporate managers and self-interest. A duty exists to examine such a takeover offer on its own merits and to make an independent decision. The guiding principle is the appropriateness of the investment decision to the pension plan, not whether the decision benefits Wiley or the company that hired him.

Example 2: JNI, a successful investment counseling firm, serves as investment manager for the pension plans of several large, regionally based companies. Its trading activities generate a significant amount of commission-related business. JNI uses the brokerage and research services of many firms, but most of its trading activity is handled through a large brokerage company, Thompson, Inc., principally because of close personal relationships between the executives of the two firms. Thompson's commission structure is high in comparison with charges for similar brokerage services from other firms. JNI considers Thompson's research services and execution capabilities average. In exchange for JNI directing its brokerage to Thompson, Thompson absorbs a number of JNI overhead expenses, including those for rent.

Comment: JNI executives breached their fiduciary duty by using client brokerage for services that do not benefit JNI clients and by not obtaining best price and execution for their clients. Because JNI executives failed to uphold their duty of loyalty, they violated Standard III(A).

Example 3: Charlotte Everett, a struggling independent investment advisor, serves as investment manager for the pension plans of several companies. One of her brokers, Scott Company, is close to consummating management agreements with prospective new clients whereby Everett would manage the new client accounts and trade the accounts exclusively through Scott. One of Everett's existing clients, Crayton Corporation, has directed Everett to place securities transactions for Crayton's account exclusively through Scott. But to induce Scott to exert efforts to land more new accounts for her, Everett also directs transactions to Scott from other clients without their knowledge.

Comment: Everett has an obligation at all times to seek best price and execution on all trades. Everett may direct new client trades exclusively through Scott Company as long as Everett receives best price and execution on the trades or receives a written statement from new clients that she is not to seek best price and execution and that they are aware of the consequence for their accounts. Everett may trade other accounts through Scott as a reward for directing clients to Everett only if the accounts receive best price and execution and the practice is disclosed to the accounts. Because Everett did not disclose the directed trading, Everett has violated Standard III(A).

Example 4: Emilie Rome is a trust officer for Paget Trust Company. Rome's supervisor is responsible for reviewing Rome's trust account transactions and her monthly reports of personal stock transactions. Rome has been using Nathan Gray, a broker, almost exclusively for trust account brokerage transactions.

Where Gray makes a market in stocks, he has been giving Rome a lower price for personal purchases and a higher price for sales than he gives to Rome's trust accounts and other investors.

> *Comment:* Rome is violating her duty of loyalty to the bank's trust accounts by using Gray for brokerage transactions simply because Gray trades Rome's personal account on favorable terms.

Example 5: Lauren Parker, an analyst with Provo Advisors, covers South American equities for the firm. She likes to travel to the markets for which she is responsible and decides to go on a briefing trip to Chile, Argentina, and Brazil. The trip is sponsored by SouthAM, Inc., a research firm with a small broker/dealer affiliate that uses the clearing facilities of a larger New York brokerage house. SouthAM specializes in arranging South American trips for analysts during which they can meet with central bank officials, government ministers, local economists, and senior executives of corporations. SouthAM accepts commission dollars at a ratio of 2 to 1 against the hard-dollar cost of the research fee for the trip. Parker is not sure that SouthAM's execution is competitive but, without informing her supervisor, directs the trading desk at Provo to start giving commission business to SouthAM so she can take the trip. SouthAM has conveniently timed the briefing trip to coincide with the beginning of Carnival season, so Parker also decides to spend five days of vacation in Rio de Janeiro at the end of the trip. Parker used commission dollars to pay for the five days of hotel expenses.

> *Comment:* Parker violated Standard III(A) by not exercising her duty of loyalty to her clients to determine whether the commissions charged by SouthAM were reasonable in relation to the benefit of the research provided by the trip and by not determining that best execution and prices can be received from SouthAM. In addition, the five extra days are not part of the research effort because they do not assist in the investment decision-making process and thus should not be paid for with client assets.

Example 6: Vida Knauss manages the portfolios of a number of high-net-worth individuals. A major part of her investment management fee is based on trading commissions. Knauss engages in extensive trading for each of her clients to ensure that she attains the minimum commission level set by her firm. While the securities purchased and sold for the clients are appropriate and fall within the acceptable asset classes for the clients, the amount of trading for each account exceeds what is necessary to accomplish the clients' investment objectives.

> *Comment:* Knauss has violated Standard III(A) because she is using the assets of her clients to benefit her firm and herself.

B. Fair Dealing

Members and candidates must deal fairly and objectively with all clients when providing investment analysis, making investment recommendations, taking investment action, or engaging in other professional activities.

Standard III(B) requires members and candidates to treat all clients fairly when disseminating investment recommendations or material changes to prior investment advice or when taking investment action with regard to general purchases, new issues, or secondary offerings. Only through the fair treatment of all parties can the investment management profession maintain the confidence of the investing public.

When an investment advisor has multiple clients, the potential exists for the advisor to favor one client over another. This favoritism may take various forms, from the quality and timing of services provided to the allocation of investment opportunities. The term "fairly" implies that the member or candidate must take care not to discriminate against any clients when disseminating investment recommendations or taking investment action. Standard III(B) does not state "equally" because members and candidates could not possibly reach all clients at exactly the same time—whether by mail, telephone, computer, facsimile, or wire. Each client has unique needs, investment criteria, and investment objectives so that not all investment opportunities are suitable for all clients. In addition, members and candidates may provide more personal, specialized, or in-depth service to clients willing to pay for premium services through higher management fees or higher levels of brokerage. Members and candidates can differentiate their services to clients, but different levels of service must not disadvantage or negatively affect clients. In addition, the different service levels should be disclosed to clients and prospective clients and be available to everyone (i.e., different service levels should not be offered selectively).

Standard III(B) covers the conduct relating to two broadly defined categories of conduct—investment recommendations and investment action.

Investment Recommendations

The first type of conduct involves members and candidates whose primary function is the preparation of investment recommendations to be disseminated either to the public or within a firm for the use of others in making investment decisions. This group includes members and candidates employed by investment counseling, advisory, or consulting firms as well as banks, brokerage firms, and insurance companies if the member's or candidate's primary responsibility is the preparation of recommendations to be acted on by others, including those in the member's or candidate's organization.

An investment recommendation is any opinion expressed by a member or candidate in regard to purchasing, selling, or holding a given security or other investment. This opinion can be disseminated to customers or clients through an initial detailed research report, through a brief update report, by addition to or deletion from a recommended list, or simply by oral communication. A recommendation that is distributed to anyone outside the organization is considered a communication for general distribution under Standard III(B).

Standard III(B) addresses the manner in which investment recommendations or changes in prior recommendations are disseminated to clients. Each member or candidate is obligated to ensure that information is disseminated in such a manner that all clients have a fair opportunity to act on every recommendation. Communicating with all clients on a uniform basis presents practical problems for members and candidates because of differences in timing and methods of communication with the various types of customers and clients. Members and candidates should encourage their firms to design an equitable system to prevent selective, discriminatory disclosure and should inform clients of what kind of communications they will receive.

The duty to clients imposed by Standard III(B) may be more critical when a member or candidate changes their recommendation than when they make an initial recommendation. Material changes in a member's or candidate's prior investment advice arising from subsequent research should be communicated to all current clients, and particularly those clients who the member or candidate knows may have acted on or been affected by the earlier advice. Clients who don't know that the member or candidate has changed a recommendation and who therefore place orders contrary to a current recommendation should be advised of the changed recommendation before the order is accepted.

Investment Actions

The second group includes those members and candidates whose primary function is taking investment action (portfolio management) based on research recommendations prepared internally or received from external sources. Investment action, like investment recommendations, can affect market value. Consequently, Standard III(B) requires that members or candidates treat all clients fairly in light of their investment objectives and circumstances. For example, when making investments in new offerings or in secondary financings, members and candidates should distribute the issues to all customers for whom the investments are appropriate in a manner consistent with the block-allocation policies of the firm. If the issue is oversubscribed, then the issue should be prorated to all subscribers. This action should be taken on a round-lot basis to avoid odd-lot distributions. In addition, if the issue is oversubscribed, members and candidates should forgo any sales to themselves or their immediate families to free up additional shares for clients.

Members and candidates must make every effort to treat all individual and institutional clients in a fair and impartial manner. A member or candidate may have multiple relationships with an institution; for example, a bank may hold many positions for a manager, such as corporate trustee, pension fund manager, manager of funds for individuals employed by the customer, loan originator, or creditor. A member or candidate must exercise care to treat clients fairly, including those with whom multiple relationships do not exist.

Members and candidates should disclose to clients and prospects the written allocation procedures they or their firms have in place and how the procedures would affect the client or prospect. The disclosure should be clear and complete so that the client can make an informed investment decision. Even when complete disclosure is made, however, members and candidates must put client interests ahead of their own. A member's or candidate's duty of fairness and loyalty to clients can never be overridden by client consent to patently unfair allocation procedures.

Treating clients fairly also means that members and candidates should not take advantage of their position in the industry to the detriment of clients. For instance, in the context of IPOs, members and candidates must make bona fide public distributions of "hot issue" securities (defined as securities of a public offering that trade at a premium in the secondary market whenever such trading commences because of the great demand for the securities). Members and candidates are prohibited from withholding such securities for their own benefit and must not use such securities as a reward or incentive to gain benefit.

Recommended Procedures for Compliance

Although Standard III(B) refers to a member's or candidate's responsibility to deal fairly and objectively with clients, members and candidates should also encourage their firms to establish compliance procedures requiring all employees who disseminate investment recommendations or take investment actions to treat customers and clients fairly. At the very least, a member or candidate should recommend appropriate procedures to management if none are in place and make management aware of possible violations of fair-dealing practices within the firm when they come to the attention of the member or candidate.

The extent of the formality and complexity of such compliance procedures depends on the nature and size of the organization and the type of securities involved. An investment advisor who is a sole proprietor and handles only discretionary accounts might not disseminate recommendations to the public, but that advisor should have formal written procedures to ensure that all clients receive fair investment action.

Good business practice dictates that initial recommendations be made available to all customers who indicate an interest. Although a member or candidate need not communicate a recommendation to all customers, the selection process by which customers receive information should be based on suitability and known interest, not on any preferred or favored status. A common practice to assure fair dealing is to communicate recommendations both within the firm and to customers—simultaneously.

Members and candidates should consider the following points when establishing fair-dealing compliance procedures:

Limit the Number of People Involved

Members and candidates should make reasonable efforts to limit the number of people who are privy to the fact that a recommendation is going to be disseminated.

Shorten the Time Frame between Decision and Dissemination

Members and candidates should make reasonable efforts to limit the amount of time that elapses between the decision to make an investment recommendation and the time the actual recommendation is disseminated. If a detailed institutional recommendation is in preparation that might take two or three weeks to publish, a short summary report including the conclusion might be published in advance. In an organization where both a research committee and investment policy committee must approve a recommendation, the meetings should be held on the same day if possible. The process of reviewing, printing, and mailing reports or faxing or distributing them by e-mail necessarily involves the passage of time, sometimes long periods of time. In large firms with extensive review processes, the time factor is usually not within the control of the analyst who prepares the report. Thus, many firms and their analysts communicate to customers and firm personnel the new or changed recommendations by an update or "flash" report. The communication technique might be fax, e-mail, wire, or short written report.

Publish Personnel Guidelines for Predissemination

Members and candidates should establish guidelines that prohibit personnel who have prior knowledge of an investment recommendation from discussing or taking any action on the pending recommendation.

Simultaneous Dissemination

Members and candidates should establish procedures for dissemination of investment recommendations so that all clients are treated fairly—that is, with the goal of informing them at approximately the same time. For example, if a firm is going to announce a new recommendation, supervisory personnel should time the announcement to avoid placing any client or group of clients at unfair advantage relative to other clients. A communication to all branch offices should be sent at the time of the general announcement. When appropriate, the firm should accompany the announcement of a new recommendation with a statement that trading restrictions for the firm's employees are now in effect. The trading restrictions should stay in effect until the recommendation is widely distributed by communicating the information to all relevant clients. Once this has occurred, the member or candidate may follow up separately with individual clients, but members and candidates should not give favored clients advanced information when such prenotification may disadvantage other clients.

Maintain a List of Clients and Their Holdings

Members and candidates should maintain a list of all clients and the securities or other investments each client holds in order to facilitate notification of customers or clients of a change in an investment recommendation. If a particular security or other investment is to be sold, such a list could be used to ensure that all holders are treated fairly in the liquidation of that particular investment.

Develop Written Trade Allocation Procedures

When formulating procedures for allocating trades, members and candidates should develop a set of guiding principles that ensure:

- ▶ fairness to advisory clients, both in priority of execution of orders and in the allocation of the price obtained in execution on block orders or trades;
- ▶ timeliness and efficiency in the execution of orders;
- ▶ accuracy of the member's or candidate's records as to trade orders and client account positions.

With these principles in mind, members and candidates should develop or encourage their firm to develop written allocation procedures, with particular attention to procedures for block trades and new issues. Members and candidates should consider the following procedures:

- ▶ requiring orders and modifications or cancellations of orders to be in writing and time stamped;
- ▶ processing and executing orders on a first-in, first-out basis;
- ▶ developing a policy to address such issues as calculating execution prices and "partial fills" when trades are grouped, or blocked, for efficiency purposes;
- ▶ giving all client accounts participating in a block trade the same execution price and charging the same commission;
- ▶ when the full amount of the block order is not executed, allocating partially executed orders among the participating client accounts pro rata on the basis of order size;
- ▶ when allocating trades for new issues, obtaining advance indications of interest, allocating securities by client (rather than portfolio manager), and providing for a method for calculating allocations.

Disclose Trade Allocation Procedures

Members and candidates should disclose to clients and prospective clients how they select accounts to participate in an order and how they determine the amount of securities each account will buy or sell. Trade allocation procedures must be fair and equitable, and disclosure of inequitable allocation methods does not relieve this obligation.

Establish Systematic Account Review

Member and candidate supervisors should review each account on a regular basis to ensure that no client or customer is being given preferential treatment and that the investment actions taken for each account are suitable for the account's objectives. Because investments should be based on individual needs and circumstances, an investment manager may have good reasons for placing a given security or other investment in one account while selling it from another account. However, members and candidates should encourage firms to establish review procedures to detect whether trading in one account is being used to benefit a favored client.

Disclose Levels of Service

Members and candidates should disclose to all clients whether or not the organization offers different levels of service to clients for the same fee or different fees. Different levels of service should not be offered to clients selectively.

Application of the Standard

Example 1: Bradley Ames, a well-known and respected analyst, follows the computer industry. In the course of his research, he finds that a small, relatively unknown company whose shares are traded over the counter has just signed significant contracts with some of the companies he follows. After a considerable amount of investigation, Ames decides to write a research report on the company and recommend purchase. While the report is being reviewed by the company for factual accuracy, Ames schedules a luncheon with several of his best clients to discuss the company. At the luncheon, he mentions the purchase recommendation scheduled to be sent early the following week to all the firm's clients.

> *Comment:* Ames violated Standard III(B) by disseminating the purchase recommendation to the clients with whom he had lunch a week before the recommendation was sent to all clients.

Example 2: Spencer Rivers, president of XYZ Corporation, moves his company's growth-oriented pension fund to a particular bank primarily because of the excellent investment performance achieved by the bank's commingled fund for the prior five-year period. A few years later, Rivers compares the results of his pension fund with those of the bank's commingled fund. He is startled to learn that, even though the two accounts have the same investment objectives and similar portfolios, his company's pension fund has significantly underperformed the bank's commingled fund. Questioning this result at his next meeting with the pension fund's manager, Rivers is told that, as a matter of policy, when a new security is placed on the recommended list, Morgan Jackson, the pension fund manager, first purchases the security for the commingled account and then purchases it on a pro rata basis for all other pension fund accounts. Similarly, when a sale is recommended, the security is sold first from the commingled account and then sold on a pro rata basis from all other accounts. Rivers also learns that if the bank cannot get enough shares (especially the hot issues) to be meaningful to all the accounts, its policy is to place the new issues only in the commingled account.

Seeing that Rivers is neither satisfied nor pleased by the explanation, Jackson quickly adds that nondiscretionary pension accounts and personal trust accounts have a lower priority on purchase and sale recommendations than discretionary pension fund accounts. Furthermore, Jackson states, the company's pension fund had the opportunity to invest up to 5 percent in the commingled fund.

Comment: The bank's policy did not treat all customers fairly, and Jackson violated her duty to her clients by giving priority to the growth-oriented commingled fund over all other funds and to discretionary accounts over nondiscretionary accounts. Jackson must execute orders on a systematic basis that is fair to all clients. In addition, trade allocation procedures should be disclosed to all clients from the beginning. Of course, in this case, disclosure of the bank's policy would not change the fact that the policy is unfair.

Example 3: Dominic Morris works for a small regional securities firm. His work consists of corporate finance activities and investing for institutional clients. Arena, Ltd., is planning to go public. The partners have secured rights to buy an arena football league franchise and are planning to use the funds from the issue to complete the purchase. Because arena football is the current rage, Morris believes he has a hot issue on his hands. He has quietly negotiated some options for himself for helping convince Arena to do the financing. When he seeks expressions of interest, the institutional buyers oversubscribe the issue. Morris, assuming that the institutions have the financial clout to drive the stock up, then fills all orders (including his own) and cuts back the institutional blocks.

Comment: Morris has violated Standard III(B) by not treating all customers fairly. He should not have taken any shares himself and should have prorated the shares offered among all clients. In addition, he should have disclosed to his firm and to his clients that he had received options as part of the deal [see Standard VI(A)—Disclosure of Conflicts].

Example 4: Eleanor Preston, the chief investment officer of Porter Williams Investments (PWI), a medium-sized money management firm, has been trying to retain a difficult client, Colby Company. Management at the disgruntled client, which accounts for almost half of PWI's revenues, recently told Preston that if the performance of its account did not improve, it would find a new money manager. Shortly after this threat, Preston purchases mortgage-backed securities (MBS) for several accounts, including Colby's. Preston is busy with a number of transactions that day, so she fails to allocate the trades immediately or write up the trade tickets. A few days later, when Preston is allocating trades, she notes that some of the MBS have significantly increased in price and some have dropped. Preston decides to allocate the profitable trades to Colby and spread the losing trades among several other PWI accounts.

Comment: Preston violated Standard III(B) by failing to deal fairly with her clients in taking these investment actions. Preston should have allocated the trades prior to executing the orders, or she should have had a systematic approach to allocating the trades, such as pro rata, as soon after they were executed as practicable. Among other things, Preston must disclose to the client that the advisor may act as broker for, receive commissions from, and have a potential conflict of interest regarding both parties in agency cross-transactions. After the disclosure, she should obtain from the client consent authorizing such transactions in advance.

Example 5: Saunders Industrial Waste Management (SIWM) publicly indicates to analysts that it is comfortable with the somewhat disappointing earnings per share projection of $1.15 for the quarter. Bernard Roberts, an analyst at Coffey Investments, is confident that SIWM management has understated the forecasted earnings so that the real announcement would cause an "upside surprise" and boost the price of SIWM stock. The "whisper number" estimate based on extensive research and discussed among knowledgeable analysts is higher than $1.15. Roberts repeats the $1.15 figure in his research report to all Coffey clients but informally tells his larger clients that he expects the earnings per share to be higher, making SIWM a good buy.

> *Comment:* By not sharing his opinion regarding the potential for a significant upside earnings surprise with all clients, Roberts is not treating all clients fairly and has violated Standard III(B).

Example 6: Jenpin Weng uses e-mail to issue a new recommendation to all his clients. He then calls his three biggest institutional clients to discuss the recommendation in detail.

> *Comment:* Weng has not violated Standard III(B) because he widely disseminated the recommendation and provided the information to all his clients prior to discussing it with a select few. Weng's larger clients received additional personal service that they presumably pay for through bigger fees or because they have a large amount of assets under Weng's management. Weng would have violated Standard III(B) if he had discussed the report with a select group of clients prior to distributing it to all his clients.

C. Suitability

1. **When members and candidates are in an advisory relationship with a client, they must:**
   a. **Make a reasonable inquiry into a client's or prospective client's investment experience, risk and return objectives, and financial constraints prior to making any investment recommendation or taking investment action and must reassess and update this information regularly.**
   b. **Determine that an investment is suitable to the client's financial situation and consistent with the client's written objectives, mandates, and constraints prior to making an investment recommendation or taking investment action.**
   c. **Judge the suitability of investments in the context of the client's total portfolio.**
2. **When members and candidates are responsible for managing a portfolio to a specific mandate, strategy, or style, they must only make investment recommendations or take investment actions that are consistent with the stated objectives and constraints of the portfolio.**

Standard III(C) requires that members and candidates who are in an investment advisory relationship with clients consider carefully the needs, circumstances, and objectives of the clients when determining the appropriateness and suitability of a given investment or course of investment action.

The responsibilities conferred upon members and candidates to gather information and make a suitability analysis prior to making a recommendation or taking investment action falls on those members and candidates who provide investment advice in the course of an advisory relationship with a client. Other members and candidates often are simply executing specific instructions for retail clients when buying or selling securities, such as shares in mutual funds. These members and candidates and others, such as sell-side analysts, may not have the opportunity to judge the suitability of the particular investment for the person or entity. In cases of unsolicited trade requests that a member or candidate knows are unsuitable for the client, the member or candidate should refrain from making the trade or seek an affirmative statement from the client that suitability is not a consideration.

When an advisory relationship exists, members and candidates must gather client information at the inception of the relationship. Such information includes the client's financial circumstances, personal data (such as age and occupation) that are relevant to investment decisions, attitudes toward risk, and objectives in investing. This information should be incorporated into a written investment policy statement (IPS) that addresses the client's risk tolerance, return requirements, and all investment constraints (including time horizon, liquidity needs, tax concerns, legal and regulatory factors, and unique circumstances). Without identifying such client factors, members and candidates cannot judge whether a particular investment or strategy is suitable for a particular client. The IPS also should identify and describe the roles and responsibilities of the parties to the advisory relationship and investment process, as well as schedules for review and evaluation. After formulating long-term capital market expectations, members and clients can assist in developing an appropriate strategic asset allocation and investment program for the client, whether these are presented in separate documents or incorporated in the IPS or in appendices to the IPS.

Such an inquiry should be repeated at least annually and prior to material changes to any specific investment recommendations or decisions on behalf of the client. The effort to determine the needs and circumstances of each client is not a one-time occurrence. Investment recommendations or decisions are usually part of an ongoing process that takes into account the diversity and changing nature of portfolio and client characteristics. The passage of time is bound to produce changes that are important with respect to investment objectives.

For an individual client, such changes might include the number of dependents, personal tax status, health, liquidity needs, risk tolerance, the amount of wealth beyond that represented in the portfolio, and the extent to which compensation and other income provide for current income needs. With respect to an institutional client, such changes might relate to the magnitude of unfunded liabilities in a pension fund, the withdrawal privileges in an employee's savings plan, or the distribution requirements of a charitable foundation. Without efforts to update information concerning client factors, one or more factors could change without the investment manager's knowledge.

Suitability review can be done effectively only if the client fully discloses his or her complete financial portfolio, including those portions not managed by the member or candidate. If clients withhold information about their financial portfolio, the suitability analysis conducted by members and candidates cannot be expected to be complete but must be done based on the information provided.

One of the most important factors to be considered in matching appropriateness and suitability of an investment with a client's needs and circumstances is measuring that client's tolerance for risk. The investment professional must consider the possibilities of rapidly changing investment environments and their likely impact on a client's holdings, both individual securities and the collective portfolio. The risk of many investment strategies can and should be analyzed and quantified in advance.

The use of synthetic investment vehicles and derivative investment products has introduced particular issues of risk. Members and candidates should pay careful attention to the leverage often inherent in such vehicles or products when considering them for use in a client's investment program. Such leverage and limited liquidity, depending on the degree to which they are hedged, bear directly on the issue of suitability for the client.

The investment profession has long recognized that the combination of several different investments is likely to provide a more acceptable level of risk exposure than having all assets in a single investment. The unique characteristics (or risks) of an individual investment may become partially or entirely neutralized when combined with other individual investments within a portfolio. Some

the mandate or is within the realm of investments allowable under the disclosures of the fund, Perkowski has violated Standard III(C).

Example 5: Max Gubler, CIO of a property/casualty insurance subsidiary of a large financial conglomerate, wants to better diversify the company's investment portfolio and increase its returns. The company's investment policy statement (IPS) provides for highly liquid investments, such as large-caps, governments, and supra-nationals, as well as corporate bonds with a minimum credit rating of AA– and maturity of no more than five years. In a recent presentation, a venture capital group offered very attractive prospective returns on some of their private equity funds providing seed capital. An exit strategy is already contemplated but investors will first have to observe a minimum three-year lock-up period, with a subsequent laddered exit option for a maximum of one-third of shares per year. Gubler does not want to miss this opportunity, and after an extensive analysis and optimization of this asset class with the company's current portfolio, he invests 4 percent in this seed fund, leaving the portfolio's total equity exposure still well below its upper limit.

> *Comment:* Gubler violates Standards III(A) and III(C). His new investment locks up part of the company's assets for at least three and for up to as many as five years and possibly beyond. Since the IPS requires investments in highly liquid investments and describes accepted asset classes, private equity investments with a lock-up period certainly do not qualify. Even without such a lock-up period, an asset class with only an occasional, and thus implicitly illiquid, market may not be suitable. Although an IPS typically describes objectives and constraints in great detail, the manager must make every effort to understand the client's business and circumstances. Doing so should also enable the manager to recognize, understand, and discuss with the client other factors that may be or may become material in the investment management process.

D. Performance Presentation

When communicating investment performance information, members and candidates must make reasonable efforts to make sure that it is fair, accurate, and complete.

Standard III(D) requires members and candidates to provide credible performance information to clients and prospective clients and to avoid misstating performance or misleading clients and prospective clients about the investment performance of members or candidates or their firms. This standard encourages full disclosure of investment performance data to clients and prospective clients.

Standard III(D) covers any practice that would lead to misrepresentation of a member's or candidate's performance record, whether the practice involves performance presentation or performance measurement. This standard prohibits misrepresentations of past performance or reasonably expected performance. A member or candidate must give a fair and complete presentation of performance information whenever communicating data with respect to the performance history of individual accounts, composites of groups of accounts, or composites of an analyst's or firm's performance results. Further, members and candidates should not state or imply that clients will obtain or benefit from a rate of return that was generated in the past.

The requirements of this standard are not limited to members and candidates managing separate accounts. Anytime a member or candidate provides performance information for which the manager is claiming responsibility, such as for pooled funds, the history must be accurate. Research analysts promoting the success or accuracy of their recommendations must ensure that their claims are fair, accurate, and complete.

If the presentation is brief, the member or candidate must make available to clients and prospects, upon request, the detailed information supporting that communication.

Recommended Procedures for Compliance

For members and candidates seeking to show the performance history of the assets they manage, compliance with the Global Investment Performance Standards (GIPS) is the best method to meet their obligations under Standard III(D). Members and candidates should encourage their firms to adhere to the GIPS standards.

Members and candidates can also meet their obligations under Standard III(D) by:

▶ considering the knowledge and sophistication of the audience to whom a performance presentation is addressed;

▶ presenting the performance of the weighted composite of similar portfolios rather than using a single representative account;

▶ including terminated accounts as part of performance history;

▶ including disclosures that would fully explain the performance results being reported (for example, stating, when appropriate, that results are simulated when model results are used, clearly indicating when the performance record is that of a prior entity, or disclosing whether the performance is gross of fees, net of fees, or after tax); and

▶ maintaining the data and records used to calculate the performance being presented.

Application of the Standard

Example 1: Kyle Taylor of Taylor Trust Company, noting the performance of Taylor's common trust fund for the past two years, states in a brochure sent to his potential clients that "You can expect steady 25 percent annual compound growth of the value of your investments over the year." Taylor Trust's common trust fund did increase at the rate of 25 percent per annum for the past year, which mirrored the increase of the entire market. The fund, however, never averaged that growth for more than one year, and the average rate of growth of all of its trust accounts for five years was 5 percent per annum.

> *Comment:* Taylor's brochure is in violation of Standard III(D). Taylor should have disclosed that the 25 percent growth occurred only in one year. Additionally, Taylor did not include client accounts other than those in the firm's common trust fund. A general claim of firm performance should take into account the performance of all categories of accounts. Finally, by stating that clients can expect a steady 25 percent annual compound growth rate, Taylor also violated Standard I(C), which prohibits statements of assurances or guarantees regarding an investment.

Example 2: Anna Judd, a senior partner of Alexander Capital Management, circulates a performance sheet listing performance figures for capital appreciation accounts for the years 1988 through 2004 and claiming compliance with the Global Investment Performance Standards (GIPS). Returns are not calculated in accordance with the Global Investment Performance Standards (GIPS) because the composites are not asset weighted, which is a violation of GIPS.

> *Comment:* Judd is in violation of Standard III(D). When claiming compliance with GIPS, firms must meet all the requirements and mandatory disclosures and any other additional requirements or disclosures necessary to that firm's specific situation. Judd's violation is not from any misuse of the data but from a false claim of GIPS compliance.

Example 3: Aaron McCoy is vice president and managing partner of the equity investment group of Mastermind Financial Advisors, a new business. Mastermind recruited McCoy because he had a proven six-year track record with G&P Financial. In developing Mastermind's advertising and marketing campaign, McCoy prepared an advertisement that included the equity investment performance he achieved at G&P Financial. The advertisement for Mastermind did not identify the equity performance as being earned while at G&P. The advertisement was distributed to existing clients and prospective clients of Mastermind.

> *Comment:* McCoy violated Standard III(D) by distributing an advertisement that contained material misrepresentations regarding the historical performance of Mastermind. Standard III(D) requires that members and candidates make every reasonable effort to ensure that performance information is a fair, accurate, and complete representation of an individual's or firm's performance. As a general matter, this standard does not prohibit showing past performance of funds managed at a prior firm as part of a performance track record so long as it is accompanied by appropriate disclosures detailing where the performance comes from and the person's specific role in achieving that performance. If McCoy chooses to use his past performance from G&P in Mastermind's advertising, he should make full disclosure as to the source of the historical performance.

Example 4: Jed Davis developed a mutual fund selection product based on historical information from the 1990–95 period. Davis tested his methodology by applying it retroactively to data from the 1996–2003 period, thus producing simulated performance results for those years. In January 2004, Davis's employer decided to offer the product, and Davis began promoting it through trade journal advertisements and direct dissemination to clients. The advertisements included the performance results for the 1996–2003 period but did not indicate that the results were simulated.

> *Comment:* Davis violated Standard III(D) by failing to clearly identify simulated performance results. Standard III(D) prohibits members and candidates from making any statements that misrepresent the performance achieved by them or their firms and requires members and candidates to make every reasonable effort to ensure that performance information presented to clients is fair, accurate, and complete. Use of the simulated results should be accompanied by full disclosure as to the source of the performance data, including the fact that the results from 1995 through 2003 were the result of applying the model retroactively to that time period.

Example 5: In a presentation prepared for prospective clients, William Kilmer shows the rates of return realized over a five-year period by a "composite" of his firm's discretionary accounts with a balanced objective. This "composite," however, consisted of only a few of the accounts that met the balanced criteria set by the firm, excluded accounts under a certain asset level without disclosing the fact of their exclusion, and included nonbalanced accounts that would boost investment results. In addition, to achieve better results, Kilmer manipulated the narrow range of accounts included in the composite by changing the accounts that made up the composite over time.

> *Comment:* Kilmer violated Standard III(D) by misrepresenting the facts in the promotional material sent to prospective clients, distorting his firm's performance record, and failing to include disclosure that would have clarified the presentation.

E. Preservation of Confidentiality

Members and candidates must keep information about current, former, and prospective clients confidential unless:

1. The information concerns illegal activities on the part of the client;
2. Disclosure is required by law; or
3. The client or prospective client permits disclosure of the information.

Standard III(E) requires that members and candidates preserve the confidentiality of information communicated to them by their clients, prospective clients, and former clients. This standard is applicable when (1) the member or candidate receives information on the basis of his or her special ability to conduct a portion of the client's business or personal affairs and (2) the member or candidate receives information that arises from or is relevant to that portion of the client's business that is the subject of the special or confidential relationship. If disclosure of the information is required by law or the information concerns illegal activities by the client, however, the member or candidate may have an obligation to report the activities to the appropriate authorities.

As a general matter, members and candidates must comply with applicable law. If applicable law requires disclosure of client information in certain circumstances, members and candidates must comply with the law. Similarly, if applicable law requires members and candidates to maintain confidentiality, even if the information concerns illegal activities on the part of the client, members and candidates should not disclose such information. When in doubt, members and candidates should consult with their employer's compliance personnel or outside counsel before disclosing confidential information about clients.

This standard protects the confidentiality of client information even if the person or entity is no longer a client of the member or candidate. Therefore, members and candidates must continue to maintain the confidentiality of client records even after the client relationship has ended. However, if a client or former client expressly authorizes the member or candidate to disclose information, the member or candidate may follow the terms of the authorization and provide the information.

Professional Conduct Investigations by CFA Institute

The requirements of Standard III(E) are not intended to prevent members and candidates from cooperating with an investigation by the CFA Institute Professional Conduct Program (PCP). When permissible under applicable law members and candidates shall consider the PCP an extension of themselves when requested to provide information about a client in support of a PCP investigation into their own conduct. Members and candidates are encouraged to cooperate with investigations into the conduct of others. Any information turned over to the PCP is kept in the strictest confidence.

Recommended Procedures for Compliance

The simplest, most conservative, and most effective way to comply with Standard III(E) is to avoid disclosing any information received from a client except to authorized fellow employees who are also working for the client. In some instances, however, a member or candidate may want to disclose information received from clients that is outside the scope of the confidential relationship and does not involve illegal activities. Before making such a disclosure, a member or candidate should ask the following:

▶ In what context was the information disclosed? If disclosed in a discussion of work being performed for the client, is the information relevant to the work?

▶ Is the information background material that, if disclosed, will enable the member or candidate to improve service to the client?

Application of the Standard

Example 1: Sarah Connor, a financial analyst employed by Johnson Investment Counselors, Inc., provides investment advice to the trustees of City Medical Center. The trustees have given her a number of internal reports concerning City Medical's needs for physical plant renovation and expansion. They have asked Connor to recommend investments that would generate capital appreciation in endowment funds to meet projected capital expenditures. Connor is approached by a local businessman, Thomas Kasey, who is considering a substantial contribution either to City Medical Center or to another local hospital. Kasey wants to find out the building plans of both institutions before making a decision, but he does not want to speak to the trustees.

> *Comment:* The trustees gave Connor the internal reports so she could advise them on how to manage their endowment funds. Because the information in the reports is clearly both confidential and within the scope of the confidential relationship, Standard III(E) requires that Connor refuse to divulge information to Kasey.

Example 2: Lynn Moody is an investment officer at the Lester Trust Company. She has an advisory customer who has talked to her about giving approximately $50,000 to charity to reduce her income taxes. Moody is also treasurer of the Home for Indigent Widows (HIW), which is planning its annual giving campaign. HIW hopes to expand its list of prospects, particularly those capable of substantial gifts. Moody recommends that HIW's vice president for corporate gifts call on her customer and ask for a donation in the $50,000 range.

> *Comment:* Even though the attempt to help the Home for Indigent Widows was well intended, Moody violated Standard III(E) by revealing confidential information about her client.

Example 3: Government officials approach Casey Samuel, the portfolio manager for Garcia Company's pension plan, to examine pension fund records. They tell her that Garcia's corporate tax returns are being audited and the pension fund reviewed. Two days earlier Samuel learned in a regular investment review meeting with Garcia officers that potentially excessive and improper charges are being made to the pension plan by Garcia. Samuel consults her employer's general counsel and is advised that Garcia has probably violated tax and fiduciary regulations and laws.

Comment: Samuel should inform her supervisor of these activities, and her employer should take steps, with Garcia, to remedy the violations. If that approach is not successful, Samuel and her employer should seek advice of legal counsel to determine the appropriate steps to be taken. Samuel may well have a duty to disclose the evidence she has of the continuing legal violations and to resign as asset manager for Garcia.

Example 4: David Bradford manages money for a family-owned real estate development corporation. He also manages the individual portfolios of several of the family members and officers of the corporation, including the chief financial officer (CFO). Based on the financial records from the corporation, as well as some questionable practices of the CFO that he has observed, Bradford believes that the CFO is embezzling money from the corporation and putting it into his personal investment account.

Comment: Bradford should check with his firm's compliance department as well as outside counsel to determine whether applicable securities regulations require reporting the CFO's financial records.

STANDARD IV—DUTIES TO EMPLOYERS

A. Loyalty

In matters related to their employment, members and candidates must act for the benefit of their employer and not deprive their employer of the advantage of their skills and abilities, divulge confidential information, or otherwise cause harm to their employer.

Standard IV(A) requires members and candidates to protect the interests of their firm by refraining from any conduct that would injure the firm, deprive it of profit, or deprive it of the advantage of the member's or candidate's skills and ability. Members and candidates must always place the interests of clients above the interests of their employer. Otherwise, in matters related to their employment, members and candidates must not engage in conduct that harms the interests of the employer. Implicit in this standard is the obligation of members and candidates to comply with the policies and procedures established by their employers that govern the employer-employee relationship—to the extent that such policies and procedures do not conflict with applicable laws, rules, regulations, or the Code and Standards.

This standard is not meant to be a blanket requirement to place employer interests ahead of personal interests in all matters. This standard does not require members and candidates to subordinate important personal and family obligations to their work. Members and candidates should enter into a dialogue with their employer about balancing personal and employment obligations when personal matters may interfere with their work on a regular or significant basis.

In addition, the employer-employee relationship imposes duties and responsibilities on both parties. Employers must adhere to the duties and responsibilities that they owe to their employees if they expect to have contented and productive employees.

Independent Practice

Included in Standard IV(A) is the requirement that members and candidates abstain from independent competitive activity that could conflict with the interests of their employer. Although Standard IV(A) does not preclude members or candidates from entering into an independent business while still employed, members and candidates who plan to engage in independent practice for compensation must provide notification to their employer describing the types of service the members or candidates will render to prospective independent clients, the expected duration of the services, and the compensation for the services. Members and candidates should not render services until receiving consent from their employer to all of the terms of the arrangement. "Practice" means any service that the employer currently makes available for remuneration. "Undertaking independent practice" means engaging in competitive business, as opposed to making preparations to begin such practice.

Leaving an Employer

When investment professionals plan to leave their current employer, they must continue to act in the employer's best interest and must not engage in any activities that would conflict with this duty until their resignation becomes effective. It is difficult to define specific guidelines for those members and candidates who plan to compete with their employer as part of a new venture. The circumstances of each situation must be reviewed to distinguish permissible preparations from violations of duty. Activities that might constitute a violation, especially in combination, include the following:

► misappropriation of trade secrets,

► misuse of confidential information,

► solicitation of employer's clients prior to cessation of employment,

► self-dealing (appropriating for one's own property a business opportunity, or information belonging to one's employer),

► misappropriation of clients or client lists.

A departing employee is generally free to make arrangements or preparations to go into a competitive business before terminating the relationship with his or her employer provided that such preparations do not breach the employee's duty of loyalty. However, members and candidates contemplating seeking other employment must not contact existing clients or potential clients prior to leaving their employer for purposes of soliciting their business for the new employer. In addition, they must not take records or files to a new employer without the written permission of the previous employer.

Once an employee has left the firm, the skills and experience that an employee obtains while employed are not "confidential" or "privileged" information. Similarly, simple knowledge of the names and existence of former clients is generally not confidential information unless deemed such by an agreement or by law. Standard IV(A) does not impose a prohibition on the use of experience or knowledge gained at one employer from being used at another employer. However, firm records or work performed on behalf of the firm stored on a home computer for the member's or candidate's convenience while employed should be erased or returned to the employer unless the firm gives permission to keep those records after employment ends.

Nor does the standard prohibit former employees from contacting clients of their previous firm so long as the contact information does not come from the records of the former employer or violate an applicable non-compete agreement. Members and candidates are free to use public information about their former firm after departing to contact former clients without violating Standard IV(A), absent a specific agreement not to do so.

Employers often require employees to sign "non-compete" agreements that preclude a departing employee from engaging in certain conduct. Members and candidates should take care to review the terms of any such agreements when leaving their employer to determine what, if any, conduct those agreements may prohibit.

Whistleblowing

A member's or candidate's personal interests, as well as the interests of his or her employer, are secondary to protecting the integrity of capital markets and the interests of the clients. Therefore, there may be circumstances in which members and candidates act contrary to their employer interests in an effort to comply with their duties to the market and clients (e.g., when an employer is engaged in illegal or unethical activity). In such instances, activities that would normally violate a member's or candidate's duty to his or her employer (such as contradicting employer instructions, violating certain policies and procedures, or preserving a record by copying employer records) may be justified. Such action would be permitted only if the intent is clearly aimed at protecting clients or the integrity of the market and not for personal gain.

Nature of Employment

A wide variety of business relationships exist within the investment industry. For instance, a member or candidate can be retained as an employee or independent contractor. Members and candidates must determine whether they are employees or independent contractors in order to determine the applicability of Standard IV(A). This issue will be decided largely by the degree of control exercised by the employing entity over the member or candidate. Factors determining control include whether the member's or candidate's hours, work location, and other parameters of the job are set; whether facilities are provided to the member or candidate; whether the member's or candidate's expenses are reimbursed; whether the member or candidate holds himself or herself out to other employers for additional work; and the number of clients or employers the member or candidate works for.

A member's or candidate's duties within an independent contractor relationship are governed by the oral or written agreement between the member and the client. Members and candidates should take care to define clearly the scope of their responsibilities and the expectations of each client within the context of each relationship. Once the member or candidate establishes a relationship with a client, they have a duty to abide by the terms of the agreement.

Application of the Standard

Example 1: Samuel Magee manages pension accounts for Trust Assets, Inc., but has become frustrated with the working environment and has been offered a position with Fiduciary Management. Before resigning from Trust Assets, Magee asks four big accounts to leave that firm and open accounts with Fiduciary. Magee also persuades several prospective clients to sign agreements with Fiduciary Management. Magee had previously made presentations to these prospects on behalf of Trust Assets, Inc.

Comment: Magee violated the employee-employer principle requiring him to act solely for his employer's benefit. Magee's duty is to Trust Assets as long as he is employed there. The solicitation of Trust Assets' current clients and prospective clients is unethical and violates Standard IV(A).

Example 2: James Hightower has been employed by Jason Investment Management Corporation for 15 years. He began as an analyst but assumed increasing responsibilities and is now a senior portfolio manager and a member of the firm's investment policy committee. Hightower has decided to leave Jason Investment and start his own investment management business. He has been careful not to tell any of Jason's clients that he is leaving, because he does not want to be accused of breaching his duty to Jason by soliciting Jason's clients before his departure. Hightower is planning to copy and take with him the following documents and information he developed or worked on while at Jason: (1) the client list, with addresses, telephone numbers, and other pertinent client information; (2) client account statements; (3) sample marketing presentations to prospective clients containing Jason's performance record; (4) Jason's recommended list of securities; (5) computer models to determine asset allocations for accounts with different objectives; (6) computer models for stock selection; and (7) personal computer spreadsheets for Hightower's major corporate recommendations which he developed when he was an analyst.

Comment: Except with the consent of their employer, departing employees may not take employer property, which includes books, records, reports, and other materials, and may not interfere with their employer's business opportunities. Taking any employer records, even those the member or candidate prepared, violates Standard IV(A).

Example 3: Rueben Winston manages all-equity portfolios at Target Asset Management (TAM), a large, established investment counselor. Ten years ago, Philpott & Company, which manages a family of global bond mutual funds, acquired TAM in a diversification move. After the merger, the combined operations prospered in the fixed-income business while the equity management business at TAM languished. Lately, a few of the equity pension accounts that had been with TAM before the merger have terminated their relationships with TAM. One day, Winston finds on his voice mail a message from a concerned client, "Hey! I just heard that Philpott is close to announcing the sale of your firm's equity management business to Rugged Life. What is going on?" Not being aware of any such deal, Winston and his associates are stunned. Their internal inquiries are met with denials from Philpott management, but the rumors persist. Feeling left in the dark, Winston contemplates leading an employee buyout of TAM's equity management business.

Comment: An employee-led buyout of TAM's equity asset management business would be consistent with Standard IV(A) because it would rest on the permission of the employer and, ultimately, the clients. In this case, however, in which employees suspect the senior managers or principals are not truthful or forthcoming, members should consult legal counsel to determine appropriate action.

Example 4: Laura Clay, who is unemployed, wants part-time consulting work while seeking a full-time analyst position. During an interview at Phere Associates, a large institutional asset manager, Clay is told that the firm has no immediate research openings but would be willing to pay her a flat fee to complete a study of the wireless communications industry within a given period of time. Clay would be allowed unlimited access to Phere's research files and would be welcome to come to the offices and use whatever support facilities are available during normal working hours. Phere's research director does not seek any exclusivity for Clay's output, and the two agree to the arrangement on a handshake. As Clay nears completion of the study, she is offered an analyst job in the research department of Dowt & Company, a brokerage firm, and she is pondering submitting the draft of her wireless study for publication by Dowt.

Comment: Although she is under no written contractual obligation to Phere, Clay has an obligation to let Phere act on the output of her study before Dowt & Company or Clay uses the information to its own advantage. That is, unless Phere gives permission to Clay waiving rights to her wireless report, Clay would be in violation of Standard IV(A) if she were to immediately recommend to Dowt the same transactions recommended in the report to Phere. Furthermore, Clay must not take from Phere any research file material or other property that she may have used.

Example 5: Emma Madeline, a recent college graduate and a candidate in the CFA Program, spends her summer as an unpaid intern at Murdoch and Lowell. Murdoch and Lowell is attempting to bring the firm into compliance with the GIPS standards, and Madeline is assigned to assist in its efforts. Two months into her internship, Madeline applies for a job at McMillan & Company, which has plans to become GIPS compliant. Madeline accepts the job with McMillan. Before leaving Murdoch, she copies the firm's software that she helped develop, as she believes this software will assist her in her new position.

Comment: Even though Madeline does not receive monetary compensation for her services at Murdoch, she has used firm resources in creating the software and she is considered an employee because she receives compensation and benefits in the form of work experience and knowledge. By copying the software, Madeline violated Standard IV(A) because she misappropriated Murdoch's property without permission.

Example 6: Dennis Elliot has hired Sam Chisolm who previously worked for a competing firm. Chisolm left his former firm after 18 years of employment. When Chisolm begins working for Elliot, he wants to contact his former clients because he knows them well and is certain that many will follow him to his new employer. Is Chisolm in violation of the Standard IV(A) if he contacts his former clients?

Comment: Because client records are the property of the firm, contacting former clients for any reason through the use of client lists or other information taken from a former employer without permission would be a violation of Standard IV(A). In addition, the nature and extent of the contact with former clients may be governed by the terms of any non-compete agreement signed by the employee and the former employer that covers contact with former clients after employment.

But, simple knowledge of the names and existence of former clients is not confidential information, just as skills or experience that an employee obtains while employed is not "confidential" or "privileged" information. The Code and Standards do not impose a prohibition on the use of experience or knowledge gained at one employer from being used at another employer. The Code and Standards also do not prohibit former employees from contacting clients of their previous firm, absent a non-compete agreement. Members and candidates are free to use public information about their former firm after departing to contact former clients without violating Standard IV(A).

In the absence of a non-compete agreement, as long as Chisolm maintains his duty of loyalty to his employer before joining Elliot's firm, does not take steps to solicit clients until he has left his former firm, and does not make use of material from his former employer without its permission after he has left, he would not be in violation of the Code and Standards.

Example 7: Gardner Allen currently works at a registered investment company as an equity analyst. Without notice to her employer, she registers with government authorities to start an investment company that will compete with her employer. However, she has not actively sought clients. Does registration of this competing company with the appropriate regulatory authorities constitute a violation of Standard IV(A)?

> *Comment:* Allen's preparations for the new business by registering with the regulatory authorities do not conflict with the work for her employer if the preparations have been done on Allen's own time outside of the office and if Allen will not be getting clients for the business or otherwise operating the new company until she has left her current employer.

Example 8: Several employees are planning to depart their current employer within a few weeks and have been careful to not engage in any activities that would conflict with their duty to their current employer. They have just learned that one of their employer's clients has undertaken a request for proposal (RFP) to review and possibly hire a new investment consultant. The RFP has been sent to the employer and all of its competitors. The group believes that the new entity to be formed would be qualified to respond to the RFP and eligible for the business. The RFP submission period is likely to conclude before the employees' resignations are effective. Is it permissible for the group of departing employees to respond to the RFP under their anticipated new firm?

> *Comment:* A group of employees responding to an RFP that their employer is also responding to would lead to direct competition between the employees and the employer. Such conduct would violate Standard IV(A) unless the group of employees received permission from their employer as well as the entity sending out the RFP.

Example 9: Alfonso Mota is a research analyst with Tyson Investments. He works part time as a mayor for his hometown, a position for which he receives compensation. Must Mota seek permission from Tyson to serve as mayor?

> *Comment:* If Mota's mayoral duties are so extensive and time consuming that they might detract from his ability to fulfill his responsibilities at Tyson, he should discuss his outside activities with his employer and come to a mutual agreement regarding how to manage his personal commitments with his responsibilities to his employer.

Example 10: After leaving her employer, Shawna McQuillen establishes her own money management business. While with her former employer, she did not sign a non-compete agreement that would have prevented her from soliciting former clients. Upon her departure, she does not take any of her client lists or contact information and clears her personal computer of any employer records, including client contact information. She obtains the phone numbers of her former clients through public records and contacts them to solicit their business.

> *Comment:* McQuillen is not in violation of Standard IV(A) because she has not used information or records from her former employer and is not prevented by an agreement with her former employer from soliciting her former clients.

B. Additional Compensation Arrangements

Members and candidates must not accept gifts, benefits, compensation, or consideration that competes with, or might reasonably be expected to create a conflict of interest with, their employers' interest unless they obtain written consent from all parties involved.

Standard IV(B) requires members and candidates to obtain permission from their employer before accepting compensation or other benefits from third parties for the services rendered to the employer or for any services that might create a conflict of interest with their employers' interest. Compensation and benefits include direct compensation by the client and any indirect compensation or other benefits received from third parties. "Written consent" includes any form of communication that can be documented (for example, communication via computer e-mail that can be retrieved and documented).

Members and candidates must obtain permission for additional compensation/benefits because such arrangements may affect loyalties and objectivity and create potential conflicts of interest. Disclosure allows an employer to consider the outside arrangements when evaluating the actions and motivations of members and candidates. Moreover, the employer is entitled to have full knowledge of compensation/benefit arrangements to assess the true cost of the services members or candidates are providing.

Recommended Procedures for Compliance

Members and candidates should make an immediate written report to their employers specifying any compensation they propose to receive for services in addition to the compensation or benefits received from their employers. This written report should state the terms of any agreement under which a member or candidate will receive additional compensation; terms include the nature of the compensation, the approximate amount of compensation, and the duration of the agreement.

Application of the Standard

Example 1: Geoff Whitman, a portfolio analyst for Adams Trust Company, manages the account of Carol Cochran, a client. Whitman is paid a salary by his employer, and Cochran pays the trust company a standard fee based on the market value of assets in her portfolio. Cochran proposes to Whitman that "any year that my portfolio achieves at least a 15 percent return before taxes, you and your wife can fly to Monaco at my expense and use my condominium during the third week of January." Whitman does not inform his employer of the arrangement and vacations in Monaco the following January as Cochran's guest.

> *Comment:* Whitman violated Standard IV(B) by failing to inform his employer in writing of this supplemental, contingent compensation arrangement. The nature of the arrangement could have resulted in partiality to Cochran's account, which could have detracted from Whitman's performance with respect to other accounts he handles for Adams Trust. Whitman must obtain the consent of his employer to accept such a supplemental benefit.

Example 2: Terry Jones sits on the board of directors of Exercise Unlimited, Inc. In return for his services on the board, Jones receives unlimited membership privileges for his family at all Exercise Unlimited facilities. Jones purchases Exercise Unlimited stock for the client accounts for which it is appropriate.

Jones does not disclose this arrangement to his employer, as he does not receive monetary compensation for his services to the board.

> *Comment:* Jones violated Standard IV(B) by failing to disclose to his employer benefits received in exchange for his services on the board of directors.

C. Responsibilities of Supervisors

Members and candidates must make reasonable efforts to detect and prevent violations of applicable laws, rules, regulations, and the Code and Standards by anyone subject to their supervision or authority.

Standard IV(C) states that members and candidates must take steps to prevent persons acting under their supervision from violating the law, rules, regulations, or the Code and Standards.

Any investment professionals who have employees subject to their control or influence—whether or not the employees are CFA Institute members, CFA charterholders, or candidates in the CFA Program—exercise supervisory responsibility. Members and candidates acting as supervisors must have in-depth knowledge of the Code and Standards and must apply this knowledge in discharging their supervisory responsibilities.

The conduct that constitutes reasonable supervision in a particular case depends on the number of employees supervised and the work performed by those employees. Members and candidates who supervise large numbers of employees cannot personally evaluate the conduct of their employees on a continuing basis. Although these members and candidates may delegate supervisory duties, such delegation does not relieve them of their supervisory responsibility. Their responsibilities under Standard IV(C) include instructing those subordinates to whom supervision is delegated regarding methods to prevent and detect violations.

Members and candidates with supervisory responsibility must make reasonable efforts to detect violations of laws, rules, regulations, and the Code and Standards. They exercise reasonable supervision by establishing and implementing written compliance procedures and ensuring that those procedures are followed through periodic review. If a member or candidate has adopted reasonable procedures and taken steps to institute an effective compliance program, then the member or candidate may not be in violation of Standard IV(C) if they do not detect violations that occur despite these efforts. The fact that violations do occur may indicate, however, that the compliance procedures are inadequate. In addition, in some cases, merely enacting such procedures may not be sufficient to fulfill the duty required by Standard IV(C). A member or candidate may be in violation of Standard IV(C) if he or she knows or should know that the procedures designed to detect and prevent violations are not being followed.

Compliance Procedures

Members and candidates with supervisory responsibility also must understand what constitutes an adequate compliance system for their firms and make reasonable efforts to see that appropriate compliance procedures are established, documented, communicated to covered personnel, and followed. "Adequate" procedures are those designed to meet industry standards, regulatory requirements, the requirements of the Code and Standards, and the circumstances of the firm. Once compliance procedures are established, the supervisor must also make reasonable efforts to ensure that the procedures are monitored and enforced.

To be effective, compliance procedures must be in place prior to the occurrence of a violation of the law or the Code and Standards. Although compliance procedures cannot be designed to anticipate every potential violation, they should be designed to anticipate the activities most likely to result in misconduct. Each compliance program must be appropriate for the size and nature of the organization. Model compliance procedures or other industry programs should be reviewed to ensure that procedures meet the minimum industry standards.

A member or candidate with supervisory responsibility should bring an inadequate compliance system to the attention of the firm's senior managers and recommend corrective action. If the member or candidate clearly cannot discharge supervisory responsibilities because of the absence of a compliance system or because of an inadequate compliance system, the member or candidate should decline in writing to accept supervisory responsibility until the firm adopts reasonable procedures to allow them to adequately exercise such responsibility.

Once a supervisor learns that an employee has violated or may have violated the law or the Code and Standards, the supervisor must promptly initiate an investigation to ascertain the extent of the wrongdoing. Relying on an employee's statements about the extent of the violation or assurances that the wrongdoing will not reoccur is not enough. Reporting the misconduct up the chain of command and warning the employee to cease the activity are also not enough. Pending the outcome of the investigation, a supervisor should take steps to ensure the violations will not be repeated, such as placing limits on the employee's activities or increasing the monitoring of the employee's activities.

Recommended Procedures for Compliance

Members and candidates are encouraged to recommend that their employers adopt a code of ethics. Adoption of a code of ethics is critical to establishing a strong ethical foundation for investment adviser firms and their employees. Codes of ethics formally emphasize and reinforce the fiduciary responsibilities of investment firm personnel, protect investing clients by deterring misconduct, and protect the firm's reputation for integrity.

There is a distinction between codes of ethics and the necessary specific policies and procedures needed to ensure compliance with the code of conduct and securities laws and regulations. While both are important, codes of ethics should consist of fundamental, principle-based ethical and fiduciary concepts that are applicable to all of the firm's employees. In this way, firms can best convey to employees and clients the ethical ideals that investment advisers strive to achieve. These concepts can then be implemented by detailed, firmwide compliance policies and procedures. Compliance procedures will assist the firm's personnel in fulfilling the responsibilities enumerated in the code of ethics and ensure that the ideals expressed in the code of ethics are adhered to in the day-to-day operation of the firm.

Commingling compliance procedures in the firm's code of ethics will diminish the goal of reinforcing with the firm's employees their ethical obligations. Stand-alone codes of ethics should be written in plain language and address general fiduciary concepts, unencumbered by numerous detailed procedures directed to the day-to-day operation of the firm. In this way codes will be most effective in stressing to employees that they are in positions of trust and must act with integrity at all times.

Separating the codes of ethics from compliance procedures will also reduce, if not eliminate, the legal terminology and boilerplate language that can make the underlying ethical principles incomprehensible to the average person. Above all, the principles in the codes of ethics must be accessible and understandable to everyone in the firm to ensure that a culture of ethics and integrity is created rather than merely a focus on attention to the rules.

In addition, members and candidates should encourage their employers to provide their codes of ethics to clients. But only simple, straightforward codes of ethics will be understandable to clients and thus be effective in conveying the message that the firm is committed to conducting business in an ethical manner and in the best interests of the clients.

A supervisor complies with Standard IV(C) by identifying situations in which legal violations or violations of the Code and Standards are likely to occur and by establishing and enforcing compliance procedures to prevent such violations. Adequate compliance procedures should:

▶ be contained in a clearly written and accessible manual that is tailored to the member's or candidate's operations;

▶ be drafted so that the procedures are easy to understand;

▶ designate a compliance officer whose authority and responsibility are clearly defined and who has the necessary resources and authority to implement the firm's compliance procedures;

▶ describe the hierarchy of supervision and assign duties among supervisors;

▶ implement a system of checks and balances;

▶ outline the scope of the procedures;

▶ outline procedures to document the monitoring and testing of compliance procedures;

▶ outline permissible conduct; and

▶ delineate procedures for reporting violations and sanctions.

Once a compliance program is in place, a supervisor should:

▶ disseminate the contents of the program to appropriate personnel;

▶ periodically update procedures to ensure that the measures are adequate under the law;

▶ continually educate personnel regarding the compliance procedures;

▶ issue periodic reminders of the procedures to appropriate personnel;

▶ incorporate a professional conduct evaluation as part of an employee's performance review;

▶ review the actions of employees to ensure compliance and identify violators; and

▶ take the necessary steps to enforce the procedures once a violation has occurred.

Once a violation is discovered, a supervisor should:

▶ respond promptly;

▶ conduct a thorough investigation of the activities to determine the scope of the wrongdoing; and

▶ increase supervision or place appropriate limitations on the wrongdoer pending the outcome of the investigation.

Application of the Standard

Example 1: Jane Mattock, senior vice president and head of the research department of H&V, Inc., a regional brokerage firm, has decided to change her recommendation for Timber Products from buy to sell. In line with H&V's procedures, she orally advises certain other H&V executives of her proposed actions before the report is prepared for publication. As a result of his conversation with Mattock, Dieter Frampton, one of the executives of H&V accountable to Mattock, immediately sells Timber's stock from his own account and from certain discretionary client accounts. In addition, other personnel inform certain institutional customers of the changed recommendation before it is printed and disseminated to all H&V customers who have received previous Timber reports.

> *Comment:* Mattock failed to supervise reasonably and adequately the actions of those accountable to her. She did not prevent or establish reasonable procedures designed to prevent dissemination of or trading on the information by those who knew of her changed recommendation. She must ensure that her firm has procedures for reviewing or recording trading in the stock of any corporation that has been the subject of an unpublished change in recommendation. Adequate procedures would have informed the subordinates of their duties and detected sales by Frampton and selected customers.

Example 2: Deion Miller is the research director for Jamestown Investment Programs. The portfolio managers have become critical of Miller and his staff because the Jamestown portfolios do not include any stock that has been the subject of a merger or tender offer. Georgia Ginn, a member of Miller's staff, tells Miller that she has been studying a local company, Excelsior, Inc., and recommends its purchase. Ginn adds that the company has been widely rumored to be the subject of a merger study by a well-known conglomerate and discussions between them are under way. At Miller's request, Ginn prepares a memo recommending the stock. Miller passes along Ginn's memo to the portfolio managers prior to leaving for vacation, noting that he has not reviewed the memo. As a result of the memo, the portfolio managers buy Excelsior stock immediately. The day Miller returns to the office, Miller learns that Ginn's only sources for the report were her brother, who is an acquisitions analyst with Acme Industries and the "well-known conglomerate" and that the merger discussions were planned but not held.

> *Comment:* Miller violated Standard IV(C) by not exercising reasonable supervision when he disseminated the memo without checking to ensure that Ginn had a reasonable and adequate basis for her recommendations and that Ginn was not relying on material nonpublic information.

Example 3: David Edwards, a trainee trader at Wheeler & Company, a major national brokerage firm, assists a customer in paying for the securities of Highland, Inc., by using anticipated profits from the immediate sale of the same securities. Despite the fact that Highland is not on Wheeler's recommended list, a large volume of its stock is traded through Wheeler in this manner. Roberta Ann Mason is a Wheeler vice president responsible for supervising compliance with the securities laws in the trading department. Part of her compensation from Wheeler is based on commission revenues from the trading department. Although she notices the increased trading activity, she does nothing to investigate or halt it.

> *Comment:* Mason's failure to adequately review and investigate purchase orders in Highland stock executed by Edwards and her failure to supervise the trainee's activities violated Standard IV(C). Supervisors should be especially sensitive to actual or potential conflicts between their own self-interests and their supervisory responsibilities.

Example 4: Samantha Tabbing is senior vice president and portfolio manager for Crozet, Inc., a registered investment advisory and registered broker/dealer firm. She reports to Charles Henry, the president of Crozet. Crozet serves as the investment advisor and principal underwriter for ABC and XYZ public mutual funds. The two funds' prospectuses allow Crozet to trade financial futures for the funds for the limited purpose of hedging against market risks. Henry, extremely impressed with Tabbing's performance in the past two years, directs Tabbing to act as portfolio manager for the funds. For the benefit of its employees, Crozet has also organized the Crozet Employee Profit-Sharing Plan (CEPSP), a defined-contribution retirement plan. Henry assigns Tabbing to manage 20 percent of the assets of CEPSP. Tabbing's investment objective for her portion of CEPSP's assets is aggressive growth. Unbeknownst to Henry, Tabbing frequently places S&P 500 Index purchase and sale orders for the funds and the CEPSP without providing the futures commission merchants (FCMs) who take the orders with any prior or simultaneous designation of the account for which the trade has been placed. Frequently, neither Tabbing nor anyone else at Crozet completes an internal trade ticket to record the time an order was placed or the specific account for which the order was intended. FCMs often designate a specific account only after the trade, when Tabbing provides such designation. Crozet has no written operating procedures or compliance manual concerning its futures trading, and its compliance department does not review such trading. After observing the market's movement, Tabbing assigns to CEPSP the S&P 500 positions with more-favorable execution prices and assigns positions with less-favorable execution prices to the funds.

> *Comment:* Henry violated Standard IV(C) by failing to adequately supervise Tabbing with respect to her S&P 500 trading. Henry further violated Standard IV(C) by failing to establish record-keeping and reporting procedures to prevent or detect Tabbing's violations.

STANDARD V—INVESTMENT ANALYSIS, RECOMMENDATIONS, AND ACTIONS

A. Diligence and Reasonable Basis

Members and candidates must:
1. **Exercise diligence, independence, and thoroughness in analyzing investments, making investment recommendations, and taking investment actions.**
2. **Have a reasonable and adequate basis, supported by appropriate research and investigation, for any investment analysis, recommendation, or action.**

The application of Standard V(A) is dependent on the investment philosophy followed, the role of the member or candidate in the investment decision-making process, and the support and resources provided by the member's or candidate's employer. These factors will dictate the nature of the diligence, thoroughness of the research, and level of investigation required by Standard V(A).

The requirements for issuing conclusions on research will vary based on the member's or candidate's role in the investment decision-making process, but the member or candidate must make reasonable efforts to cover all pertinent issues when arriving at the recommendation. Members and candidates enhance transparency by providing or offering to provide supporting information to clients when recommending a purchase or sale or when changing a recommendation.

Using Secondary or Third-Party Research

If members and candidates rely on secondary or third-party research, they must make reasonable and diligent efforts to determine whether such research is sound. Secondary research is defined as research conducted by someone else in the member's or candidate's firm. Third-party research is research conducted by entities outside the member's or candidate's firm, such as a brokerage firm, bank, or research firm. If a member or candidate has reason to suspect that either secondary or third-party research or information comes from a source that lacks a sound basis, the member or candidate must refrain from relying on that information. This requirement also applies in situations involving quantitatively oriented research, such as computer-generated screening or ranking of universes of equity securities based on various sets of prescribed criteria. Examples of criteria that a member or candidate can use in forming his or her opinion that research is sound include:

- ▶ review of the assumptions used,
- ▶ rigor of analysis performed,
- ▶ date/timeliness of the research,
- ▶ evaluation of the objectivity and independence of recommendations.

When a member or candidate relies on others within his or her firm to determine whether secondary or third-party research is sound, the information can be used in good faith unless the member or candidate has reason to question its validity or the processes and procedures used by those responsible for the investigation. An example of this situation would be a portfolio manager who does not have a choice over a data source because the firm's senior management conducted due diligence to determine which vendor would provide services.

Group Research and Decision Making

Commonly, members and candidates may be part of a group or team that is collectively responsible for producing investment analysis or research. The conclusions or recommendations of the report represent the consensus of the group and are not necessarily the views of the member or candidate, even though the name of the member or candidate is included on the report. There may be many instances when the member or candidate does not agree with the independent and objective view of the group. If the member or candidate believes that consensus opinion has a reasonable and adequate basis, then the member or candidate does not necessarily have to decline to be identified with the report. There should be a presumption that the group members are independent and objective and have a reasonable basis for the opinions. If the member or candidate is confident in the process, the member or candidate does not have to dissociate from the report if it does not reflect his or her opinion. The member or candidate should, however, document his or her difference of opinion with the team.

Recommended Procedures for Compliance

Members and candidates should encourage their firms to consider the following policies and procedures to support the principles of Standard V(A):

- ▶ Establish a policy requiring that research reports and recommendations have a basis that can be substantiated as reasonable and adequate. An individual employee (supervisory analyst) or a group of employees (review committee) should be appointed to review and approve all research reports and recommendations to determine whether they meet the criteria as established in the policy.

▶ Develop detailed, written guidance for research analysts, supervisory analysts, and review committees that establishes due-diligence procedures for judging whether a particular recommendation has a reasonable and adequate basis.

▶ Develop measurable criteria for assessing the quality of research, including the reasonableness and adequacy of the basis for any recommendation and the accuracy of recommendations over time, and implement compensation arrangements that depend on these measurable criteria and that are applied consistently to all research analysts.

Application of the Standard

Example 1: Helen Hawke manages the corporate finance department of Sarkozi Securities, Ltd. The firm is anticipating that the government will soon close a tax loophole that currently allows oil and gas exploration companies to pass on drilling expenses to holders of a certain class of shares. Because market demand for this tax-advantaged class of stock is currently high, Sarkozi convinces several companies to undertake new equity financings at once before the loophole closes. Time is of the essence, but Sarkozi lacks sufficient resources to conduct adequate research on all the prospective issuing companies. Hawke decides to estimate the IPO prices based on the relative size of each company and to justify the pricing later when her staff has time.

Comment: Sarkozi should have taken on only the work that it could adequately handle. By categorizing the issuers as to general size, Hawke has bypassed researching all the other relevant aspects that should be considered when pricing new issues and thus has not performed sufficient due diligence. Such an omission can result in investors purchasing shares at prices that have no actual basis. Hawke has violated Standard V(A).

Example 2: Babu Dhaliwal works for Heinrich Brokerage in the corporate finance group. He has just persuaded Feggans Resources, Ltd., to allow his firm to do a secondary equity financing at Feggans Resources' current stock price. Because the stock has been trading at higher multiples than similar companies with equivalent production, Dhaliwal presses the Feggans Resources managers to project what would be the maximum production they could achieve in an optimal scenario. Based on these numbers, he is able to justify the price his firm will be asking for the secondary issue. During a sales pitch to the brokers, Dhaliwal then uses these numbers as the base-case production levels that Feggans Resources will achieve.

Comment: When presenting information to the brokers, Dhaliwal should have given a range of production scenarios and the probability of Feggans Resources achieving each level. By giving the maximum production level as the likely level of production, he has misrepresented the chances of achieving that production level and seriously misled the brokers.

Example 3: Brendan Witt creates an Internet site with a chat-room area to publish his stock recommendations. He views the site as a chance to attract new clients. In the chat room, he almost always writes positively about technology stocks and recommends purchasing based on what the conventional wisdom of the markets has deemed the "hot" securities of the day.

Comment: Witt's exuberance about technology and the conventional wisdom of the markets, without more information, do not constitute a reasonable and adequate basis, supported by appropriate research and investigation, on which to base a recommendation. Therefore, Witt has violated Standard V(A).

Example 4: Carsten Dunlop is an investment consultant in the London office of EFG, a major global investment consultant firm. One of her U.K. pension funds has decided to appoint a specialist U.S. equity manager. EFG's global manager research relies on local consultants to cover managers within their region and, after conducting thorough due diligence, post their views and ratings on EFG's manager database. Dunlop accesses EFG's global manager research database and conducts a screen of all U.S. equity managers based on the client's desired match for philosophy/style, performance, and tracking-error targets and those that are rated "buy." She selects the five managers meeting these criteria and puts them in a briefing report that is delivered to the client 10 days later. In between the time of Dunlop's database search and delivery of the report to the client, EFG updated the database with the information that one of the firms that Dunlop has recommended for consideration lost its chief investment officer, head of U.S. equity research, and the majority of portfolio managers on the U.S. equity product—all of whom have left to establish their own firm, and she does not provide the client with this updated information. Although EFG has updated its database, Dunlop's report to the client does not reflect this new information.

Comment: Dunlop has failed to satisfy the requirement of Standard V(A) by not checking the database in a timely manner and updating her report to the client. Although EFG updated the manager ratings to reflect the personnel turnover at the firm, Dunlop did not update her report to reflect the new information.

Example 5: Evelyn Mastakis is a junior analyst asked by her firm to write a research report predicting the expected interest rate for residential mortgages over the next six months. Mastakis submits her report to the fixed-income investment committee of her firm for review, as required by firm procedures. Although some committee members support Mastakis's conclusion, the majority of the committee disagrees with her conclusion, and the report is significantly changed to indicate that interest rates are likely to increase more than originally predicted by Mastakis.

Comment: The results of research are not always clear, and different people may have different opinions based on the same factual evidence. In this case, the majority of the committee may have valid reasons for issuing a report that differs from the analyst's original research. The firm can issue a report different from the original report of the analyst as long as there is a reasonable or adequate basis for its conclusions. Generally, analysts must write research reports that reflect their own opinion and can ask the firm not to put their name on reports that ultimately differ from that opinion. When the work is a group effort, however, not all members of the team may agree with all aspects of the report. Ultimately, members and candidates can ask to have their names removed from the report, but if they are satisfied that the process has produced results or conclusions that have a reasonable or adequate basis, members or candidates do not have to dissociate from the report even when they do not agree with its contents. The member or candidate should document the difference of opinion and any request to remove his or her name from the report.

Example 6: Gary McDermott runs a small, two-person investment management firm. McDermott's firm subscribes to a service from a large investment research firm that provides research reports. McDermott's firm makes investment recommendations based on these reports.

> *Comment:* Members and candidates can rely on third-party research but must make reasonable and diligent efforts to determine that such research is sound. If McDermott undertakes due diligence efforts on a regular basis to ensure that the research produced by the large firm is objective and reasonably based, McDermott can rely on that research when making investment recommendations to clients.

B. Communication with Clients and Prospective Clients

Members and candidates must:

1. **Disclose to clients and prospective clients the basic format and general principles of the investment processes used to analyze investments, select securities, and construct portfolios and must promptly disclose any changes that might materially affect those processes.**

2. **Use reasonable judgment in identifying which factors are important to their investment analyses, recommendations, or actions and include those factors in communications with clients and prospective clients.**

3. **Distinguish between fact and opinion in the presentation of investment analysis and recommendations.**

Standard V(B) addresses members' and candidates' conduct with respect to communicating with clients. Developing and maintaining clear, frequent, and thorough communication practices is critical to providing high-quality financial services to clients. When clients can understand the information communicated to them, they also can understand exactly how members and candidates are acting on their behalf, which gives clients the opportunity to make well-informed decisions regarding their investments. Such understanding can be accomplished only through clear communication.

Standard V(B) states the responsibility of members and candidates to include in their communications those key factors that are instrumental to the investment recommendation presented. A critical part of this requirement is to distinguish clearly between opinions and facts. In preparing a research report, the member or candidate must present the basic characteristics of the security being analyzed, which will allow the reader to evaluate the report and incorporate information the reader deems relevant to his or her investment decision-making process.

Members and candidates must adequately illustrate to clients and prospective clients the manner in which the member or candidate conducts the investment decision-making process. The member or candidate must keep existing clients and other interested parties informed with respect to changes to the chosen investment process on an ongoing basis. Only by thoroughly understanding the nature of the investment product or service can a client determine whether changes to that product or service could materially affect the client's investment objectives.

Understanding the basic characteristics of the investment is of great importance in judging the suitability of each investment on a stand-alone basis, but it is especially important in determining the impact each investment will have on the characteristics of the portfolio. For instance, although the risk and return characteristics of shares of a common stock might seem to be essentially the same for any investor when the stock is viewed in isolation, the implications of such an investment vary greatly depending on the other investments held. If the particular stock represents 90 percent of an individual's investments, the stock's importance in the portfolio is vastly different from what it would be to an investor who holds the same amount of the stock in a highly diversified portfolio in which the stock represents only 2 percent of the holdings.

For purposes of Standard V(B), communication is not confined to a written report of the type traditionally generated by an analyst researching a particular security, company, or industry. A presentation of information can be made via any means of communication, including in-person recommendation, telephone conversation, media broadcast, or transmission by computer (e.g., on the Internet). Furthermore, the nature of these communications is highly diverse—from one word ("buy" or "sell") to in-depth reports of more than 100 pages. Brief communications must be supported by background reports or data that can be made available to interested parties on request.

A communication may contain a general recommendation about the market, asset allocation, or classes of investments (e.g., stocks, bonds, real estate) or relate to a specific security. If recommendations are contained in capsule form (such as a recommended stock list), members and candidates should notify clients that additional information and analyses are available from the producer of the report. Investment advice based on quantitative research and analysis must be supported by readily available reference material and should be applied in a manner consistent with previously applied methodology or with changes in methodology highlighted. Members and candidates should outline known limitations of the analysis and conclusions contained in their investment analysis. In evaluating the basic characteristics of the investment being recommended, members and candidates should consider in the report the principal risks inherent in the expected cash returns, which may include credit risk, financial risk (specifically the use of leverage or financial derivatives), and overall market risk.

Once the process has been completed, the member or candidate who prepares the report must include those elements important to the analysis and conclusions of the report so that the user can follow and challenge the report's reasoning. A report writer who has done adequate investigation may emphasize certain areas, touch briefly on others, and omit certain aspects deemed unimportant. For instance, a report may dwell on a quarterly earnings release or new-product introduction at the sacrifice of examining other fundamental matters in depth so long as the analyst clearly stipulates the limits to the scope of the report.

Standard V(B) requires that opinion be separated from fact. Violations are most likely to occur when reports fail to separate the past from the future by not indicating that earnings estimates, changes in the outlook for dividends, and/or future market price information are opinions subject to future circumstances. In the case of complex quantitative analysis, analysts must clearly separate fact from statistical conjecture and should identify the known limitations of the analysis.

Recommended Procedures for Compliance

Because the selection of relevant factors is an analytical skill, determination of whether a member or candidate has used reasonable judgment in excluding and including information in research reports depends heavily on case-by-case review rather than a specific checklist. To assist in the after-the-fact review of a report, the member or candidate must maintain records indicating the nature of the research and should, if asked, be able to supply additional information to the client (or any user of the report) covering factors not included.

Application of the Standard

Example 1: Sarah Williamson, director of marketing for Country Technicians, Inc., is convinced that she has found the perfect formula for increasing Country Technicians' income and diversifying its product base. Williamson plans to build on Country Technicians' reputation as a leading money manager by marketing an exclusive and expensive investment advice letter to high-net-worth individuals. One hitch in the plan is the complexity of Country Technicians' investment system—a combination of technical trading rules (based on historical price and volume fluctuations) and portfolio-construction rules designed to minimize risk. To simplify the newsletter, she decides to include only each week's top-five buy and sell recommendations and to leave out details of the valuation models and the portfolio-structuring scheme.

> *Comment:* Williamson's plans for the newsletter violate Standard V(B). Williamson need not describe the investment system in detail in order to implement the advice effectively, clients must be informed of Country Technicians' basic process and logic. Without understanding the basis for a recommendation, clients cannot possibly understand its limitations or its inherent risks.

Example 2: Richard Dox is a mining analyst for East Bank Securities. He has just finished his report on Boisy Bay Minerals. Included in his report is his own assessment of the geological extent of mineral reserves likely to be found on the company's land. Dox completed this calculation based on the core samples from the company's latest drilling. According to Dox's calculations, the company has in excess of 500,000 ounces of gold on the property. Dox concludes his research report as follows: "Based on the fact that the company has 500,000 ounces of gold to be mined, I recommend a strong BUY."

> *Comment:* If Dox issues the report as written, he will violate Standard V(B). His calculation of the total gold reserves for the property is an opinion not a fact. Opinion must be distinguished from fact in research reports.

Example 3: Olivia Thomas, an analyst at Government Brokers, Inc., which is a brokerage firm specializing in government bond trading, has produced a report that describes an investment strategy designed to benefit from an expected decline in U.S. interest rates. The firm's derivative products group has designed a structured product that will allow the firm's clients to benefit from this strategy. Thomas's report describing the strategy indicates that high returns are possible if various scenarios for declining interest rates are assumed. Citing the proprietary nature of the structured product underlying the strategy, the report does not describe in detail how the firm is able to offer such returns in the scenarios, nor does the report address the likely returns of the strategy if, contrary to expectations, interest rates rise.

> *Comment:* Thomas has violated Standard V(B) because her report fails to describe properly the basic characteristics of the investment strategy, including how the structure was created and the degree to which leverage was embedded in the structure. The report should include a balanced discussion of how the strategy would perform in the case of rising as well as falling interest rates.

Example 4: May & Associates is an aggressive growth manager that has represented itself since its inception as a specialist at investing in small-capitalization domestic stocks. One of May's selection criteria is a maximum capitalization of $250 million for any given company. After a string of successful years of superior relative performance, May expanded its client base significantly, to the point at which assets under management now exceed $3 billion. For liquidity purposes, May's chief investment officer (CIO) decides to lift the maximum permissible market-cap ceiling to $500 million and change the firm's sales and marketing literature accordingly to inform prospective clients and third-party consultants.

> *Comment:* Although May's CIO is correct about informing potentially interested parties as to the change in investment process, he must also notify May's existing clients. Among the latter group might be a number of clients who not only retained May as a small-cap manager but also retained mid-cap and large-cap specialists in a multiple-manager approach. Such clients could regard May's change of criteria as a style change that could distort their overall asset allocations.

Example 5: Rather than lifting the ceiling for its universe from $250 million to $500 million, May & Associates extends its small-cap universe to include a number of non-U.S. companies.

> *Comment:* Standard V(B) requires that May's CIO advise May's clients of this change because the firm may have been retained by some clients specifically for its prowess at investing in domestic small-cap stocks. Other variations requiring client notification include introducing derivatives to emulate a certain market sector or relaxing various other constraints, such as portfolio beta. In all such cases, members and candidates must disclose changes to all interested parties.

Example 6: RJZ Capital Management is a value-style active equity manager that selects stocks using a combination of four multifactor models. Because of favorable results gained from back-testing the most recent 10 years of available market data, the president of RJZ decides to replace its simple model of price to trailing 12-months earnings with a new dividend discount model designed by the firm that is a function of projected inflation rates, earnings growth rates, and interest rates.

> *Comment:* Because the introduction of a new and different valuation model represents a material change in the investment process, RJZ's president must communicate the change to the firm's clients. RJZ is moving away from a model based on hard data toward a new model that is at least partly dependent on the firm's forecasting skills. Clients would likely view such a model as a significant change rather than a mere refinement of RJZ's process.

Example 7: RJZ Capital Management loses the chief architect of its multifactor valuation system. Without informing its clients, the president of RJZ decides to redirect the firm's talents and resources toward developing a product for passive equity management—a product that will emulate the performance of a major market index.

> *Comment:* The president of RJZ failed to disclose to clients a substantial change to its investment process, which is a violation of Standard V(B).

Example 8: At Fundamental Asset Management, Inc., the responsibility for selecting stocks for addition to the firm's "approved" list has just shifted from individual security analysts to a committee consisting of the research director and three senior portfolio managers. Eleanor Morales, a portfolio manager with Fundamental Asset Management, fails to notify her clients of the change.

> *Comment:* Morales must disclose the process change to all her clients. Some of Fundamental's clients might be concerned about the morale and motivation among the firm's best research analysts following the change. Moreover, clients might challenge the stock-picking track record of the portfolio managers and might even want to monitor the situation closely.

C. Record Retention

Members and candidates must develop and maintain appropriate records to support their investment analysis, recommendations, actions, and other investment-related communications with clients and prospective clients.

Members and candidates must retain records that substantiate the scope of their research and reasons for their actions or conclusions. The records required to support recommendations and/or investment actions depend on the role of the member or candidate in the investment decision-making process. Records can be maintained either in hard copy or electronic form.

As a general matter, records created as part of a member's or candidate's professional activity on behalf of his or her employer are the property of the member's or candidate's firm. When a member or candidate leaves a firm to seek other employment, the member or candidate cannot take the property of the firm, including originals or copies of supporting records of the member's or candidate's work, to the new employer without the express consent of the previous employer. Without re-creating the records at the new firm, the member or candidate cannot use historical recommendations or research reports created at the previous firm because the supporting documentation is unavailable.

Local regulators often impose requirements on members, candidates, and their firms related to record retention that must be followed. Fulfilling such regulatory requirements also may satisfy the requirements of Standard V(C), but members and candidates must explicitly determine whether it does. In the absence of regulatory guidance, CFA Institute recommends maintaining records for at least seven years.

Recommended Procedures for Compliance

The responsibility to maintain records that support investment action generally falls with the firm rather than individuals. However, members and candidates must retain research notes and other documents supporting current investment-related communications to assist their firms in complying with internal or external record preservation requirements.

Application of the Standard

Example 1: One of Nikolas Lindstrom's clients is upset by the negative investment returns in his equity portfolio. The investment policy statement for the client requires that the portfolio manager follow a benchmark-oriented approach. The benchmark for the client included a 35 percent investment allocation in the technology sector, which the client acknowledged was appropriate. Over the past three years, the portion put into the segment of technology stocks suffered severe losses. The client complains to the investment manager that so much money was allocated to this sector.

> *Comment:* For Lindstrom, it is important to have appropriate records to show that over the past three years the percentage of technology stocks in the benchmark index was 35 percent. Therefore, the amount of money invested in the technology sector was appropriate according to the investment policy statement. Lindstrom should also have the investment policy statement for the client stating that the benchmark was appropriate for the client's investment objectives. He should also have records indicating that the investment had been explained appropriately to the client and that the investment policy statement was updated on a regular basis.

Example 2: Malcolm Young is a research analyst who writes numerous reports rating companies in the luxury retail industry. His reports are based on a variety of sources, including interviews with company management, manufacturers, and economists; onsite company visits; customer surveys; and secondary research from analysts covering related industries.

> *Comment:* Young must carefully document and keep copies of all the information that goes into his report, including the secondary or third-party research of other analysts.

Example 3: Martin Blank develops an analytical model while employed by Grosse Point Investment Management, LLP (GPIM). While at the firm, he systematically documents the assumptions that make up the model as well as his reasoning for the assumptions. As the result of the success of his model, Blank is hired to be the head of the research department of one of GPIM's competitors. Blank takes copies of the records supporting his model to his new firm.

> *Comment:* The records created by Blank supporting the research model he developed at GPIM are the records of GPIM. He cannot take the documents with him to his new employer without GPIM's permission. Blank must re-create the records supporting his model at the new firm.

STANDARD VI—CONFLICTS OF INTEREST

A. Disclosure of Conflicts

Members and candidates must make full and fair disclosure of all matters that could reasonably be expected to impair their independence and objectivity or interfere with respective duties to their clients, prospective clients, and their employer. Members and candidates must ensure that such disclosures are prominent, are delivered in plain language, and communicate the relevant information effectively.

Conflicts of interest often arise in the investment management profession. Conflicts can occur between the interests of clients, the interests of employers, and the member's or candidate's own personal interest. Managing these conflicts is a critical part of working in the investment industry and can take many forms. Best practice is to avoid conflicts of interest when possible. When conflicts cannot be reasonably avoided, disclosure of their existence is necessary.

Standard VI(A) protects investors and employers by requiring members and candidates to fully disclose to clients, potential clients, and employers all actual and potential conflicts of interest. Once a member or candidate has made full disclosure, the member's or candidate's employer, clients, and prospects will have the information needed to evaluate the objectivity of the investment advice or action taken on their behalf.

To be effective, disclosures must be prominent and must be made in plain language and in a manner designed to effectively communicate the information to clients and prospective clients. It is up to members and candidates to determine how often, in what manner, or under what particular circumstances disclosure of conflicts must be made. Members and candidates have the responsibility to assess when and how they meet their obligations under this standard in each particular case. Members and candidates should err on the side of caution or repetition to ensure that conflicts of interest are effectively communicated.

Disclosure to Clients

Members and candidates must maintain their objectivity when rendering investment advice or taking investment action. Investment advice or actions may be perceived to be tainted in numerous situations. Can a member or candidate remain objective if, on behalf of the firm, the member or candidate obtains or assists in obtaining fees for services? Can a member or candidate give objective advice if he or she owns stock in the company that is the subject of an investment recommendation or if the member or candidate has a close personal relationship with the company managers? Requiring members and candidates to disclose all matters that reasonably could be expected to impair the member's or candidate's objectivity allows clients and prospects to judge motives and possible biases for themselves.

In the investment industry, a conflict, or the perception of a conflict, often cannot be avoided. The most obvious conflicts of interest, which should always be disclosed, are relationships between the member, candidate, or their firm and an issuer (such as a directorship or consultancy), investment banking, underwriting and financial relationships, broker/dealer market-making activities, and material beneficial ownership of stock. A member or candidate must take reasonable steps to determine if a conflict of interest exists and disclose to clients any conflicts of the member's or candidate's firm when known. Disclosure of broker/dealer market-making activities alerts clients that a purchase or sale might be made from or to the firm's principal account and that the firm has a special interest in the price of the stock.

Service as a director poses three basic conflicts of interest. First, a conflict may exist between the duties owed to clients and the duties owed to shareholders of the company. Second, investment personnel who serve as directors may receive the securities or the option to purchase securities of the company as compensation for serving on the board, which could raise questions about trading actions that could increase the value of those securities. Third, board service creates the opportunity to receive material nonpublic information involving the company. Even though the information is confidential, the perception could be that information not available to the public might be communicated to a director's firm—whether a broker, investment advisor, or other type of organization. When members or candidates providing investment services also serve as directors, they should be isolated from those making investment decisions by the use of firewalls or similar restrictions.

Many other circumstances give rise to actual or potential conflicts of interest. For instance, a sell-side analyst working for a broker/dealer may be encouraged, not only by members of her or his own firm but by corporate issuers themselves, to write research reports about particular companies. The buy-side analyst is likely to be faced with similar conflicts as banks exercise their underwriting and securities-dealing powers. The marketing division may ask an analyst to recommend the stock of a certain company in order to obtain business from that company.

The potential for conflicts of interest also exists with broker-sponsored limited partnerships formed to invest venture capital. Increasingly, members and candidates are expected not only to follow issues from these partnerships once they are offered to the public but also to promote the issues in the secondary market after public offerings. Members, candidates, and their firms should attempt to resolve situations presenting potential conflicts of interest or disclose them in accordance with the principles set forth in Standard VI(A).

The most prevalent conflict requiring disclosure under Standard VI(A) is a member's or candidate's ownership of stock in companies that they recommend to clients and/or that clients hold. Clearly, the easiest method for preventing a conflict is to prohibit members and candidates from owning any such securities, but this approach is over burdensome and discriminates against members and candidates. Therefore, sell-side members and candidates should disclose any materially beneficial ownership interest in a security or other investment that the member or candidate is recommending. Buy-side members and candidates should disclose their procedures for reporting requirements for personal transactions. For the purposes of Standard VI(A), members and candidates beneficially own securities or other investments if they have a direct or indirect pecuniary interest in the securities; have the power to vote or direct the voting of the shares of the securities or investments; or have the power to dispose or direct the disposition of the security or investment. Conflicts arising from personal investing are discussed more fully in the guidance for Standard VI(B)—Priority of Transactions.

Disclosure of Conflicts to Employers

Disclosure of conflicts to employers may also be appropriate in many instances. When reporting conflicts of interest to employers, members and candidates should give their employer enough information to assess the impact of the conflict. By complying with employer guidelines, members and candidates allow their employers to avoid potentially embarrassing and costly ethical or regulatory violations.

Reportable situations include conflicts that would interfere with rendering unbiased investment advice and conflicts that would cause a member or candidate not to act in the employer's best interest. The same circumstances that generate conflicts to be reported to clients and prospects also would dictate reporting to employers. Ownership of stocks analyzed or recommended, participation in outside boards, and financial and other pressures that may influence a decision are to be promptly reported to the employer so that their impact can be assessed and a decision made on how to resolve the conflict.

The mere appearance of conflict of interest may create problems for members, candidates, and their employers. Therefore, many of the conflicts previously mentioned could be explicitly prohibited by the employer. For example, many employers restrict personal trading, outside board membership, and related activities to prevent situations that might not normally be considered problematic from a conflict-of-interest point of view but that could give the appearance of a conflict of interest. Members and candidates must comply with these restrictions. Members and candidates must take reasonable steps to avoid conflicts and, if they occur inadvertently, must report them promptly so that the employer and the member or candidate can resolve them as quickly and effectively as possible.

Standard VI(A) also deals with a member's and candidate's conflicts of interest that might be detrimental to the employer's business. Any potential conflict situation that could prevent clear judgment in or full commitment to the execution of the member's or candidate's duties to the employer should be reported to the member's or candidate's employer and promptly resolved.

Recommended Procedures for Compliance

Members or candidates should disclose special compensation arrangements with the employer that might conflict with client interests, such as bonuses based on short-term performance criteria, commissions, incentive fees, performance fees, and referral fees. If the member's or candidate's firm does not permit such disclosure, the member or candidate should document the request and may consider dissociating from the activity.

Members' or candidates' firms are encouraged to include information on compensation packages in firms' promotional literature. If a member or candidate manages a portfolio for which the fee is based on a share of capital gains or capital appreciation (a performance fee), this information should be disclosed to clients. If a member, candidate, or a member's or candidate's firm has outstanding agent options to buy stock as part of the compensation package for corporate financing activities, the amount and expiration date of these options should be disclosed as a footnote to any research report published by the member's or candidate's firm.

Application of the Standard

Example 1: Hunter Weiss is a research analyst with Farmington Company, a broker and investment-banking firm. Farmington's merger and acquisition department has represented Vimco, a conglomerate, in all of its acquisitions for 20 years. From time to time, Farmington officers sit on the boards of directors of various Vimco subsidiaries. Weiss is writing a research report on Vimco.

> *Comment:* Weiss must disclose in his research report Farmington's special relationship with Vimco. Broker/dealer management of and participation in public offerings must be disclosed in research reports. Because the position of underwriter to a company presents a special past and potential future relationship with a company that is the subject of investment advice, it threatens the independence and objectivity of the report and must be disclosed.

Example 2: The investment management firm of Dover & Roe sells a 25 percent interest in its partnership to a multinational bank holding company, First of New York. Immediately thereafter, Margaret Hobbs, president of Dover & Roe, changes her recommendation of First of New York's common stock from "sell" to "buy" and adds First of New York's commercial paper to Dover & Roe's approved list for purchase.

> *Comment:* Hobbs must disclose the new relationship with First of New York to all Dover & Roe clients. This relationship must also be disclosed to clients by the firm's portfolio managers when they make specific investment recommendations or take investment actions with respect to First of New York's securities.

Example 3: Carl Fargmon, a research analyst who follows firms producing office equipment, has been recommending purchase of Kincaid Printing because of its innovative new line of copiers. After his initial report on the company, Fargmon's wife inherits from a distant relative $3 million of Kincaid stock. He has been asked to write a follow-up report on Kincaid.

> *Comment:* Fargmon must disclose his wife's ownership of the Kincaid stock to his employer and in his follow-up report. Best practice would be to avoid the conflict by asking his employer to assign another analyst to draft the follow-up report.

Example 4: Betty Roberts is speculating in penny stocks for her own account and purchases 100,000 shares of Drew Mining, Inc., for 30 cents a share. She intends to sell these shares at the sign of any substantial upward price movement of the stock. A week later, her employer asks her to write a report on penny stocks in the mining industry to be published in two weeks. Even without owning the Drew stock, Roberts would recommend it in her report as a "buy." A surge of the price of the stock to the $2 range is likely to result once the report is issued.

> *Comment:* Although this holding may not be material, Roberts must disclose it in the report and to her employer before writing the report because the gain for her will be substantial if the market responds strongly to her recommendation. The fact that she has only recently purchased the stock adds to the appearance that she is not entirely objective.

Example 5: Samantha Dyson, a portfolio manager for Thomas Investment Counsel, Inc., specializes in managing defined-benefit pension plan accounts, all of which are in the accumulative phase and have long-term investment objectives. A year ago, Dyson's employer, in an attempt to motivate and retain key investment professionals, introduced a bonus compensation system that rewards portfolio managers on the basis of quarterly performance relative to their peers and certain benchmark indexes. Dyson changes her investment strategy and purchases several high-beta stocks for client portfolios in an attempt to improve short-term performance. These purchases are seemingly contrary to the client investment policy statement. Now, an officer of Griffin Corporation, one of Dyson's pension fund clients, asks why Griffin Corporation's portfolio seems to be dominated by high-beta stocks of companies that often appear among the most actively traded issues. No change in objective or strategy has been recommended by Dyson during the year.

Comment: Dyson violated Standard VI(A) by failing to inform her clients of the changes in her compensation arrangement with her employer that created a conflict of interest. Firms may pay employees on the basis of performance, but pressure by Thomas Investment Counsel to achieve short-term performance goals is in basic conflict with the objectives of Dyson's accounts.

Example 6: Wayland Securities works with small companies doing IPOs and/or secondary offerings. Typically, these deals are in the $10 million to $50 million range and, as a result, the corporate finance fees are quite small. In order to compensate for the small fees, Wayland Securities usually takes "agents options"—that is, rights (exercisable within a two-year time frame) to acquire up to an additional 10 percent of the current offering. Following an IPO performed by Wayland for Falk Resources, Ltd., Darcy Hunter, the head of corporate finance at Wayland, is concerned about receiving value for her Falk Resources options. The options are one month from expiring, and the stock is not doing well. She contacts John Fitzpatrick in the research department of Wayland Securities, reminds him that he is eligible for 30 percent of these options and indicates that now would be a good time to give some additional coverage to Falk Resources. Fitzpatrick agrees and immediately issues a favorable report.

Comment: In order for Fitzpatrick not to be in violation of Standard VI(A), he must indicate in the report the volume and expiration date of agent options outstanding. Furthermore, because he is personally eligible for some of the options, Fitzpatrick must disclose the extent of this compensation. He also must be careful that he does not violate his duty of independence and objectivity under Standard I(B).

Example 7: Gary Carter is a representative with Bengal International, a registered broker/dealer. Carter is approached by a stock promoter for Badger Company, who offers to pay Carter additional compensation for sales to his clients of Badger Company's stock. Carter accepts the stock promoter's offer but does not disclose the arrangements to his clients or to his employer. Carter sells shares of the stock to his clients.

Comment: Carter has violated Standard VI(A) by failing to disclose to clients that he was receiving additional compensation for recommending and selling Badger stock. Because he did not disclose the arrangement with Badger to his clients, the clients were unable to evaluate whether Carter's recommendations to buy Badger were affected by this arrangement. Carter's conduct also violated Standard VI(A) by failing to disclose to his employer monetary compensation received in addition to the compensation and benefits conferred by his employer. Carter was required by Standard VI(A) to disclose the arrangement with Badger to his employer so that his employer could evaluate whether the arrangement affected his objectivity and loyalty.

Example 8: Carol Corky, a senior portfolio manager for Universal Management, recently became involved as a trustee with the Chelsea Foundation, a very large not-for-profit foundation in her hometown. Universal is a small money manager (with assets under management of approximately $100 million) that caters to individual investors. Chelsea has assets in excess of $2 billion. Corky does not believe informing Universal of her involvement with Chelsea is necessary.

> *Comment:* By failing to inform Universal of her involvement with Chelsea, Corky violated Standard VI(A). Given the large size of the endowment at Chelsea, Corky's new role as a trustee can reasonably be expected to be time-consuming, to the possible detriment of Corky's portfolio responsibilities with Universal. As a trustee, Corky also may become involved with the investment decisions at Chelsea. Therefore, Standard VI(A) obligates Corky to discuss becoming a trustee at Chelsea with her compliance officer or supervisor at Universal before accepting the position, and she should have disclosed the degree to which she would be involved in investment decisions at Chelsea.

Example 9: Bruce Smith covers East European equities for Marlborough investments, an investment management firm with a strong presence in emerging markets. While on a business trip to Russia, Smith learns that investing in Russian equity directly is difficult but that equity-linked notes that replicate the performance of the underlying Russian equity can be purchased from a New York-based investment bank. Believing that his firm would not be interested in such a security, Smith purchases a note linked to a Russian telecommunications company for his own account without informing Marlborough. A month later, Smith decides that the firm should consider investing in Russian equities using equity-linked notes, and he prepares a write-up on the market that concludes with a recommendation to purchase several of the notes. One note recommended is linked to the same Russian telecom company that Smith holds in his personal account.

> *Comment:* Smith violated Standard VI(A) by failing to disclose his ownership of the note linked to the Russian telecom company. Smith is required by the standard to disclose the investment opportunity to his employer and look to his company's policies on personal trading to determine whether it was proper for him to purchase the note for his own account. By purchasing the note, Smith may or may not have impaired his ability to make an unbiased and objective assessment of the appropriateness of the derivative instrument for his firm, but Smith's failure to disclose the purchase to his employer impaired his employer's ability to render an opinion regarding whether the ownership of the security constituted a conflict of interest that might have affected future recommendations. Once he recommended the notes to his firm, Smith compounded his problems by not disclosing that he owned the notes in his personal account—a clear conflict of interest.

B. Priority of Transactions

Investment transactions for clients and employers must have priority over investment transactions in which a member or candidate is the beneficial owner.

Standard VI(B) reinforces the responsibility of members and candidates to give the interests of their clients and employers priority over their personal financial interests. This standard is designed to prevent any potential conflict of interest or the appearance of a conflict of interest with respect to personal transactions. Client interests have priority. Client transactions must take precedence over transactions made on behalf of the member's or candidate's firm or personal transactions.

Standard VI(B) states that transactions for clients and employers must have priority over transactions in securities or other investments of which a member or candidate is the beneficial owner so that such personal transactions do not adversely affect the interests of their clients or employers. For purposes of the Code and Standards, a member or candidate is a "beneficial owner" if the member or candidate has a direct or indirect personal interest in the securities. A member or candidate having the same investment positions or being coinvested with their clients does not always create a conflict. Some clients in certain investment situations require members or candidates to have aligned interests. However, personal investment positions or transactions of a member or candidate or their firm should never adversely affect client investments.

Conflicts between the client's interest and an investment professional's personal interest may occur. Although conflicts of interest exist, there is nothing inherently unethical about individual managers, advisors, or mutual fund employees making money from personal investments as long as (1) the client is not disadvantaged by the trade, (2) the investment professional does not benefit personally from trades undertaken for clients, and (3) the investment professional complies with applicable regulatory requirements.

Standard VI(B) covers the activities of all members and candidates who have knowledge of pending transactions that may be made on behalf of their clients or employers. Standard VI(B) also applies to members and candidates who have access to information during the normal preparation of research recommendations or who take investment actions. Members and candidates are prohibited from conveying such information to any person whose relationship to the member or candidate makes the member or candidate a beneficial owner of the person's securities. Members and candidates must not convey this information to any other person if the information can be deemed material nonpublic information.

Members or candidates may undertake transactions in accounts for which they are a beneficial owner only after their clients and employers have had an adequate opportunity to act on the recommendation. Personal transactions include those made for the member's or candidate's own account, for family (including spouse, children, and other immediate family members) accounts, and for accounts in which the member or candidate has a direct or indirect pecuniary interest, such as a trust or retirement account. Family accounts that are client accounts should be treated like any other firm account and should neither be given special treatment nor be disadvantaged because of an existing family relationship with the member or candidate. If a member or candidate has a beneficial ownership in the account, however, the member or candidate may still be subject to preclearance or reporting requirements of their employer or applicable law.

Recommended Procedures for Compliance

Policies and procedures designed to prevent potential conflicts of interest, or even the appearance of a conflict of interest, with respect to personal transactions are critical to establishing investor confidence in the securities industry. Because investment firms vary greatly in assets under management, types of clients, number of employees, and so on, each firm should establish policies regarding personal investing that are best suited to the firm. Members and candidates should then prominently disclose those policies to clients and prospective clients.

The specific provisions of each firm's standards will vary, but all firms should adopt certain basic procedures to address the conflict areas created by personal investing. These include:

Limited Participation in Equity IPOs

Some eagerly awaited IPOs may significantly rise in value shortly after the issue is brought to market. Because the new issue may be highly attractive and sought after, the opportunity to participate in the IPO may be limited. Therefore, purchases of IPOs by investment personnel create conflicts of interest in two principal ways. First, participation in an IPO may have the appearance of appropriating an attractive investment opportunity from clients for personal gain—a clear breach of the duty of loyalty to clients. Second, because opportunities to participate in IPOs are limited, there may be an appearance that the investment opportunity is being bestowed as an incentive to make future investment decisions for the benefit of the party providing the opportunity. Members and candidates can avoid these conflicts or the appearance of a conflict of interest by not participating in IPOs.

Reliable and systematic review procedures should be established to ensure that conflicts relating to IPOs are identified and appropriately dealt with by supervisors. Members and candidates should preclear their participation in IPOs, even in situations were there are no conflicts of interest between a member's or candidate's participation in an IPO and the client's interests. Members and candidates should not benefit from the position that their clients occupy in the marketplace—through preferred trading, the allocation of limited offerings, and/or oversubscription.

Restrictions on Private Placements

Strict limits should be placed on investment personnel acquiring securities in private placements, and appropriate supervisory and review procedures should be established to prevent noncompliance.

Firms do not routinely use private placements for clients (e.g., venture capital deals) because of the high risk associated with them. Conflicts relating to private placements are more significant to members and candidates who manage large pools of assets or act as plan sponsors because these managers may be offered special opportunities, such as private placements, as a reward or an enticement for continuing to do business with a particular broker.

Participation in private placements raises conflict-of-interest issues that are similar to issues surrounding IPOs. Investment personnel should not be involved in transactions, including (but not limited to) private placements that could be perceived as favors or gifts that seem designed to influence future judgment or to reward past business deals.

Whether the venture eventually proves to be good or bad, managers have an immediate conflict concerning private placement opportunities. Participants in private placements have an incentive to recommend these investments to clients if and when they go public, regardless of the suitability of the investments for their clients, in order to increase the value of the participants' personal portfolios.

Establish Blackout/Restricted Periods

Investment personnel involved in the investment decision-making process should establish blackout periods prior to trades for clients so that managers cannot take advantage of their knowledge of client activity by "front-running" client trades.

Individual firms must decide who within the firm should be required to comply with the trading restrictions. At a minimum, all individuals who are involved in the investment decision-making process should be subject to the same restricted period. Each firm must determine specific requirements relating to blackout and restricted periods that are most relevant to the firm while ensuring that the procedures are governed by the guiding principles set forth in the Code and Standards. Size of firm and type of securities purchased are relevant factors. For example, in a large firm, a blackout requirement is, in effect, a total trading ban because the firm is continually trading in most securities. In a small firm, the blackout period is more likely to prevent the investment manager from front-running.

Reporting Requirements

Supervisors should establish reporting procedures for investment personnel, including duplicate confirmations, disclosure of personal holdings/beneficial ownerships, and preclearance procedures. Once trading restrictions are in place, they must be enforced. The best method for monitoring and enforcing procedures established to eliminate conflicts of interest relating to personal trading is through reporting requirements, including the following:

▶ Disclosure of holdings in which the employee has a beneficial interest. Disclosure by investment personnel to the firm should be made upon commencement of the employment relationship and at least annually thereafter. To address privacy considerations, disclosure of personal holdings should be handled in a confidential manner by the firm.

▶ Providing duplicate confirmations of transactions. Investment personnel should be required to direct their brokers to supply duplicate copies or confirmations to their firms of all their personal securities transactions and copies of periodic statements for all securities accounts. Firms should establish additional reporting requirements, including the frequency of such reporting, that emphasize the firm's intention to promote full and complete disclosure and that explain the role and responsibilities of supervisors. The duplicate confirmation requirement has two purposes: (1) The requirement sends a message that "people are looking" and makes it difficult for an individual to act unethically, and (2) it enables verification of the accounting of the flow of personal investments that cannot be determined from merely looking at transactions or holdings.

▶ Preclearance procedures. Investment personnel should clear all personal investments to identify possible conflicts prior to the execution of personal trades. Preclearance procedures are designed to identify possible conflicts before a problem arises. Preclearance procedures are consistent with the CFA Institute Code and Standards and demonstrate that members, candidates, and their firms place the interests of their clients ahead of their own personal investing interests.

Disclosure of Policies

Upon request, members and candidates should fully disclose to investors their firms' personal investing policies. The infusion of information on employees' personal investment activities and policies into the marketplace will foster an atmosphere of full and complete disclosure and calm the public's legitimate concerns about the conflicts of interest posed by investment personnel's personal trading. The disclosure must be helpful to investors, however, not simply boiler-plate language containing some vague admonition that investment personnel are "subject to policies and procedures regarding their personal trading."

Application of the Standard

Example 1: A research analyst, Marlon Long, does not recommend purchase of a common stock for his employer's account because he wants to purchase the stock personally and does not want to wait until the recommendation is approved and the stock purchased by his employer.

> *Comment:* Long violated Standard VI(B) by taking advantage of his knowledge of the stock's value before allowing his employer to benefit from that information.

Example 2: Carol Baker, the portfolio manager of an aggressive-growth mutual fund, maintains an account in her husband's name at several brokerage firms with which the fund and a number of Baker's other individual clients do a substantial amount of business. Whenever a new hot issue becomes available, she instructs the brokers to buy it for her husband's account. Because such issues normally are scarce, Baker often acquires shares while her clients are not able to participate.

> *Comment:* Baker must acquire shares for her mutual fund first and, only after doing so, acquire them for her husband's account, even though she might miss out on participating in new issues via her husband's account. She also must disclose the trading for her husband's account to her employer because this activity creates a conflict between her personal interests and her employer's interests [Standard VI(A)—Disclosure of Conflicts].

Example 3: Erin Toffler, a portfolio manager at Esposito Investments, manages the retirement account established with the firm by her parents. Whenever IPOs become available, she first allocates shares to all her other clients for whom the investment is appropriate; only then does she place any remaining portion in her parents' account, if the issue is appropriate for them. She has adopted this procedure so that no one can accuse her of favoring her parents.

> *Comment:* Toffler has breached her duty to her parents by treating them differently from her other accounts simply because of the family relationship. As fee-paying clients of Esposito Investments, Toffler's parents are entitled to the same treatment as any other client of the firm. If Toffler has beneficial ownership in the account, however, and Esposito Investments has preclearance and reporting requirements for personal transactions, she may have to preclear the trades and report the transactions to Esposito.

Example 4: Gary Michaels is an entry-level employee who holds a relatively low-paying job serving both the research and investment management departments of an active investment management company. He purchases a sports car and begins to wear expensive clothes after only a year of employment with the firm. The director of the investment management department, who has responsibility for monitoring the personal stock transactions of all employees, investigates and discovers that Michaels has made substantial investment gains by purchasing stocks just before they were put on the firm's recommended purchase list. Michaels was regularly given the firm's quarterly personal transaction form but declined to complete it.

> *Comment:* Michaels violated Standard VI(B) by placing personal transactions ahead of client transactions. In addition, his supervisor violated the

Standards by permitting Michaels to continue to perform his assigned tasks without first having signed the quarterly personal transaction form [Standard IV(C)—Responsibilities of Supervisors]. Note also that if Michaels had communicated information about the firm's recommendations to a person who traded the security, that action would be a misappropriation of the information and a violation of Standard II(A)—Material Nonpublic Information.

Example 5: A brokerage's insurance analyst, Denise Wilson, makes a closed-circuit report to her firm's branches around the country. During the broadcast, she includes negative comments about a major company within the industry. The following day, Wilson's report is printed and distributed to the sales force and public customers. The report recommends that both short-term traders and intermediate investors take profits by selling that company's stocks. Seven minutes after the broadcast, Ellen Riley, head of the firm's trading department, closes out a long call position in the stock. Shortly thereafter, Riley establishes a sizable "put" position in the stock. Riley claims she took this action to facilitate anticipated sales by institutional clients.

> *Comment:* Riley expected that both the stock and option markets would respond to the "sell" recommendation, but she did not give customers an opportunity to buy or sell in the options market before the firm itself did. By taking action before the report was disseminated, Riley's firm could have depressed the price of the "calls" and increased the price of the "puts." The firm could have avoided a conflict of interest if it had waited to trade for its own account until its clients had an opportunity to receive and assimilate Wilson's recommendations. As it is, Riley's actions violated Standard VI(B).

C. Referral Fees

Members and candidates must disclose to their employer, clients, and prospective clients, as appropriate, any compensation, consideration, or benefit received from, or paid to, others for the recommendation of products or services.

Standard VI(C) states the responsibility of members and candidates to inform employer, clients, and prospective clients of any benefit received for referrals of customers and clients. Such disclosure will allow the client or employer to evaluate (1) any partiality shown in any recommendation of services and (2) the full cost of the services.

Appropriate disclosure means that members and candidates must advise the client or prospective client, before entry into any formal agreement for services, of any benefit given or received for the recommendation of any services provided by the member or candidate. In addition, the member or candidate must disclose the nature of the consideration or benefit—for example, flat fee or percentage basis, one-time or continuing benefit, based on performance, benefit in the form of provision of research or other noncash benefit—together with the estimated dollar value. Consideration includes all fees, whether paid in cash, in soft dollars, or in kind.

Application of the Standard

Example 1: Brady Securities, Inc., a broker/dealer, has established a referral arrangement with Lewis Brothers, Ltd., an investment counseling firm. Under this arrangement, Brady Securities refers all prospective tax-exempt accounts,

▶ providing confidential program information to candidates or the public;

▶ disregarding or attempting to circumvent security measures established by CFA Institute for the CFA examination;

▶ improperly using the CFA designation or other association with CFA Institute to further personal or professional goals; and

▶ misrepresenting information on the Professional Conduct Statement or the CFA Institute Professional Development Program.

This standard does not cover expressing opinions regarding the CFA Program or CFA Institute. Members and candidates are free to disagree and express their disagreement with CFA Institute on its policies, procedures, or any advocacy positions taken by the organization.

Application of the Standard

Example 1: Travis Nero serves as a proctor for the administration of the CFA examination in his city. In the course of his service, he reviews a copy of the Level II examination on the evening prior to the examination's administration and provides information concerning the examination questions to two candidates who use it to prepare for the exam.

> *Comment:* Nero and the two candidates violated Standard VII(A). By giving information concerning the examination questions to two candidates, Nero provided an unfair advantage to the two candidates and undermined the integrity and validity of the Level II examination as an accurate measure of the knowledge, skills, and abilities necessary to earn the right to use the CFA designation. By accepting the information, the candidates also compromised the integrity and validity of the Level II examination and undermined the ethical framework that is a key part of the designation.

Example 2: Loren Sullivan is enrolled to take the Level II CFA examination. He has been having difficulty remembering a particular formula, so prior to entering the examination room, he writes the formula on the palm of his hand. During the afternoon section of the examination, a proctor notices Sullivan looking at the palm of his hand. She asks to see his hand and finds the formula to be a bit smudged but readable.

> *Comment:* Because Sullivan wrote down information from the Candidate Body of Knowledge and took that written information into the examination, his conduct compromised the validity of his examination and violated Standard VII(A). Sullivan's conduct was also in direct contradiction of the rules and regulations of the CFA Program, the Candidate Pledge, and the CFA Institute Code and Standards.

Example 3: Prior to participating in the CFA Examination Grading Program, Wesley Whitcomb is required to sign a CFA Institute Grader Agreement. As part of the Grader Agreement, Whitcomb agrees not to reveal or discuss the examination materials with anyone except CFA Institute staff or other graders. Several weeks after the conclusion of the CFA examination grading, Whitcomb tells several colleagues who are candidates in the CFA Program which question he graded. He also discusses the guideline answer and adds that few candidates scored well on the question.

> *Comment:* Whitcomb violated Standard VII(A) by breaking the Grader Agreement and disclosing information related to a specific question on the examination, which compromised the integrity of the examination process.

Example 4: At the conclusion of the morning section of the Level I CFA examination, the proctors announce that all candidates are to stop writing immediately. John Davis has not completed the examination, so he continues to randomly fill in ovals on his answer sheet. A proctor approaches Davis's desk and reminds him that he should stop writing immediately; Davis, however, continues to complete the answer sheet. After the proctor asks him to stop writing two additional times, Davis finally puts down his pencil.

Comment: By continuing to complete his examination after time was called, Davis violated Standard VII(A). By continuing to write, Davis had an unfair advantage over other candidates, and his conduct compromised the validity of his examination. Additionally, by not heeding the proctor's repeated instructions, Davis violated the rules and regulations of the CFA Program.

Example 5: Ashlie Hocking is writing Level II of the CFA examination in London. After completing the exam, she immediately attempts to contact her friend in Sydney, Australia, to tip him off to specific questions on the exam.

Comment: Hocking has violated Standard VII(A) by attempting to give her friend an unfair advantage, thereby compromising the integrity of the CFA examination process.

Example 6: Jose Ramirez is an investment-relations consultant for several small companies that are seeking greater exposure to investors. He is also the program chair for the CFA Institute society in the city where he works. To the exclusion of other companies, Ramirez only schedules companies that are his clients to make presentations to the society.

Comment: Ramirez, by using his volunteer position at CFA Institute to benefit himself and his clients, compromises the reputation and integrity of CFA Institute and, thus, violates Standard VII(A).

Example 7: Marguerite Warrenski is a member of the CFA Institute Investment Performance Council (IPC), which oversees the creation, implementation, and revision of the CFA Institute performance presentation standards: the AIMR-PPS and GIPS. As a member of the IPC, she has advance knowledge of confidential information regarding both standards, including any new or revised standards the committee is considering. She tells her clients that her IPC membership will allow her to assist her clients in keeping up with changes to the standards and facilitating their compliance with the changes.

Comment: Warrenski, by using her volunteer position at CFA Institute to benefit herself and her clients, compromises the reputation and integrity of CFA Institute and, thus, violates Standard VII(A).

B. Reference to CFA Institute, the CFA Designation, and the CFA Program

When referring to CFA Institute, CFA Institute membership, the CFA designation, or candidacy in the CFA Program, members and candidates must not misrepresent or exaggerate the meaning or implications of membership in CFA Institute, holding the CFA designation, or candidacy in the CFA Program.

Individuals may reference their CFA designation, CFA Institute membership, or candidacy in the CFA Program but must not exaggerate the meaning or implications of membership in CFA Institute, holding the CFA designation, or candidacy in the CFA Program.

This standard is intended to prevent promotional efforts that make promises or guarantees that are tied to the designation. Statements referencing CFA Institute, the CFA designation, or the CFA Program must not:

► over-promise the competency of an individual, or

► over-promise future investment results (e.g., higher performance, lower risk).

Statements that highlight or emphasize the commitment of CFA Institute members, CFA charterholders, and CFA candidates to ethical and professional conduct as well as the thoroughness and rigor of the CFA Program are appropriate. Members and candidates may make claims about the relative merits of CFA Institute, the CFA Program, or the Code of Ethics as long as those statements are the opinion of the speaker, whether implicitly or explicitly stated as opinion. Otherwise, statements that do not express opinion have to be supported by facts.

Standard VII(B) applies to any form of communication, including but not limited to that made in electronic or written form (such as on firm letterhead, business cards, professional biographies, directory listings, printed advertising, firm brochures, or personal resumes) and oral statements made to the public, clients, or prospects.

CFA Institute Membership

The term "CFA Institute members" refers to Regular and Affiliate members of CFA Institute who have met the membership requirements as defined in the CFA Institute Bylaws. Once accepted as a CFA Institute member, the member must satisfy the following requirements to maintain his or her status:

► remit annually to CFA Institute a completed Professional Conduct Statement, which renews the commitment to abide by the requirements of the CFA Institute Code of Ethics and Standards of Professional Conduct and the CFA Institute Professional Conduct Program, and

► pay applicable CFA Institute membership dues on an annual basis.

If a CFA Institute member fails to meet any one of the requirements listed above, then the individual is no longer considered an active member. Until their membership is reactivated, individuals must not hold themselves out as active members. They may state, for example, that they were CFA Institute members in the past or reference the years when their membership was active.

Using the Chartered Financial Analyst Designation

Those who have earned the right to use the Chartered Financial Analyst designation may use the marks "Chartered Financial Analyst" or "CFA" and are encouraged to do so but only in a manner that does not misrepresent or exaggerate the meaning or implications of the designation. The use of the designation may be accompanied by an accurate explanation of the requirements that have been met to earn the right to use the designation.

"CFA charterholders" are those individuals who have earned the right to use the Chartered Financial Analyst designation granted by CFA Institute. These are people who have satisfied certain requirements, including completion of the CFA Program and required years of acceptable work experience. Once granted the right to use the designation, individuals must also satisfy the CFA Institute membership requirements (see above) to maintain their right to use the designation.

If a CFA charterholder fails to meet any one of the membership requirements, he or she forfeits the right to use the CFA designation. Until reactivated, individuals must not hold themselves out as CFA charterholders. They may state, for example, that they were charterholders in the past.

Referencing Candidacy in the CFA Program

Candidates in the CFA Program may reference their participation in the CFA Program, but the reference must clearly state that an individual is a candidate in the CFA Program and must not imply that the candidate has achieved any type of partial designation. A person is a candidate in the CFA Program if:

► the person's application for registration in the CFA Program has been accepted by CFA Institute, as evidenced by issuance of a notice of acceptance, and the person is enrolled to sit for a specified examination; or

► the registered person has sat for a specified examination but exam results have not yet been received.

If an individual is registered for the CFA Program but declines to sit for an exam or otherwise does not meet the definition of a candidate as described in the CFA Institute Bylaws, then that individual is no longer considered an active candidate. Once the person is enrolled to sit for a future examination, his or her CFA candidacy resumes.

CFA candidates must never state or imply a partial designation for passing one or more levels or cite an expected completion date of any level of the CFA Program. Final award of the charter is subject to meeting the CFA Program requirements and approval by the CFA Institute Board.

If a candidate passes each level of the exam on the first try and wants to state that he or she did so, that is not a violation of Standard VII(B) because it is a statement of fact. If the candidate then goes on to claim or imply superior ability by obtaining the designation in only three years, he or she is in violation of the standard.

The following statements and Exhibit 2 (on pp. 106–107) illustrate proper and improper references to the CFA designation:

Improper References

► "CFA charterholders achieve better performance results."

► "John Smith is among the elite, having passed all three CFA examinations in three consecutive attempts."

► "As a CFA charterholder, I am the most qualified to manage client investments."

► "CFA, Level II."

► "CFA, Expected 2005."

Proper References

► "Completion of the CFA Program has enhanced my portfolio management skills."

► "John Smith passed all three CFA examinations in three consecutive years."

► "The CFA designation is globally recognized and attests to a charterholder's success in a rigorous and comprehensive study program in the field of investment management and research analysis."

EXHIBIT 2	Correct and Incorrect Use of the Chartered Financial Analyst and CFA Marks

Incorrect	Principle	Correct
He is one of two CFAs in the company. He is a Chartered Financial Analyst.	The CFA and Chartered Financial Analyst designations must always be used as adjectives, never as nouns or common names.	He is one of two CFA charterholders in the company. He earned the right to use the Chartered Financial Analyst designation.
Jane Smith, C.F.A. John Doe, cfa	No periods. Always capitalize the letters "CFA".	Jane Smith, CFA
John, a CFA-type portfolio manager. The focus is on Chartered Financial Analysis. CFA-equivalent program Swiss-CFA	Do not alter the designation to create new words or phrases.	John Jones, CFA
Jones Chartered Financial Analysts, Inc.	The designation must not be used as part of the name of a firm.	John Jones, Chartered Financial Analyst
Jane Smith, **CFA** John Doe, **Chartered Financial Analyst**	The CFA designation should not be given more prominence (e.g., larger, bold) than the charterholder's name.	Jane Smith, CFA John Doe, Chartered Financial Analyst
Chartered Financial Analyst (CFA), September 2007	Candidates in the CFA Program must not cite the expected date of exam completion and award of charter.	Level I candidate in the CFA Program.
CFA Level I. CFA degree expected in 2006.	No designation exists for someone who has passed Level I, Level II, or Level III of the exam. The CFA designation should not be referred to as a degree.	Passed Level I of the CFA examination in 2002.
CFA (Passed Finalist)	A candidate who has passed Level III but has not yet received his or her charter cannot use the CFA or Chartered Financial Analyst designation.	I have passed all three levels of the CFA Program and may be eligible for the CFA charter upon completion of the required work experience.

(Exhibit continued on next page …)

EXHIBIT 2	(continued)

CFA, 2001, UK Society of Investment Professionals	In citing the designation in a resume, a charterholder should use the date that he or she received the designation and should cite CFA Institute as the conferring body.	CFA, 2001, CFA Institute (optional: Charlottesville, Virginia, USA)

▶ "The credibility that the CFA designation affords and the skills the CFA Program cultivates are key assets for my future career development."

▶ "As a CFA charterholder, I am committed to the highest ethical standards."

▶ "I enrolled in the CFA Program to obtain the highest set of credentials in the global investment management industry."

▶ "I passed Level I of the CFA examination."

▶ "I am a 2003 Level III CFA candidate."

▶ "I passed all three levels of the CFA Program and will be eligible for the CFA charter upon completion of the required work experience."

Proper Usage of the CFA Marks

Upon obtaining the CFA charter from CFA Institute, charterholders are given the right to use the CFA trademarks, including Chartered Financial Analyst®, CFA®, and the CFA Logo (a certification mark). These trademarks are registered by CFA Institute in countries around the world.

▶ The Chartered Financial Analyst and CFA marks must always be used either after a charterholder's name or as adjectives (never as nouns) in written documents or oral conversations. For example, to refer to oneself as "a CFA" or "a Chartered Financial Analyst" is improper.

▶ The CFA Logo certification mark is used by charterholders as a distinctive visual symbol of the CFA designation that can be easily recognized by employers, colleagues, and clients. As a certification mark, it must only be used to directly reference an individual charterholder or group of charterholders.

CFA charterholders should refer to guidelines published by CFA Institute that provide additional information and examples illustrating proper and improper use of the CFA Logo, Chartered Financial Analyst, and CFA marks. These guidelines and the CFA Logo are available on the CFA Institute website at www.cfainstitute.org/memservices/cfaguide.html.

Recommended Procedures for Compliance

It is common for references to a member's CFA designation or CFA candidacy to be misused or improperly referenced by others within a member's or candidate's firm who do not possess knowledge of the requirements of Standard VII(B). As an appropriate step to reduce this risk, members and candidates should disseminate written information on Standard VII(B) and the accompanying guidance to their firm's legal, compliance, public relations, and marketing departments. Information on proper use of the designation can be found on the CFA Institute website at: www.cfainstitute.org/memservices/pdf/trademark_usage.pdf. For materials that reference employees' affiliation with CFA Institute, members and candidates should encourage their firms to create templates that are approved by a central authority (such as the compliance department) as being consistent with Standard VII(B). This practice would promote consistency and accuracy of references to CFA Institute membership, the CFA designation, and CFA candidacy within the firm.

Application of the Standard

Example 1: An advertisement for AZ Investment Advisors states that all the firm's principals are CFA charterholders and all passed the three examinations on their first attempt. The advertisement prominently links this fact to the notion that AZ's mutual funds have achieved superior performance.

> *Comment:* AZ may state that all principals passed the three examinations on the first try as long as this statement is true and is not linked to performance or does not imply superior ability. Implying that (1) CFA charterholders achieve better investment results and (2) those who pass the exams on the first try may be more successful than those who do not violates Standard VII(B).

Example 2: Five years after receiving his CFA charter, Louis Vasseur resigns his position as an investment analyst and spends the next two years traveling abroad. Because he is not actively engaged in the investment profession, he does not file a completed Professional Conduct Statement with CFA Institute and does not pay his CFA Institute membership dues. At the conclusion of his travels, Vasseur becomes a self-employed analyst, accepting assignments as an independent contractor. Without reinstating his CFA Institute membership by filing his Professional Conduct Statement and paying his dues, he prints business cards that display "CFA" after his name.

> *Comment:* Vasseur has violated Standard VII(B) because Vasseur's right to use the CFA designation was suspended when he failed to file his Professional Conduct Statement and stopped paying dues. Therefore, he no longer is able to state or imply that he is an active CFA charterholder. When Vasseur files his Professional Conduct Statement and resumes paying CFA Institute dues to activate his membership, he will be eligible to use the CFA designation upon satisfactory completion of CFA Institute reinstatement procedures.

Example 3: After a 25-year career, James Simpson retires from his firm. Because he is not actively engaged in the investment profession, he does not file a completed Professional Conduct Statement with CFA Institute and does not pay his CFA Institute membership dues. Simpson designs a plain business card (without a corporate logo) to hand out to friends with his new contact details, and he continues to put "CFA" after his name.

> *Comment:* Simpson has violated Standard VII(B). If he wants to obtain "retired" status in terms of his CFA Institute membership and CFA charter status, he needs to file the appropriate paperwork with CFA Institute to be recognized as such. By failing to file his Professional Conduct Statement and ceasing to pay dues, his membership is suspended and he gives up his right to use the CFA designation. When Simpson receives his notification from

CFA Institute that his membership has been reclassified as "retired" and he resumes paying reduced dues, his membership will be reactivated and his right to use the CFA designation will be reinstated.

Example 4: Asia Futures Ltd. is a small quantitative investment advisory firm. The firm takes great pride in the fact that all its employees are CFA charterholders. To underscore this fact, the firm's senior partner is proposing to change the firm's letterhead to include the following:

Asia Futures Ltd.

Comment: The CFA Logo is a certification mark intended to identify individual charterholders and must not be incorporated into a company name, confused with a company logo, or placed in such close proximity to a company name or logo as to give the reader the idea that the certification mark certifies the company. It would only be appropriate to use the CFA Logo on the business card or letterhead of each individual CFA charterholder.

Example 5: Rhonda Reese has been a CFA charterholder since 2000. In a conversation with a friend who is considering enrolling in the CFA Program, she states that she has learned a great deal from the CFA Program and that many firms require their employees to be CFA charterholders. She would recommend the CFA Program to anyone pursuing a career in investment management.

Comment: Reese's comments comply with Standard VII(B). Her statements refer to enhanced knowledge and the fact that many firms require the CFA designation for their investment professionals.

Example 6: Tatiana Prittima has earned both her CFA designation and a Ph.D. in finance. She would like to cite both her accomplishments on her business card but is unsure of the proper method for doing so.

Comment: The order of designations cited on such items as resumes and business cards is a matter of personal preference. Prittima is free to cite the CFA designation either before or after listing her Ph.D.

PRACTICE PROBLEMS FOR READING 2

Unless otherwise stated in the question, all individuals in the following questions are CFA Institute members or candidates in the CFA program and, therefore, are subject to the CFA Institute Code of Ethics and Standards of Professional Conduct.

1. Smith, a research analyst with a brokerage firm, decides to change his recommendation on the common stock of Green Company, Inc., from a buy to a sell. He mails this change in investment advice to all the firm's clients on Wednesday. The day after the mailing, a client calls with a buy order for 500 shares of Green Company. In this circumstance, Smith should:

   A. accept the order.

   B. advise the customer of the change in recommendation before accepting the order.

   C. not accept the order until five days have elapsed after the communication of the change in recommendation.

   D. not accept the order because it is contrary to the firm's recommendation.

2. All of the following statements about a manager's use of clients' brokerage commissions are true *except*:

   A. a client may direct a manager to use that client's brokerage commissions to purchase goods and services for that client.

   B. client brokerage commissions may be used by the manager to pay for securities research used in managing the client's portfolio.

   C. client brokerage commissions should be used to benefit the client and should be commensurate with the value of the brokerage and research services received.

   D. client brokerage commissions may be directed to pay for the investment manager's operating expenses.

3. Jamison is a junior research analyst with Howard & Howard, a brokerage and investment-banking firm. Howard & Howard's mergers and acquisitions department has represented the Britland Company in all of its acquisitions for the past 20 years. Two of Howard & Howard's senior officers are directors of various Britland subsidiaries. Jamison has been asked to write a research report on Britland. What is the best course of action for her to follow?

   A. Jamison may write the report but must refrain from expressing any opinions because of the special relationships between the two companies.

   B. Jamison may write the report so long as the officers agree not to alter it.

   C. Jamison may write the report if she discloses the special relationships with the company in the report.

   D. Jamison should not write the report because the two Howard & Howard officers are constructive insiders.

4. Which of the following statements clearly *conflicts* with the recommended procedures for compliance presented in the CFA Institute *Standards of Practice Handbook?*

A. Firms should disclose to clients the personal investing policies and procedures established for their employees.

B. Prior approval must be obtained for the personal investment transactions of all employees.

C. For confidentiality reasons, personal transactions and holdings should not be reported to employers unless mandated by regulatory organizations.

D. Personal transactions should be defined as including transactions in securities owned by the employee and members of his or her immediate family and transactions involving securities in which the employee has a beneficial interest.

5. Bronson provides investment advice to the board of trustees of a private university endowment fund. The trustees have provided Bronson with the fund's financial information, including planned expenditures. Bronson receives a phone call on Friday afternoon from Murdock, a prominent alumnus, requesting that Bronson fax him comprehensive financial information about the fund. According to Murdock, he has a potential contributor but needs the information that day to close the deal and cannot contact any of the trustees. Based on CFA Institute Standards, Bronson should:

A. send Murdock the information because disclosure would benefit the client.

B. not send Murdock the information to preserve confidentiality.

C. send Murdock the information, provided Bronson promptly notifies the trustees.

D. send Murdock the information because it is not material nonpublic information.

6. Miller heads the research department of a large brokerage firm. The firm has many analysts, some of whom are subject to the Code and Standards. If Miller delegates some supervisory duties, which statement best describes her responsibilities under the Code and Standards?

A. Miller's supervisory responsibilities do not apply to those subordinates who are not subject to the Code and Standards.

B. Miller no longer has supervisory responsibility for those duties delegated to her subordinates.

C. Miller retains supervisory responsibility for all subordinates despite her delegation of some duties.

D. CFA Institute Standards prevent Miller from delegating supervisory duties to subordinates.

7. Willier is the research analyst responsible for following Company X. All the information he has accumulated and documented suggests that the outlook for the company's new products is poor, so the stock should be rated a weak hold. During lunch, however, Willier overhears a financial analyst from another firm whom he respects offer opinions that conflict with Willier's forecasts and expectations. Upon returning to his office, Willier releases a strong buy recommendation to the public. Willier:

   A. was in full compliance with the Standards.

   B. violated the Standards by failing to distinguish between facts and opinions in his recommendation.

   C. violated the Standards because he did not seek approval of the change from his firm's compliance department.

   D. violated the Standards because he did not have a reasonable and adequate basis for his recommendation.

8. An investment management firm has been hired by ETV Corporation to work on an initial public offering for the company. The firm's brokerage unit now has a sell recommendation on ETV, but the head of the investment-banking department has asked the head of the brokerage unit to change the recommendation from sell to buy. According to the Standards, the head of the brokerage unit would be permitted to:

   A. increase the recommendation by no more than one increment (in this case, to a hold recommendation).

   B. place the company on a restricted list and give only factual information about the company.

   C. assign a new analyst to decide if the stock deserves a higher rating.

   D. reassign responsibility for rating the stock to the head of the investment-banking unit.

9. Albert and Tye, who recently started their own investment advisory business, have registered to take the Level III CFA examination. Albert's business card reads, "Judy Albert, CFA Level II." Tye has not put anything about the CFA designation on his business card, but promotional material that he designed for the business describes the CFA requirements and indicates that Tye participates in the CFA Program and has completed Levels I and II. According to the Standards:

   A. Albert has violated the Standards but Tye has not.

   B. Tye has violated the Standards but Albert has not.

   C. both Albert and Tye have violated the Standards.

   D. neither Albert nor Tye has violated the Standards.

10. Scott works for a regional brokerage firm. He estimates that Walkton Industries will increase its dividend by $1.50 a share during the next year. He realizes that this increase is contingent on pending legislation that would, if enacted, give Walkton a substantial tax break. The U.S. representative for Walkton's home district has told Scott that, although she is lobbying hard for the bill and prospects for passage look good, Congress's concern over the federal deficit could cause the tax bill to be voted down. Walkton has not made any statements regarding a change in dividend policy. Scott writes in his research report, "We expect Walkton's stock price to rise by at least $8.00 a share by the end of the year. Because the dividend will increase by $1.50 a share, the stock price gain will be fueled, in large part, by the increase in the dividend. Investors buying the stock at the current time should expect to realize a total return of at least 15 percent on the stock." According to the Standards:

   A. Scott violated the Standards because he used material inside information.

   B. Scott violated the Standards because he failed to separate opinion from fact.

   C. Scott violated the Standards by basing his research on uncertain predictions of future government action.

   D. Scott did not violate the Standards.

11. Which *one* of the following actions will *not* help to ensure the fair treatment of brokerage firm clients when a new investment recommendation is made?

   A. Limit the number of people in the firm who are aware in advance that a recommendation is to be disseminated.

   B. Distribute recommendations to institutional clients prior to individual accounts.

   C. Minimize elapsed time between the decision and the dissemination of a recommendation.

   D. Monitor the trading activities of firm personnel.

12. The mosaic theory holds that an analyst:

   A. violates the Code and Standards if the analyst fails to have knowledge of and comply with applicable laws.

   B. can use material public information or nonmaterial nonpublic information in the analyst's analysis.

   C. should use all available and relevant information in support of an investment recommendation.

   D. should distinguish between facts and opinions in research reports.

13. Jurgens is a portfolio manager. One of her firm's clients has told Jurgens that he will compensate her beyond that provided by her firm on the basis of the capital appreciation of his portfolio each year. Jurgens should:

   A. turn down the additional compensation because it will result in conflicts with the interests of other clients' accounts.

   B. receive permission from CFA Institute for the compensation arrangement.

   C. obtain permission from her employer prior to accepting the compensation arrangement.

   D. turn down the additional compensation because it will create undue pressure on her to achieve strong short-term performance.

Use the following information to answer Questions 26–31

Elias Nano, a recent MBA graduate and a CFA Level II candidate, is an unpaid summer intern with Patriarch Investment Counsel and expects to be offered a full-time paid position in the fall. Through his efforts, he is able to convince some family members and friends to become clients of the firm, and he now assists with the management of their accounts. His supervisor congratulates him and states: "These clients are the foundation from which you will be able to build your career as an investment advisor." After working hard all summer, Nano is told that Patriarch will not be able to offer him a paid position.

Nano interviews with a number of firms, and tells each one about the accounts that he is managing and expects to be able to bring with him. Because he was merely an intern at Patriarch, he does not think he owes any particular loyalty to Patriarch. He gains further assurance that he can keep the clients from the fact that his former supervisor implied that these were Nano's clients.

Nano subsequently joins Markoe Advisors as an assistant director with supervisory responsibilities. Markoe Advisors is an investment management firm that advertises that it provides customized portfolio solutions for individual and institutional clients. As a matter of policy, Markoe does not reject as a client any individual meeting the account minimum size. Markoe has two strategies—aggressive growth equity and growth equity—and is always fully invested. Nano asks his family and friends to transfer their accounts from Patriarch to Markoe.

As the first CFA candidate to be employed by Markoe, Nano has been asked to head a team that is reviewing the firm's compliance policies and procedures, which Nano considers inadequate and incomplete. He states his concerns to President Markoe: "Although Markoe Advisors, as a firm, cannot adopt the CFA Institute Code of Ethics and Standards of Professional Conduct, the firm can adopt the CFA Institute Asset Manager Code of Professional Conduct." President Markoe tells Nano that the firm is considering acquiring another advisory firm that has similar compliance policies and procedures. Markoe says: "We are not going to consider any compliance changes at this time."

Nano decides to draft a model compliance document to guide discussions about compliance issues at the firm in the future. Nano's initial draft includes the following components of a compliance policy statement:

1. Performance Presentation

   Performance data must be documented for each of Markoe Advisors' active accounts, be disclosed upon request, and be compared with the firm's composite, which is composed of active accounts only. Performance data must be presented on a before-tax basis to all clients, with the disclosure that all performance data are presented gross of fees.

2. Suitability of Investments

   Markoe Advisors, to maintain consistency of performance, assigns each client to one of the firm's two portfolios. Both of these portfolios are sufficiently broadly diversified to meet the investment objectives of all of our clients.

3. Disclosures of Conflicts

   Markoe Advisors encourages its staff to be involved in the business and civic community. Only business or civic interests that relate to current portfolio holdings need to be reported to the firm.

4. <u>Violations</u>

Any violation of the Markoe Advisors compliance policy statement will be reported to the president, and employees will receive an official warning.

5. <u>Compensation</u>

All staff members of Markoe Advisors will discuss with their supervisor all outside compensation that they are receiving or may receive.

26. Does Nano comply with CFA Institute Standards of Professional Conduct when he asks his clients to transfer their accounts to Markoe Advisors?

  A. No.

  B. Yes, because he contacted the clients after leaving Patriarch.

  C. Yes, because he was an intern and not a paid employee of Patriarch.

27. Is Nano's statement with respect to adoption of the CFA Institute Code of Ethics and Standards of Professional Conduct and the CFA Institute Asset Manager Code of Professional Conduct, respectively, correct?

	CFA Institute Code and Standards	CFA Institute Asset Manager Code of Professional Conduct
A.	No	No
B.	No	Yes
C.	Yes	No

28. According to the CFA Institute Code and Standards, what action should Nano take after discussing the firm's compliance policy with President Markoe? Nano should:

  A. resign from the firm.

  B. notify the board of directors.

  C. decline to accept supervisory responsibilities.

29. Does Nano's draft compliance policy statement conform to CFA Institute Code and Standards with respect to performance presentation?

  A. No, because terminated accounts are excluded.

  B. No, because performance is reported to all clients gross of fees.

  C. No, because performance data are presented on a before-tax basis.

30. Does Nano's draft compliance policy statement conform to CFA Institute Code and Standards with respect to:

	suitability of investments?	disclosures of conflicts?
A.	No	No
B.	No	Yes
C.	Yes	No

31. Does Nano's draft compliance policy statement conform to the CFA Institute Code and Standards with respect to:

	violations?	compensation?
A.	No	No
B.	No	Yes
C.	Yes	No

Use the following information to answer Questions 32–37

Patricia Jollie, CFA, is the fixed-income analyst and portfolio manager at Mahsud Financial Corporation, a small investment firm.

On 5 April, a friend who works for a bond-rating agency mentions to Jollie that a bond the agency is analyzing will experience a rating change. That bond also happens to be in Mahsud Financial's portfolios. Not wanting to trade ahead of the rating change announcement, Jollie decides to wait for distribution of the information through her friend's scheduled interview on a business television program the afternoon of 8 April. On the morning of 8 April, the information is released on a worldwide financial news service. Jollie immediately changes her mind about waiting for the interview and trades the bonds in Mahsud Financial's portfolios.

On 8 April, Jollie also trades a second bond to rebalance one of Mahsud Financial's portfolios. Jollie knows before executing her transaction that the bond is thinly traded. Although Jollie's trade will materially affect the bond's market price, it is not her intention to create price movement. A colleague witnesses the trade and large bond price change and says, "What a market overreaction; the bond price appears to be distorted now!" The colleague also points out to Jollie that Mahsud Financial's policy on market manipulation states: "Mahsud Financial employees must refrain from making transactions that distort security prices or volume with the intent to mislead market participants."

In conducting fixed-income research, Jollie believes that insight into prospective corporate bond returns can be derived from information that is also relevant to a company's stock. She spends several hours a week in equity investment chat rooms on the Internet, and she pays particular attention to the research reports posted by Jill Dean, CFA, a self-employed analyst, on www.Jill_Dean_the_Independent_Analyst.com. Prior to writing each report, Dean is paid a flat fee by the companies whose stocks she researches, but she does not reveal this fact to readers of her reports. She produces reports only for those companies whose stocks she can legitimately give "buy" recommendations after conducting a thorough analysis. Otherwise, she returns the flat fee. Investors have come to recognize all her "buy" ratings as having a sound and reasonable basis.

Jollie considers Dean's summaries and forecasts to be very well-crafted. Dean has given Jollie written permission to use her summaries and forecasts, word for word and without attribution, in her own bond analysis reports. On occasion, Jollie has done so. In Dean's other Internet postings, she reports the results of relevant academic finance studies. Once Jollie learns of a study by reading Dean's postings, she often reads the original study and mentions the results in her own reports. Jollie always cites the original study only and does not reveal that she learned of the study through Dean.

Mahsud Financial occasionally sponsors seminars on ethics. In the most recent seminar, the main speaker made statements about the relationship between ethics and the law, and also about potential sources of conflict of interest for research analysts. The seminar speaker's statements were:

Statement 1: An illegal action is unethical, and actions that are legal are ethically sound.

Statement 2: For analysts, a major source of conflict of interest is potential profit resulting from a weak barrier between the employer's research department and investment banking department.

Statement 3: For situations in which conflicts of interest cannot be avoided, Mahsud Financial's written compliance policy should include the following component: "For unavoidable conflicts of interest that the employee judges to be material, employees must disclose the conflicts of interest to clients prominently, and in plain language."

Statement 4: On the matter of gifts that might impair employees' objectivity, Mahsud Financial's written compliance policy should also include the following component: "Employees must disclose to Mahsud Financial all client gifts regardless of value."

32. Does Jollie violate CFA Institute Standards of Professional Conduct by trading on the news of the bond rating change?

   A. No.

   B. Yes, only because she possessed material nonpublic information.

   C. Yes, only because she should have waited to trade until after her friend's television interview took place.

33. Are Jollie's 8 April trade of the second bond and Mahsud Financial's policy on market manipulation, respectively, consistent with CFA Institute Standards on market manipulation?

   A. Both Jollie's 8 April trade of the second bond and Mahsud Financial's policy on market manipulation are consistent with CFA Institute Standards.

   B. Jollie's 8 April trade of the second bond is inconsistent and Mahsud Financial's policy on market manipulation is consistent with CFA Institute Standards.

   C. Jollie's 8 April trade of the second bond is consistent and Mahsud Financial's policy on market manipulation is inconsistent with CFA Institute Standards.

34. Does Dean violate CFA Institute Standards in preparing and disseminating her equity reports?

   A. No.

   B. Yes, only by misrepresenting her recommendations as independent.

   C. Yes, only by accepting payment from the companies on which she produces reports.

35. In preparing investment reports, does Jollie violate CFA Institute Standards with respect to her:

	use of Dean's summaries and forecasts?	citation of studies found in Dean's Internet postings?
A.	No	Yes
B.	Yes	No
C.	Yes	Yes

36. Are the seminar speaker's statements #1 and #2, respectively, correct?

	Statement #1	Statement #2
A.	No	No
B.	No	Yes
C.	Yes	No

37. Are the seminar speaker's statements #3 and #4, respectively, sufficient to meet the requirements of related CFA Institute Standards?

	Statement #3	Statement #4
A.	No	No
B.	No	Yes
C.	Yes	No

Harvest Financial[1]

Stacia Finnegan, CFA, manages a regional office of Harvest Financial's brokerage business. Her responsibilities include training all personnel in compliance with the firm's standards, policies, procedures, and applicable laws and regulations.

Finnegan is currently providing training on the firm's new PlusAccount, a comprehensive fee-based brokerage account. "PlusAccounts," she tells the brokers, "are an excellent way to ensure that the financial advisor does not recommend trades for the purpose of generating commissions. The advisor and client's interests are aligned." She continues, "You will find that many clients will benefit from converting a traditional brokerage account to a PlusAccount. Be aware, however, that PlusAccounts are not appropriate for all categories of investors, including buy-and-hold clients and certain clients with assets less than $50,000." Finnegan distributes written compliance procedures for establishing and maintaining PlusAccounts. She carefully explains that regulatory rules "require that we have reasonable grounds for believing that the PlusAccount is appropriate for a particular customer. Additionally, we must review each account on an annual basis to determine whether PlusAccount status remains appropriate. The policies outlined in these documents are designed to ensure compliance with industry standards and regulatory requirements. You must follow these compliance procedures exactly."

[1] This case was written by Dorothy C. Kelly, CFA.

Finnegan then distributes and explains the sales and disclosure materials for clients. The materials include the following fee structure:

PlusAccount Annual Fee (as a Percent of Assets)*		
Account Asset Level	**Equity**	**Mutual Fund/Fixed Income**
From 0–$250,000	2.00%	1.00%
Next $250,000	1.50%	1.00%
Next $250,000	1.25%	1.00%
Next $250,000	1.00%	1.00%
More than $1 million	0.75%	0.75%

*Minimum annual fee of $1,000 billed quarterly.

Finnegan spends the rest of the afternoon training the staff on detailed procedures and answering their questions.

Chris Klein is a registered broker and financial advisor with Harvest. He is also a Level II Candidate in the CFA Program. Klein is excited about the new PlusAccounts and believes that they will be attractive for many clients.

One of Klein's clients is Elaine Vanderon, who contributes weekly to her brokerage account. Under Vanderon's directions, Klein invests the weekly contributions in actively managed mutual funds (unit trusts). The funds have below-average management fees and average returns. Commissions for Vanderon average $35 per transaction.

When Vanderon's account reaches $50,000 in assets, Klein recommends conversion to a PlusAccount. He carefully explains that in a PlusAccount, both the cost of investment advice and many implementation costs are wrapped into the management fee billed on a quarterly basis. Stock and bond commissions, he tells Vanderon, are discounted by 70%. Klein informs Vanderon that in a PlusAccount, she can buy or sell thousands of mutual funds or unit trusts (including those in which she invests) for no commissions or transaction charges. He explains that PlusAccounts are ideal for clients who trade often—or as part of a periodic investment program such as hers. Vanderon reads through the disclosure material provided by Klein and accepts his recommendation.

Klein routinely informs clients about the benefits of PlusAccount status and presents them with all the disclosure materials. Another client Klein encourages to open a PlusAccount is Lee Brown. Brown has accumulated stock holdings of $300,000 and trades equities almost daily. His annual commissions for the previous twelve months equal $9,100. His portfolio is well-diversified. He has a high risk tolerance and prefers growth stocks. After explaining the fee structure, Klein tells Brown "The PlusAccount is ideal for an active trader like you."

One year later, Finnegan is promoted. She delegates supervisory responsibility for Klein and 15 other brokers to her assistant branch manager.

The same month, Klein meets with Vanderon and Brown to review their portfolios and financial situations. Both clients are happy with their PlusAccounts. Vanderon's commission costs have declined to zero. Her account continues to grow in line with her plans and expectations. Brown is also happy with his account. His annual commission costs have declined 70% to $2,700.

Two months later, Vanderon receives a $1 million inheritance and places it in her PlusAccount. Although he conducted a full review two months earlier, Klein meets with Vanderon to review her financial situation and discuss potential changes to her investment policy. During their meeting, Klein mentions that he has completed Level III of the CFA examination. He informs Vanderon "Completion of the CFA Program has enhanced my portfolio management skills." He tells Vanderon "As a CFA charterholder, I am the best qualified to manage your investments." Vanderon congratulates Klein on his accomplishment and agrees to consider any changes he recommends to her PlusAccount.

The following month, Klein telephones Vanderon to recommend a highly-rated mutual fund. Klein states "The fund has an excellent performance history and is ranked in the top decile of comparable funds. For the past three- and five-year periods, its average annual return has exceeded the benchmark by 90 basis points. Of course, past performance is no guarantee of future returns, but several of my clients hold this fund and they are all very happy with it. One of them invested $50,000 five years ago. That investment is worth more than $100,000 today." When Vanderon asks about fees, Klein explains that the fund's management fees are 25 basis points higher than those of her existing investments. He adds "Because of your PlusAccount status, you won't incur a brokerage commission for this transaction even though I will receive a referral fee if you invest in the fund."

Six months later, Brown suffers serious medical and financial problems and stops trading. Klein telephones him to review his financial situation. Brown insists that he will make a full recovery and that he will be trading again shortly. During the next twelve months, Brown is too ill to trade. His growing expenses force him to withdraw large amounts from his PlusAccount. Within another 18 months, his PlusAccount value is less than $50,000.

38. When recommending Vanderon convert to a PlusAccount, does Klein violate any CFA Institute Standards of Professional Conduct?

   A. No.

   B. Yes, because he does not have a reasonable basis.

   C. Yes, because the account is unsuitable for Vanderon.

39. When recommending Brown convert to a PlusAccount, does Klein violate any CFA Institute Standards?

   A. No.

   B. Yes, relating to suitability.

   C. Yes, relating to reasonable basis.

40. When meeting with Vanderon, does Klein violate any CFA Standards?

   A. No.

   B. Yes, because he improperly references the CFA designation.

   C. Yes, because he claims enhanced portfolio management skills.

41. When recommending the mutual fund to Vanderon, does Klein violate any CFA Standards?

   A. No.

   B. Yes, relating to suitability.

   C. Yes, relating to referral fees.

42. In the eighteen months following Brown's change in financial situation, Klein is *least likely* to have violated the Standard relating to:

   A. loyalty, prudence, and care.

   B. diligence and reasonable basis.

   C. communication with clients and prospective clients.

43. In her supervisory duties, does Finnegan violate any CFA Standards?

   A. No.

   B. Yes, because she fails to ensure that compliance procedures are enforced.

   C. Yes, because she delegates supervisory authority to her assistant branch manager.

Khadri and Vinken[2]

A. J. Vinken, CFA, manages the Stonebridge Fund at Silk Road Capital Management. He develops a growth-stock selection model which produces highly favorable simulated performance results. He would like to employ the model in managing the Stonebridge Fund, a large-capitalization equity fund. He drafts a letter for distribution to all shareholders. In it, he discusses in detail his approach to equity selection using the model. He includes both the actual and simulated performance results of the Stonebridge Fund for the past three years as seen in Exhibit 1:

EXHIBIT 1	Stonebridge Fund Annual Returns	
Year	Stonebridge Fund (Simulated)	Stonebridge Fund (Actual)
1	10.71%	9.22%
2	2.83%	−4.13%
3	22.23%	22.23%
Average annual return	11.92%	9.11%

Vinken writes, "Using the proprietary selection model for the past three years, the Stonebridge Fund would have earned an average annual return of almost 300 basis points in excess of the fund's actual return. Based on these simulated results, I am confident that employing the model will yield better performance results in the future; however, Silk Road Capital Management can make no statement of assurances or guarantee regarding future investment returns."

D.S. Khadri, CFA, is also a portfolio manager at Silk Road. She recently assumed management of the small-cap Westlake Fund from Vinken.

Khadri implements an electronic record-retention policy when she becomes the Westlake manager. In accordance with her policy, all records for the fund, including investment analyses, transactions, and investment-related communications with clients and prospective clients, are scanned and electronically stored. Vinken maintained the same records in hard-copy format

---

[2] This case was written by David S. Krause, PhD, and Dorothy C. Kelly, CFA.

strategies; market opportunities; potential clients; and current and prospective fund managers. For his role on the board, Riser would receive an annual payment directly from the subsidiary equivalent to 5% of his total portfolio manager salary in Switzerland.

The following month, Riser accepts the position on the board. The subsidiary registers each new fund-of-funds product with regulatory authorities in Luxembourg and discloses Riser's role as a board member in the required filings, which are public and readily available.

Riser serves as the contact person for the subsidiary's institutional clients in Switzerland and participates in the subsidiary's road shows in Switzerland. His role during these road shows varies. On some occasions, he simply attends the presentations while the operating management sells the products; on others he gives the actual presentation promoting the products. Riser's name does not appear in the promotional material distributed at the road shows.

Alexander Komm, a long-time colleague of Riser, is the founder of Komm Private Management, which provides asset management, advisory, and trust services to high-net-worth individuals. The firm has several well-managed proprietary funds. Komm offers Riser a position with the firm as managing partner. Riser is flattered, but declines the offer, explaining that he is very happy working at Swibank.

That same week, the subsidiary informs Riser that it needs an experienced fund manager to manage a new publicly-traded Japanese equity product. Riser is convinced that Komm Private Management would be qualified and recommends the firm for the new product. After a thorough search process, the subsidiary hires Komm Private Management for the new product.

Six months later, after numerous discussions, Komm finally convinces Riser to join Komm Private Management as a managing partner. The following week, Riser submits his resignation at the private bank. His position on the board of the subsidiary is not dependent on his employment at the bank, and he agrees to serve the remaining three years of his term.

After signing and submitting his employment contract to Komm, Riser takes three weeks of vacation before starting his new position. During this time he purchases 2,000 shares of the new Japanese equity product for his private account. When he begins working at Komm Private Management, he purchases a large block of shares in the Japanese equity product, which he allocates according to internal procedures to all accounts for which it is suitable.

56. According to the CFA Institute Standards of Professional Conduct, before accepting the position on the board of the subsidiary, Riser should:

    A. receive verbal consent from Swibank.

    B. receive verbal consent from his clients.

    C. disclose to his employer the financial compensation proposed by the subsidiary.

57. When participating in the road shows in Switzerland, Riser *least likely* violates the Standard relating to:

    A. Disclosure of Conflicts.

    B. Independence and Objectivity.

    C. Additional Compensation Arrangements.

58. When recommending Komm, does Riser violate any CFA Institute Standards?

    A. No.

    B. Yes, relating to duties to employer.

    C. Yes, relating to disclosure of conflicts.

59. When resigning from Swibank, does Riser violate any CFA Institute Standards?

    A. No.

    B. Yes, because he breaches his duty of loyalty to his employer.

    C. Yes, because he does not resign his position with the Luxembourg subsidiary.

60. In his original purchase of 2,000 shares of the Japanese equity product, Riser *least likely* violates the Standard relating to:

    A. Suitability.

    B. Priority of Transactions.

    C. Integrity of Capital Markets.

61. According to CFA Institute Standards, Riser is not required to disclose to clients his:

    A. holdings of the Japanese equity product.

    B. relationship with the Swibank subsidiary.

    C. compensation from the Swibank subsidiary.

STUDY SESSION 2
ETHICAL AND PROFESSIONAL STANDARDS IN PRACTICE

Using examples and case studies, the readings in this study session show the use of the CFA Institute Code of Ethics and Standards of Professional Conduct as a body of principles for ethical reasoning and decision making. The readings serve as effective aids in understanding and internalizing the values and standards presented in the CFA Institute *Standards of Practice Handbook*. By applying the Code and Standards to case study conflicts, the candidate will gain experience identifying and explaining fundamental principles of conduct, which then become tools for dealing with real world challenges.

The Asset Manager Code of Professional Conduct uses the basic tenets of the CFA Institute Code of Ethics and Standards of Professional Conduct to establish ethical and professional standards for firms managing client assets. The Asset Manager Code of Professional Conduct also extends the Code and Standards to address investment management firm practices regarding trading, compliance, security pricing, and disclosure.

READING ASSIGNMENTS

Reading 3	Ethics in Practice
	Ethics in Practice, by Philip Lawton, CFA
Reading 4	The Consultant
	Ethics Cases
Reading 5	Pearl Investment Management (A), (B), and (C)
	Ethics Cases
Reading 6	Asset Manager Code of Professional Conduct

ETHICS IN PRACTICE
by Philip Lawton, CFA

LEARNING OUTCOMES

The candidate should be able to: Mastery

a. summarize the ethical responsibilities required by each of the six   ☐
   provisions of the Code of Ethics and the seven categories of the
   Standards of Professional Conduct;

b. interpret the Code of Ethics and Standards of Professional Conduct in   ☐
   situations involving issues of professional integrity and formulate
   corrective actions where appropriate.

INTRODUCTION   1

Investment professionals often face unanticipated ethical dilemmas in their work. Training and practice can help them recognize issues, and sound, relevant principles of ethical conduct can help them make appropriate decisions. Written for investment professionals, this reading is an introduction and overview of the CFA Institute Code of Ethics and Standards of Professional Conduct (the Code and Standards), revised in 2005. Sections 2 through 4 provide a conceptual framework for reading, interpreting, and applying the Code and Standards: Section 2 discusses the criteria for a profession and the place of ethics in the investment profession; Section 3 treats the relationship between ethics and the law; and Section 4 outlines an approach to ethical reasoning, using the Code and Standards as a set of principles for ethically positive action in concrete situations. Sections 5 and 6 are devoted to the Preamble and the provisions of the Code. Section 7 introduces the Standards, and Sections 8 through 14 present and explain the provisions of the Standards with numerous practical examples. Section 15 sets up the case studies following the text as exercises in ethical reasoning. A summary is provided for review, and multiple-choice questions give readers an opportunity to test their comprehension of specific provisions of the Code and Standards. The reading is followed by an Appendix of five short case studies, lifelike situations in which investment professionals encounter ethical challenges in their work.

2   ETHICS AND THE INVESTMENT PROFESSION

What makes investment analysis a profession as opposed to a business, a trade, or a craft? There is an extensive philosophical literature on the criteria defining a profession. For the purpose of this discussion, however, there are two factors that, taken together, can be said to distinguish a profession from other forms of work:

1. an established body of knowledge
2. a commitment to a broader good than the practitioner's self-interest[1]

Investment analysis is clearly based upon a body of knowledge, including economic and financial theory, empirical findings, and analytical techniques. The rigorous curriculum of the CFA Program is accordingly designed to equip practitioners with the concepts and skills to meet the actual demands of their work. In addition to ethical and professional standards, the CFA body of knowledge includes quantitative methods; economics; financial statement analysis; corporate finance; the analysis of equity, debt, derivative, and alternative investment instruments; and portfolio management, including performance evaluation and presentation. There is, moreover, general agreement on the scope of this body of knowledge. With the likely exception of industry-specific ethical standards of practice, much the same list of technical topics would be covered in a graduate business school course of study centering on investments. Investment analysis patently satisfies the first criterion for a profession: It rests upon an established body of knowledge, one that continues to grow as new insights are published.

This is enough to characterize investment analysis as a trade or a craft (admittedly a highly advanced craft) but not yet as a profession; taken singly, the criteria mentioned above are necessary but not sufficient conditions.

The many ways in which the discipline of investment analysis may serve the practitioner's self-interest are readily apparent. A career in investment analysis offers extraordinary opportunities for intellectual development, creativity, and prestige. Qualified individuals can choose to work in small firms or large national or multinational corporations. Depending upon their interests and talents, they can (among many other alternatives) value securities, make deals, or manage portfolios. They can choose a specialization rewarding superior quantitative skills or a position requiring an exceptional ability to form relationships and to explain technical matters clearly; they can stay close to home or travel frequently to distant locations. A high level of income is also a potential benefit. But, beyond the practitioner's self-interest, what broader good does investment analysis advance in the same way, for example, that medicine promotes health and at its best the law champions justice and liberty?

---

[1] These criteria are adapted from Thomas Donaldson, "Are Business Managers 'Professionals'?", *Business Ethics Quarterly*, Vol. 10, No. 1 (January 2000), pp. 83–94.

In the most general terms, for a society as a whole, investment analysis may be said to foster the creation of wealth by attending to the efficient allocation of resources in a market economy. The fundamental task of investment analysis is pricing securities in view of their riskiness, that is, estimating their present worth or intrinsic value in light of current and prospective capital market, economic, and industry conditions and the issuer's credit quality, competitive strength, and earnings outlook. Collectively, security analysts contribute to market efficiency by attempting to identify the most attractive investment opportunities, and in so doing, they improve the likelihood that prices fairly reflect the best information publicly available. Their purchase and sale recommendations influence investors' decisions and, it may be hoped, tend over the long term to channel financial assets to their most economically productive uses. *A first greater good qualifying investment analysis as a profession is the promotion of fair and efficient capital markets.*

As a practical matter, however, investment analysis is for the most part conducted on behalf of clients, institutional or individual investors. Its direct purpose is not to nurture economic expansion but to achieve the investors' financial objectives. For the trustees of a pension plan, the primary investment objective is to earn returns enabling the sponsor to maintain sufficient plan assets to meet current and projected liabilities for the benefit of plan participants. For the officers of an endowment fund or a foundation, the overriding objective is to fund the spending program without loss of principal. For the individual investor, the objective might be to produce current income or to save for the future. *A second broader good served by investment analysis is the clients' financial well-being.* Along with the body of knowledge, it is a dual commitment to promoting fair and efficient capital markets and to protecting and furthering the investing clients' interests that makes investment analysis a profession.

Although they are not generally identified as criteria, there are other characteristics that professions typically exhibit. One of the most noteworthy is having a code of ethics endorsed by a professional association and designed to set forth shared values such as integrity and independence of judgment.[2] These values notably include the practitioner's commitment to maintaining his or her competence (the body of knowledge) and the primacy of the clients' interests (the broader good). A code of ethics articulates the ideals to which the profession adheres. If it is thoughtfully written by experienced leaders committed to furthering the profession, and especially if it is complemented by standards of practice, a code of ethics usefully offers practitioners principled guidance on the basis of which they can make ethically sound decisions. It additionally functions as an authoritative source to which they can refer in justifying a course of action to their colleagues and managers.

Ethical values are not incidental to the profession of investment analysis, nor for that matter to any other line of work that qualifies as professional. In effect, those who identify themselves as investment professionals are making a claim, not only about their expertise but also about their commitment to a broader good than their own self-interest. They are implicitly proclaiming (or "professing") their adherence to values like honesty and diligence and to principles such as respecting the priority of the client's interests and promoting the integrity of the capital markets. CFA charterholders and candidates can look to the CFA Institute Code of Ethics and Standards of Professional Conduct for practical direction in realizing these values and actualizing these principles in their work.

---

[2] Many professions are also licensed by regulatory authorities.

3 PROFESSIONAL ETHICS AND THE LAW

Why is it not enough just to obey the law?

Certainly investment professionals are ethically obligated to be familiar with applicable laws and regulations—the rules directly governing their work. They are expected to know and understand the legal and regulatory requirements that pertain to their professional activities. In the CFA Institute Standards of Professional Conduct, this fundamental expectation appears as the first item in the first standard, Professionalism, but it could also be considered a matter of competence to practice, and to supervise others, in a given area of specialization. Unless they are responsible for their firm's compliance, investment analysts generally need not be expert in legal and regulatory matters. They do have to know enough, however, to be able to conduct their routine work by the rules and to recognize when it is appropriate to seek authoritative guidance.

Investment professionals are, furthermore, ethically obligated to abide by applicable law and regulation. Thinkers have taken many positions on the philosophical foundations of positive law, but in many societies there is a tacit presumption that illegal actions are usually unethical. The CFA Institute Standards of Professional Conduct hold that investment professionals must not only know but also comply with the laws, rules, and regulations governing their work. In general, if an action is illegal, it is also deemed unethical.

This is not to suggest that there is no such thing as an unjust law. Investment professionals are not *ethically* bound to comply with unjust laws. Nor, clearly, does the presupposition that illegal activity is unethical mean that legal action is necessarily ethical. For example, it may not be against the law to overstate one's expertise in order to win a job or a client, but it certainly conflicts with the fundamental ethical principles of honesty and integrity. There are significant ethical obligations beyond what is required by law, and it is therefore possible to be legally unassailable but ethically in the wrong, to the certain detriment of one's reputation and the possible disadvantage of others who merit honest and equitable treatment. This is why it is not enough, in striving for the ethical excellence legitimately expected of investment professionals, simply to obey the law.

4 INTERPRETING AND APPLYING THE CFA INSTITUTE CODE AND STANDARDS

Ethical reasoning is logical but not mathematically precise. The imperatives of the Code of Ethics and Standards of Professional Conduct have the general form, "Members of CFA Institute and candidates for the CFA designation must do *X*," for instance, "act with integrity." These are general orders based upon abstract concepts. Although apparently uncomplicated, words and expressions like "integrity" and "respect" and "in a professional and ethical manner" are not technical terms susceptible to clear-cut and unequivocal definition. They remain words used in ordinary language with all its ambiguity. This is not at all to suggest that they cannot be understood or that a consensus cannot be reached on their meaning. But it does mean that interpreting them may take some effort.

Consider Standard V(B.2), discussed later in this reading. It requires individuals to use "reasonable judgment" in identifying the factors that are important to their investment analysis, recommendations, or actions and to address those factors in their communications to clients and prospective clients. "Reasonable judgment" is a variant of phrases encountered elsewhere in the Code of Ethics and Standards of Professional Conduct. For example, the Code calls upon those people who are governed by its provisions to "use reasonable care and exercise independent professional judgment"; Standard I(B), Independence and Objectivity, refers to "reasonable care and judgment"; and Standard III(A), Loyalty, Prudence, and Care, requires covered persons to "act with reasonable care and exercise prudent judgment."

Let us make two observations. First, the term "judgment" is associated with "care" in the Code and Standards. Second, whether an investment professional is using "reasonable judgment" in identifying and communicating pertinent factors is itself a matter of judgment. This is not an impasse, but it is a challenge. Judgment is acquired with education and experience (and education may be seen as a means of gaining experience more systematically and rapidly than personally witnessing events would permit). The "reasonable judgment" required by the Code and Standards is the practical wisdom displayed by mature experts, competent investment professionals qualified by training and practice not only to identify relevant factors but also to evaluate their significance and to weigh their relative importance.

It is not only the words that may, despite their apparent simplicity and straightforwardness, be open to interpretation. It is, above all, the circumstances in which we find ourselves that may prove complicated and ambiguous. It is impossible, however, to anticipate every case, much less to capture the nuances of each situation. The idea of a code of ethics is to have a concise set of general principles which one can bear in mind as specific questions arise. Aristotle wrote, "The whole theory of [right] conduct is bound to be an outline only and not an exact system. . . . And if this is true of the general theory of ethics, still less is exact precision possible in dealing with particular cases of conduct, for these come under no science or professional tradition, but the agents themselves have to consider what is suited to the circumstances on each occasion, just as is the case with the art of medicine or navigation."[3] The CFA Institute Code and Standards articulate general principles and shared values to guide investment analysts, but one of the basic practical issues for ethical decision making is how to apply them correctly to complicated situations.

In any specific case, the initial and easiest step is to determine which provisions of the Code and Standards are pertinent. Consider, for example, having to explain the risks of a private equity investment opportunity to a client. The issuer, a manufacturer of capital goods, has an exciting new product but will face substantial challenges in winning acceptance in the marketplace, where competitors are entrenched and there are significant switching costs for potential buyers. How does the analyst choose the right words to characterize the risk? A relevant section of the Standards of Professional Conduct is Section I(C), Misrepresentation: "Members and candidates must not knowingly make any misrepresentations relating to investment analysis, recommendations, actions, or other professional activities." Other sections may also apply—for example, the requirements to have a reasonable and adequate basis for investment analyses and recommendations and to include the pertinent factors in client communications—but this one, prohibiting misrepresentation, is unquestionably germane.

Of course, that doesn't directly help answer the analyst's question, how to convey the riskiness of a deal when the financial projections are necessarily based upon assumptions about such matters as the future state of the economy, industrial purchasing managers' behavior, and competitors' responses. But it

---

[3] Aristotle, *Nichomachean Ethics,* II.ii.3–5. Translated by H. Rackham. Loeb Classical Library, Vol. XIX. Harvard University Press (1968), pp. 75–77.

does offer some direction. For example, characterizing the issuer's early-stage business risk as "slight" could be adjudged misrepresentation by objective, experienced investment analysts.

Interpreting the Code and Standards and applying them to actual situations, often involving real money, complex investment strategies, and several parties at interest, requires ethical wisdom. Even with a code of ethics and a set of professional standards written specifically to guide investment analysts, there aren't cookbook solutions for many concrete ethical problems. It takes training to recognize when there are ethical as opposed to "merely" technical matters to be addressed, and it takes practice to discern the principles and values at stake, to formulate the alternatives, and to decide upon the most suitable course of action in a particular situation.

Nonetheless, some general ideas, or at least some helpful questions, may be suggested. First, having identified the pertinent sections of the Code and Standards, the analyst must consider whether a course of action under consideration is consistent with their intent. Does the proposed action conform to the Code and Standards, or would another resolution be more in line with the principles and values they advance?

Second, when evaluating an alternative in view of the Code and Standards, it is useful to consider what the client would be likely to think if he were told all the circumstances. Would the client then agree that you had done the right thing? Or would the client conclude that you are untrustworthy?

Third, if your decision and the full circumstances surrounding it came to light, would your own or your firm's reputation for fair dealing be enhanced or compromised? How would it read in the press? Of course, not all journalists have the training to describe complex financial instruments and strategies correctly, but they themselves are generally subject to their own publishers' codes stressing integrity, independence, and accuracy. Assume for the present purpose that an article setting forth your action was comprehensive and factually correct. How would it sound?

Finally, is your decision commendable? Is it consistent with what one would expect of a leader? Does it set a good example for others? In a broader context, practicing the profession in an ethical manner means not merely following the rules but trying to become a person who knows and does the right thing.

Let us now turn to a survey of the Code of Ethics.

5   PREAMBLE TO THE CODE OF ETHICS

The Preamble to the CFA Institute Code of Ethics makes three points. It places the Code in the context of CFA Institute's educational mission, specifies who is bound by it, and mentions the sanctions to which violators are subject.

Throughout its long history, CFA Institute and its predecessors[4] have been dedicated to serving investors and members as a global leader in educating and examining investment managers and analysts and in sustaining high standards of professional conduct. CFA Institute's stated mission is "to lead the investment profession globally by setting the highest standards of ethics, education, and pro-

---

[4] CFA Institute is the name given the former Association for Investment Management and Research (AIMR) by vote of the membership in 2004. AIMR was founded in January 1990, when the Financial Analysts Federation (FAF) merged with the Institute of Chartered Financial Analysts (ICFA). The FAF was originally established in 1947 as a service organization for investment professionals in its societies and chapters. The ICFA was founded in 1959 to examine candidates and award the Chartered Financial Analyst (CFA) designation.

fessional excellence." It carries forward this goal not only through the CFA Program but also through conferences, publications, and the activities of its affiliated societies around the world.

Clearly, the Code of Ethics and the Standards of Professional Conduct are central to the mission of CFA Institute as a professional standard-setting association. As the Preamble mentions, the Code and the Standards were originally formulated in the 1960s. The Financial Analysts Federation first adopted a code of ethics in 1962, and the Institute of Chartered Financial Analysts adapted the FAF code in 1964.[5] The ethical standards have been expanded and clarified over time, but they have consistently emphasized certain core values such as the priority of client transactions over personal transactions. The version of the Code and Standards currently in force was revised by the members of the Standards of Practice Council in the period 2003–05.

The Code and Standards apply to all CFA Institute members, including CFA charterholders, and to candidates for the CFA designation. Upon joining CFA Institute as a member or entering the CFA program, individuals agree to be bound by the ethical standards.

The Preamble indicates that disciplinary sanctions may be imposed for violations of the Code and Standards. This position reflects the longstanding conviction of CFA Institute that breaches of ethical standards are serious matters; even the first version of the ethical guidelines, published over forty years ago, provided for terminating a violator's right to use the CFA designation. CFA Institute has developed carefully defined protocols for dealing with alleged infractions.

To remain in good standing, members of CFA Institute must submit an annual Professional Conduct Statement. Failure to file a Professional Conduct Statement can result in suspension of one's membership in CFA Institute, one's right to use the CFA designation, or both. By filing the Professional Conduct Statement, members disclose whether they have been the subject of any written complaints involving their professional conduct or of certain types of legal or regulatory action. Members additionally certify that they agree to comply with CFA Institute's Code of Ethics, Standards of Professional Conduct, Bylaws, and Rules of Procedure for Proceedings Related to Professional Conduct and to cooperate with CFA Institute in any investigation of their conduct. The current form of the Professional Conduct Statement is available on the CFA Institute website.

CFA Institute also accepts complaints from others about its members' professional conduct. Information about how to make a complaint appears on the CFA Institute website.

Investigations of alleged violations of the Code and Standards and subsequent actions including hearing panels, review panels, and the imposition of disciplinary sanctions are governed by the CFA Institute Rules of Procedure for Proceedings Related to Professional Conduct. Disciplinary sanctions may be imposed if a candidate is found to have violated the Code and Standards. Possible sanctions can include private censure, public censure, prohibition from future participation in the CFA Program, revocation of CFA Institute membership, and revocation of the right to use the CFA designation. Complete information about disciplinary procedures, including provisions for dealing with candidate misconduct during the CFA examination administration process, is available on the CFA Institute website.

---

[5] Nancy Regan, *The Institute of Chartered Financial Analysts: A Twenty-Five Year History,* The Institute of Chartered Financial Analysts (1987), pp. 50–52. The original (1964) version of the ICFA's ethical guidelines is reprinted as an appendix to Regan's history (p. 169).

take the initiative to bring up pertinent ethical issues with their managers, who might not otherwise be alert to potential missteps.

V. The fifth requirement of the Code of Ethics is to "promote the integrity of, and uphold the rules governing, global capital markets." Contributing to the fair and efficient functioning of the capital markets is one of the "greater goods" that make investment analysis a profession. Under the Code, there is a positive ethical obligation not only to respect and comply with applicable laws, rules, and regulations but to act in such a way as to foster and justify investors' trust in the equitability of the markets. Securities markets are based upon the fair pricing of risky assets and vitally dependent upon investors' confidence. In addition to causing possible economic damages to specific parties, actions intended to manipulate capital markets to the unjust advantage of certain participants undermine public trust in the fairness of market-based asset pricing. Obvious examples include unduly promoting or "hyping" stocks to trigger short-term price increases for a quick sale and circulating unfounded or exaggerated rumors to drive down the price of a stock in which one has a short position. The Code of Ethics prohibits such actions.

VI. Finally, the Code re-emphasizes the importance of professional competence by requiring covered persons to "maintain and improve their own competence and strive to maintain and improve the competence of other investment professionals." Staying intellectually fit and keeping up with advances in the field of investment analysis as well as with new investment products and strategies is mandatory if one is to make sound decisions and well-informed recommendations. The CFA curriculum and examination program are designed for generalists who are expected to be conversant with a wide range of topics. In addition, in the course of their careers members and charterholders often specialize in highly technical domains such as evaluating mortgage-backed securities or negotiating private placements, to name just a few of the possibilities. In order to maintain and enhance their expertise, investment professionals employed in these fields have to stay current with such matters as deal structures, legal developments, and market trends as well as new analytic techniques. One could make similar observations about other specialized areas of professional practice.

As noted, covered persons are further called upon to endeavor to maintain and improve other investment professionals' competence. Supervisors, of course, have particularly relevant opportunities to foster their professional staff members' continuing development through some combination of on-the-job coaching, internal educational programs, and, if possible, outside seminars or conferences. However, even "individual contributors" without managerial responsibilities can routinely share what they learn about the state of the art with their colleagues. This practice fosters excellence in the firm and contributes, however modestly and indirectly, to the repute of the investment profession.

INTRODUCTION TO THE STANDARDS OF PROFESSIONAL CONDUCT

The Standards of Professional Conduct are composed of seven sets of norms identified as:

  I Professionalism;

 II Integrity of Capital Markets;

III Duties to Clients;

IV Duties to Employers;

 V Investment Analysis, Recommendations, and Actions;

VI Conflicts of Interest; and

VII Responsibilities as a CFA Member or CFA Candidate.

The Standards complement the broad imperatives of the Code by addressing topics of concern more explicitly. We will give an overview of the Standards here, with particular attention to their rationale—the values and ideals they reflect and advance. However, we refer the reader to Reading 2 ("Guidance" for Standards I–VII) for the most authoritative and detailed direction in interpreting and applying them correctly in specific professional situations.

STANDARD I: PROFESSIONALISM 8

Under the heading of Professionalism, the first set of Standards sets forth members' and candidates' responsibilities with regard to knowledge of the law, independence and objectivity, misrepresentation, and misconduct.

Standard I(A), Knowledge of the Law, advances three ideas. First, covered persons must understand and comply with all applicable laws, rules, and regulations, including the Code and Standards themselves. Not all investment professionals are expected to have the scope and level of expertise achieved by compliance officers and attorneys specializing in securities law and regulatory matters. However, covered persons are required to have sufficient familiarity with the laws, rules, and regulations directly affecting their work to recognize covered situations and to avoid violations.

Second, in the event of a conflict between the requirements of different rule-making bodies, covered persons must comply with the more strict law, rule, or regulation. With increasing globalization, investment professionals working across borders are often subject to more than one legal system. It would not be in the spirit of meeting the highest standards to use compliance with the more liberal conventions of one country as a dodge to avoid or evade the more stringent laws and regulations of another. In addition, there may be instances when the ethical obligations imposed by the Code and Standards are more exacting than the applicable legal and regulatory requirements. In such cases, the provisions of the Code and Standards prevail.

Third, covered persons must not knowingly participate or assist in, and must dissociate themselves from, any violation of the laws, rules, or regulations governing their professional activities. "Knowingly participating or assisting" in a breach of the rules means (1) knowing the law, as required by this standard, (2) being aware of the factual situation, and (3) nonetheless playing an active or facilitating role in the commission of a violation. Covered persons must not only decline to play such a part but also take positive steps to "dissociate" or distance themselves from a transgression.

The specific steps to be taken depend upon situational factors. For example, it may suffice for investment professionals to call an actual or contemplated breach to the attention of their colleagues or manager who simply might not be aware of both the law and the facts. If the investment professionals are supervisors, however, and members of their staff engage in illegal or unethical activity, it is their responsibility to put a stop to it and to initiate corrective or disciplinary action. There may be cases when it is appropriate to contact the firm's compliance officer. There may also be cases when it becomes necessary to resign from the firm or to report the matter to the authorities. Generally, progressive escalation is a sound approach. It is prudent, moreover, to document one's efforts to correct a transgression. What is not acceptable is to allow oneself to be compromised by going along with improper practices.

Standard I(B), Independence and Objectivity, goes to the heart of the investment professional's ethical responsibilities because it requires that the clients' best interests be evaluated and served impartially. In other words, the only part investment professionals should take is the client's, and their only interest should be the client's best interest, the client's financial welfare. The standard sets forth two mandates, one positive and the other negative. First, covered persons *must* "use reasonable care and judgment to achieve and maintain independence and objectivity in their professional activities." Second, they *must not* offer or accept any sort of consideration that could be "reasonably expected" to impair their own or another's independence and objectivity.

Interestingly, observing these mandates necessarily presupposes mature professional judgment and independent thinking. For example, because the standard does not specify a monetary amount as a guideline for determining that offering or accepting a gift is improper, it is up to investment professionals to make their own decisions about a questionable exchange, with due attention to firm-specific guidelines for employee conduct. The only rule of thumb suggested in the standard is that if a consideration could sensibly be perceived as unfitting by others, notably including the client and other investment professionals committed to the value of uncompromised objectivity, then it is to be rejected. In general, ethical decision-making means not only knowing the rules but also discerning the most fitting course of action, and ethical discernment requires, in turn, a willingness and ability to think for oneself.

Security and credit analysts may be subject to pressure to conform their opinions to the desires of interested parties, usually for favorable coverage. For example, the firm that employs them may have extraneous commercial lending or investment banking relationships with issuers of publicly traded securities covered by the analyst group. The companies whose security prices are influenced by analysts' appraisals certainly prefer positive reports and recommendations, as do portfolio managers who are holding the securities. A great deal of money may ride on the analysts' opinions, and in the recent past, interested parties have been found to exert direct or indirect pressure in an attempt to influence analysts' conclusions. A well-managed firm whose organizational culture values objectivity will take steps to protect the analysts' independence, but it nonetheless remains the analysts' responsibility to be vigilant in maintaining impartiality.[6]

It is not security and credit analysts alone, of course, who are susceptible to outside influences. For instance, investment professionals working on behalf of institutional investors are no less required to uphold their independence in decision-making. Investment officers of pension plans, endowments, and foundations are often approached by service providers such as custodians, securities lending organizations, and transition managers as well as long-term investment managers seeking to win business. The influential consultants to whom plan sponsors look for sound, objective advice in structuring, implementing, and monitoring their investment program effectively serve as gatekeepers to the same service providers. Plan sponsors and investment consultants subject to the Code and Standards must take care to ensure that their actions promote the best interests of those who have a legitimate claim on their professionalism, without regard

[6] See the CFA Institute Research Objectivity Standards (2003) on the CFA Institute website.

to their own personal advantage and the desires of other parties. In the cases mentioned here, pension plan assets must be invested for the benefit of the plan participants, and endowment and foundation assets must be managed to support current and future spending in furtherance of the institution's stated objectives. Investment bankers and dealmakers are likewise required to act in the client's interest without, of course, undermining the integrity of the capital markets.

Standard I(C), Misrepresentation, holds that covered persons must not knowingly misstate facts relating to investment analysis, recommendations, actions, or "other professional activities." Misrepresentation is not merely outright falsification but also includes misleading a client or decision-maker. For instance, slanting a proposal by selectively omitting or downplaying certain factors and unduly emphasizing others so as to persuade the client to approve a preferred course of action would likely constitute misrepresentation. A key word is "knowingly." In this context, if investment professionals know *or should know under the duties of competence and diligence* that an analysis is biased and nonetheless proceed to recommend or to take inadequately supported investment action, they are in breach of the Standard. They may not have consciously and deliberately intended to mislead, although they may have acted in bad faith by not taking care to present all the facts that affect the investment characteristics to be taken into account in making an objectively defensible recommendation or decision.

Several kinds of misrepresentation merit special attention. The prohibition of misrepresentation implicitly bars covered persons from making or implying any guarantees or assurances about any investment. In other words, it is impermissible to tell clients or prospective clients that an investment cannot fail, that a positive return is assured, or that there is no possibility of an unfavorable outcome. In fact, there are no risk-free assets.[7] Nor are there risk-free strategies; even well-designed hedges structured to lock in returns regardless of interim market movements are subject to unexpected outcomes due to faulty assumptions or extraordinary events. It is a most serious violation of professional ethics to mislead a client into believing that a proposed investment is guaranteed. By extension, it is improper to understate the riskiness of a recommended course of action.

It is, however, permissible and indeed desirable to communicate accurate factual information about the characteristics, terms, and issuer's obligations under a particular instrument or type of security. For example, fixed income instruments known as Guaranteed Investment Contracts (GICs) are a form of "stable value investments." GICs are obligations of insurance companies providing a fixed interest rate and a fixed maturity. They are typically accorded amortized cost or book value accounting treatment that exempts the investor from reporting changes in market value due to fluctuations in the level of interest rates.[8] Investment advisors suggesting the use of a GIC or similar stable value instrument should clearly explain its contractual terms. They should also clarify that, despite the appearance of the word "guaranteed" in the very name of the instrument, there is credit risk, and the quality of the "guarantee" depends upon the creditworthiness of the issuer.

---

[7] Capital market theory assumes the existence of a risk-free asset (an asset with zero variance) and the ability of investors to borrow and lend at a risk-free rate of return. However, even default-free short-term securities are subject to changes in the supply and demand of capital and the expected rate of inflation. See Frank K. Reilly, CFA and Keith C. Brown, CFA, *Investment Analysis and Portfolio Management*, 7th ed., South-Western (2003), pp. 17–19.

[8] For a more complete description, see Kenneth L. Walker, "Stable Value Investments," in Frank J. Fabozzi, CFA, Ed., *The Handbook of Fixed Income Securities*, 6th ed., McGraw-Hill (2001), pp. 399–400.

prudent for professionals to document their internal and external communications on the subject, just in case their actions should come under scrutiny.

Standard II(B), Market Manipulation, prohibits engaging in "practices that distort prices or artificially inflate trading volume with the intent to mislead market participants." In this case, the practitioner's intention or purpose is the critical element for distinguishing between legitimate trading strategies and duplicitous ploys. It is permissible, for example, to sell and repurchase a holding in order to realize a gain or loss in accordance with the provisions of a tax code or to rebalance positions in different portfolios, but it is impermissible to buy and sell a security among various accounts under one's control for the purpose of running up the bid price. It would be similarly improper for a commodity trading company to enter a large volume of related-party transactions disguised as arm's-length open market trades to enhance its perceived market power or to influence the price of derivative instruments tied to the traded product.

Acceptable trading strategies with fitting and explainable business purposes may exploit asymmetrical information but are not intended to deceive counterparties or other market participants. While determining the intent of the person initiating a transaction or a series of transactions may seem to be a matter of dubious psychological inference, investment professionals who know the markets and the instruments can reliably tell the difference when all the facts are disclosed.

The twofold ethical basis for outlawing market manipulation is by now familiar. Engaging in deceptive practices in order to gain an edge over others may cause them to suffer undue financial damages and impedes the fair and efficient operation of the capital markets.

10   STANDARD III: DUTIES TO CLIENTS

Standard III addresses five areas of ethical concern. They are the loyalty, prudence, and care due to clients; fair dealing; the suitability of investments; performance presentation; and the preservation of confidentiality.

Standard III(A), Loyalty, Prudence, and Care, stresses that covered persons must not only act for the benefit of their clients but also place their clients' interests before their firm's and their own. There can be no "utilitarian calculus" where an action which is very good for the firm or the professional and "not too bad" for the client is acceptable. Under the Standard, investment professionals are obligated to act in the best interest of the client without regard to their employer's potentially divergent interests or their own advantage.

Moreover, covered persons have a "duty of loyalty" to their clients. Professional relationships are generally governed by legal contracts under which one person, the professional, consents to give another, the client, the benefit of his or her special competence in exchange for compensation during the term of the agreement. Accordingly, professional relationships are not, as a rule, personal in the sense of friendships or family ties. However, neither are they merely commercial. Investors place trust in professionals to whom they look for judicious, expert advice, and investment professionals are obligated by the nature of this relationship of trust to keep faith with their clients. They must not merely refrain from deceiving or defrauding the clients; they must ensure that the investment recommendations they offer are sound and the actions they take are well-considered.

In practical terms, this duty of loyalty to the client means using "reasonable care" and applying "prudent judgment." Acting with reasonable care implies identifying and taking into account all the factors that materially affect the investment characteristics of a security or a strategy. In the context of professional investment analysis, exercising prudent judgment reflects a high standard of care because it signifies the caution of an expert in evaluating the risk and reward characteristics of a security or a strategy. The investment professional serves the client's interests by proceeding with reasonable care and exercising prudent judgment when making recommendations and taking action.

In the language of some legal systems, the word "fiduciary" is used as a noun to identify the role and as an adjective to describe the obligations of a person to whom property or decision-making authority are entrusted on behalf of another. Fiduciaries are legally bound to act solely in the interest of the person for whose benefit they manage assets under the terms of the governing agreement. It is vitally important for investment professionals acting in a fiduciary capacity to determine to whom the duty of loyalty is owed. For example, in general corporate pension assets must be managed exclusively for the benefit of the plan's participants and beneficiaries, even though it is the plan sponsor who has the authority to hire and fire investment managers. Of course, the plan sponsor also has fiduciary obligations toward the participants and beneficiaries.

While the legal concept of fiduciary obligations is not universally applicable, under the Code and Standards, covered persons have comparable ethical responsibilities when assets are entrusted to their care. It should be observed that loyalty is owed by investment managers of a mutual fund to the shareholders of that fund just as it is owed by managers to their separate account clients.

Standard III(B), Fair Dealing, requires fair and objective treatment for all clients and prospective clients in the conduct of one's professional activities. For example, in the absence of specific client-initiated constraints, attractively priced securities must be proportionately allocated among accounts managed in the same style so as not to give preference to some clients over others. Similarly, securities held in multiple accounts should be liquidated in an orderly and equitable manner so that one client, or one group of clients, does not receive more favorable treatment than another.

Fair dealing is an area requiring particular attention, both because there have been serious abuses (for instance, in the allocation of initial public offerings) and because it may sometimes seem natural in the course of business to offer special rewards to valued clients or inducements to desirable prospects. It is improper to do so at the expense of others. In economic terms, the opportunity cost to a client denied fair access to an undervalued security is no less material than a loss unfairly apportioned. Individuals must take care to see that clients are treated fairly in all their dealings. Moreover, with regard to the examples cited above, their firms' trading processes must be designed and monitored to uphold the objective equitability of transactions. While directed primarily to the issue of "best execution," CFA Institute's Trade Management Guidelines include ensuring that all clients are treated fairly in the execution of orders and allocation of trades. It is remarked there, "The term 'fairly' implies that Firms should take care not to discriminate against clients or place the interests of some clients over those of others."[9]

Standard III(B) refers to existing clients. However, it is desirable for professionals to disclose their firm's policies and procedures for disseminating investment advice and allocating trades to prospective as well as existing clients. In addition, professionals should communicate the availability, nature, and cost of any premium services such as in-depth investment analysis. Such premium services should be designed in such a way that, while beneficial to those who are in

---

[9] CFA Institute, "Trade Management Guidelines" (2002), 1.D, p. 9.

a position to take advantage of them, they are not unfairly disadvantageous to other classes of clients.

Standard III(C), Suitability, addresses two distinct situations. In the first, professionals are providing investment advice to clients and prospective clients (typically clients whose assets are held in actively managed separate accounts); in the second, they may not have direct contact with specific clients but are responsible for managing a portfolio such as a commingled fund or a mutual fund in accordance with a stated mandate, strategy, or style. In both cases, it is the professionals' duty to ensure that investment recommendations and decisions are fitting, but the particular requirements differ.

When providing advice, covered persons are first directed to inquire about the client's investment experience, objectives, and constraints before they make any recommendations or take any action. [See Standard III(C.1.a).] A primary purpose served by asking about the client's investment experience is to determine how to communicate investment ideas most clearly and effectively. For example, an inexperienced investor with modest savings will undoubtedly need more basic education about financial instruments and strategies than a seasoned investor with extensive, diversified holdings. It might be considered questionable to place the assets of a client unfamiliar with the investment industry at risk in complex, highly leveraged derivative instruments that surpass the client's understanding.

The advisor must also ascertain the client's or prospective client's return objectives and risk tolerance. A financial planner interviewing a retail client may use a questionnaire to determine the individual's orientation toward current income or asset appreciation and to assess the client's attitudes toward financial risk-taking. A consultant advising the officers of a university's endowment fund will consider such factors as the significance of the endowment in relation to the institution's overall budget, the fund's annual spending plan, and pertinent inflation projections such as estimated tuition increases affecting future scholarship needs. The advisor must additionally establish whether there are special constraints or considerations of any sort to be taken into account in formulating an investment plan.

With this background, the advisor is further directed to determine that an investment is suitable to the client's financial situation. [See Standard III(C.1.b).] Making such a determination always requires critical thinking and often calls for superior judgment. For example, the trustees of a currently underfunded public pension plan with an aggressive, legislatively mandated timetable for achieving fully funded status might ask an investment professional for advice about investing a significant portion of the plan's assets in alternative asset classes offering high expected returns. Although it is difficult to assess the riskiness of illiquid securities, the advisor might conclude that under prevailing market conditions the return premiums appear to be in line with their perceived quality. Nonetheless, the investment professional must seriously consider if the possibility of loss is unacceptably high, potentially necessitating substantial cash infusions to sustain the plan's viability. In such a situation, it may be imprudent to attempt to achieve the target level of return, and the proposed investment program might in fact be unsuitable to the client's financial condition. This example illustrates the need not only for sound judgment but also, in some instances, for political courage. The investment advisor's best course might be to urge the trustees to seek legislative relief rather than to risk far greater financial setbacks in the pursuit of excess return.

Under the same section, covered persons must further determine that an investment under consideration is consistent with the client's objectives, mandates, and constraints.

Written investment policy statements are widely used by institutional investors such as pension plan sponsors, endowment and foundation officers, and insurance companies. Among other elements, policy statements typically set forth the investor's financial objectives, including return expectations, sensitivity to risk, and the fund's time horizon. They also identify permitted asset classes and investment vehicles and articulate portfolio constraints intended to control risk. Charles Ellis wrote, "The principal reason for articulating long-term investment policy explicitly and *in writing* is to enable the client and portfolio manager to protect the portfolio from ad hoc revisions of sound long-term policy, and to help them hold to long-term policy when short-term exigencies are most distressing and the policy is most in doubt."[10]

Investment professionals working on behalf of the institution, whether as employees or advisors, must make recommendations and decisions with the policy statement in view. Portfolio managers must not only attend to the general spirit of the policy statement, notably with regard to risk tolerance, but must also comply with its detailed provisions. For example, the policy statement may limit an individual equity portfolio's economic sector exposure to a certain percentage of portfolio assets or of the comparable benchmark weight. A fixed income portfolio may be constrained to hold no securities rated below investment grade and to maintain the portfolio's weighted average duration within a specified range, often expressed as a percentage of the benchmark duration. Such restrictions are intended to preserve the fund from a loss in value due to inadequate sector diversification, excessive credit quality risk, or unacceptable levels of interest rate risk.

It is at present less common for individuals to have written investment policy statements. Nonetheless, investment professionals are obligated under the Standards to determine that an investment is consistent with the client's objectives, mandates, and constraints before making a recommendation or taking action. The best practice is to document the client's guidelines and to follow them when offering advice and making decisions.

When providing advice to clients and prospective clients, there is a third and final directive for determining the appropriateness of an investment recommendation or action. [See Standard III(C.1.c).] Covered persons are instructed to judge the suitability of investments in the context of the client's "total portfolio," that is, the client's entire set of personal, real, and financial assets.

The principle of portfolio optimization through diversification is well established in investment theory. Given reasonable assumptions about prospective asset class returns, volatilities, and covariance, portfolio returns can be maximized for a specified level of risk, or alternately risk can be minimized for a specified target return, by aptly weighting holdings in various asset classes which do not move in concert. The Standard applies the same logic to the client's overall financial situation, with the objective of avoiding an excessive concentration of assets, and correlatively of risk, in any domain. For instance, if the client's major assets are residential real estate and the stock of a closely held specialty chemical company where the client is also employed, the client's investment program might well emphasize marketable securities issued predominately by corporations engaged in other lines of business.

To protect their privacy, some clients may refuse to disclose all their holdings to an investment advisor. In that case, it remains the advisor's responsibility to explain the importance of diversification and the nature of the investments under consideration.

---

[10] Charles D. Ellis, *Investment Policy; How to Win the Loser's Game*, Dow Jones-Irwin (1985), p. 53. Ellis's emphasis.

engaging in professional activities "on the side" in competition with one's employer. The Standard also states that confidential information is not to be disclosed. Confidential information would include, for example, client contacts, proprietary analytic techniques, and product strategies, among other things. The Standard further asserts that covered persons "must not otherwise cause harm to their employer." How is this provision to be interpreted and applied in particular situations?

Identifying so exclusively with the firm and working so single-mindedly to further the firm's interests that one neglects one's health or family is certainly not expected. When personal matters may interfere with their work on a regular or significant basis, members and candidates should enter into a dialogue with their employers about balancing personal and professional obligations.

In addition, covered persons are not expected to consent to firm policies and practices that are contrary to ethical standards. "Whistleblowers"— individuals who disclose their firm's misdeeds—are often accused of disloyalty to their colleagues and their employers, but such reactions to an individual's difficult decision to report an uncorrected wrong reflect a serious misunderstanding of the duty of loyalty. On the contrary, it may be the case that going public, or going to regulatory authorities, bespeaks the employee's commitment to the identity, culture, and values of a firm whose reputation for excellence is in jeopardy due to others' poor judgment or ethical failures.

Although their leaving might be harmful to the firm, covered persons are neither required nor expected by the Standard to remain in the firm's employ when other opportunities are more attractive. Best practice is to give advance notice of their departure and assist the firm in effecting a smooth transition. In some cases, a directly competing organization may extend an offer of employment to an individual or even to an entire team; in other cases, employees may decide to start their own business. The departing employees may attempt to rationalize clandestinely removing or copying the firm's property as the products of their own creativity, but without permission it is wrong for them to take the firm's client list, software, files, or other assets with the intention of entering into competition with their former employer.

Global competition has made attaining ever greater operational efficiency a matter of corporate survival in many industries, including financial services. Business combinations are often initiated to achieve productivity improvements through economies of scale or better cost control. "Downsizing" and "outsourcing" have entered the business vocabulary, and the nature of the relationship between employers and employees has changed. Broker/dealers have long engaged in boom-and-bust cycles of staff recruitment and termination, but traditionally stable organizations like banks and insurance companies no longer offer the job security their long-term personnel once took for granted. Employment is increasingly seen as a temporary economic arrangement for the mutual benefit of the company and the worker, and it lasts only as long as both parties find it advantageous. Examining the employer's responsibilities to employees goes beyond the scope of the present discussion. However, the employer/employee relationship imposes duties and responsibilities on both parties. If they expect to have committed and productive employees, employers should refrain from exploiting their workers' natural proclivity to identify with the firm and should reward their loyalty by recognizing their contributions and treating them with honesty and respect.

Standard IV(B), Additional Compensation Arrangements, is clear-cut. Covered persons must not accept any form of inducement or recompense—the Standard mentions "gifts, benefits, compensation, or consideration"—that competes with their employer's interest or that might reasonably be expected to produce a conflict between their own and their employer's interest, *unless* they obtain written consent from all parties involved. For example, employees must not accept a consulting assignment, an appointment to a board of directors, or a publishing contract without clearly and realistically explaining the terms of the commitment to their employer or manager and getting approval to proceed *in writing.* Similarly, they should make the other organization aware of the nature and the demands of their regular employment, and they should have written evidence that the other organization understands any limits on their ability to work on its behalf. The Standard applies to situations in which the investment professionals' compensated outside interests might interfere with their concentrating as fully as expected on their regular work as well as to situations in which they plan to engage in an activity directly competing with their firm's business. Many corporations have formal procedures for approving their staff's outside engagements.

Finally, **Standard IV(C)**, Responsibilities of Supervisors, explicitly states that covered persons in managerial positions "must make reasonable efforts to *detect and prevent* violations of applicable laws, rules, [and] regulations," as well as breaches of the Code and Standards, by persons subject to their supervision or authority. (Emphasis added.) Reasonable prevention and detection measures would include defining and documenting policies and procedures, training staff members, designing and implementing controls, and monitoring the unit's activities with an eye to spotting unethical or illegal conduct. Staff training should cover not only the firm's standards but also the applicable laws, rules, and regulations in sufficient depth to equip employees to perform their routine functions and to raise questions in doubtful cases.

It is also advisable to inform staff members about the provisions of the Code and Standards. Although they themselves may not be members or candidates, managers who are subject to the Code and Standards can be found in violation for failing to supervise the activities of those under their authority in the event of a contravention. In addition, it should be acknowledged that managers set expectations and lead by example. Along with senior management, the group or unit supervisor is responsible for establishing a culture in which ethically sound decisions are expected and rewarded.

STANDARD V: INVESTMENT ANALYSIS, RECOMMENDATIONS, AND ACTIONS

12

Standard V lies at the heart of ethical Standards for investment professionals. The Standard has three sections, addressing the requirement that investment analysis, recommendations, and decisions be based upon reasonable and adequate grounds; the norms for clear and informative client communications; and the need to retain supporting documentation.

Standard V(A), Diligence and Reasonable Basis, first reiterates the requirement that covered persons exercise diligence, independence, and thoroughness in their professional work. Diligence and the exercise of independent professional judgment figure prominently in the Code of Ethics, and independence and objectivity were addressed in connection with Standard I(B). We focus attention here on the second provision of Standard V(A). Covered persons are required to have "a reasonable and adequate basis, supported by appropriate research and investigation, for any investment analysis, recommendation, [or] action."

In investment analysis as in any other discipline, a rational, well-founded conclusion will be based upon theoretically and logically sound premises, plausibly argued, and above all supported by factual evidence.

The idea of "theoretically and logically sound premises" is not intended to preclude original work by requiring hypotheses to be consistent with conventional ideas about risk, return, or the capital markets. For example, style-based investment strategies, now widely accepted, emerged from research on stock market anomalies indicating that price/book ratios and company size were promising alternatives to beta in accounting for security returns.[13] In one view of scientific discovery, knowledge advances through what the philosopher Karl Popper called "conjectures and refutations," as individuals and groups seek to determine whether suppositions about empirical relationships withstand tests designed to disprove them.[14] Nor does the expectation that analyses be theoretically grounded and logically developed necessarily rule out approaches which do not assert causal connections between conditions or patterns and outcomes. ("Technical analysis" may be broadly characterized as such an approach.) However, when clients' assets are put at risk, there is a practical demand that investment analysis, and the recommendations and decisions to which it leads, must be explainable and defensible rather than merely reflecting an analyst's hunch. In this context, it is imperative to offer a plausible explanation of observed phenomena.

Most important—indeed, indispensable—is factual research. Analyses, recommendations, and actions *must* be predicated upon reliable, up-to-date data. The capital markets have a way of disproving hypotheses most convincingly, and the analyst's rigorously logical reasoning is no defense when he or she has misconstrued or ignored available facts that should have been taken into consideration.

This is not by any means to suggest that analysts cannot accept others' research as the basis for a conclusion. A great deal of investment analysis is dependent upon other researchers' papers, secondary sources, and commercially developed databases. In the vast majority of cases, conducting unassisted research would be inefficient to the point of impracticality. It is necessary, however, for analysts to make a reasonable inquiry into the reliability of their sources. They should be tolerably assured that the analytical techniques are solid, the quality controls are dependable, and the data are timely and accurate.

At most investment management organizations, research and analysis are conducted in a group setting. There are frequently occasions when the consensus is at variance with an individual analyst's considered position. In such cases, investment professionals must weigh the requirements for independent thinking and for well-founded decisions. If the group's decision process is rational, pertinent facts have been ascertained and evaluated, the analyst has been given a fair opportunity to express contrary views, and the conclusions are not unreasonable (although arguably incorrect), then investment professionals may justifiably acquiesce and consent to have their names associated with the group's view. Reasonable people can disagree, for example, on the timing and magnitude of a correction in the general level of interest rates or the attractiveness of an economic sector.

If, on the other hand, the process is flawed, important and undeniable facts have been disregarded, or extraneous business considerations have improperly influenced the debate, then the analysts may have to conclude that the group

---

[13] The original research by Eugene F. Fama and Kenneth R. French (1992) and others leading to the development of style-based equity investment strategies is recalled in Louis K. C. Chan and Josef Lakonishok, "Value and Growth Investing: Review and Update," *Financial Analysts Journal*, Vol. 60, No. 1 (January/February 2004), p. 71.

[14] See Karl Popper, *Conjectures and Refutations: The Growth of Scientific Knowledge*, Harper & Row (1968).

does not have a reasonable and adequate basis for its conclusions and that endorsing the outcome would compromise their integrity. In this event, the analysts are faced with a difficult decision about the best course of action. They may elect to hold their fire for a more consequential issue or to submit a dissenting opinion or to request that their name be removed from a published report. If the firm's management routinely misuses the research and analysis process to validate foregone conclusions, then the analysts will have to decide whether they can continue to meet their professional obligations in that organization.

With **Standard V(B)**, Communication with Clients and Prospective Clients, we proceed from conducting investment analysis to conveying the results of analysis to the clients and potential clients whom it may benefit.

Standard V(B.1) requires covered persons to describe their investment decision-making process. For example, one firm engaged in active equity management may conduct fundamental "economic-industry-company" analysis, while another favors enhanced indexing and focuses on the development and application of quantitative portfolio optimization techniques. These two organizations will differ substantially in the investment principles, research resources, screening techniques, decision rules, and process controls they employ. The nature of the risks to which the investor is exposed will also differ with two such dissimilar approaches. By clearly explaining the basic format and the general principles of the firm's approach to portfolio construction, the investment professional enables clients and prospective clients to determine whether the firm is well matched to their preferences for the mandate under consideration. Similarly, by promptly communicating significant modifications in the way the firm conducts research, selects securities for purchase and sale, and constructs and trims portfolios, the investment professional equips clients and prospective clients to monitor the impact of changes and to make informed decisions about their asset mix and roster of managers on the basis of up-to-date information.

Standard V(B.2) requires covered persons to use reasonable judgment in identifying the factors that are important to their investment analysis, recommendation, or actions, and to address those factors in their communications to clients and prospective clients. As we saw earlier, the "reasonable judgment" expected here is that of a knowledgeable and experienced practitioner.

Note that the factors to be communicated are the factors that were significant in conducting the analysis, formulating the recommendation, or reaching the decision. If a projection of the future course of interest rates, for example, or an appraisal of the attractiveness of an industry was an important piece of the work, then its contribution to the analyst's reasoning must be made clear. The communication should, in short, convey the "reasonable and adequate basis" or the factual and logical grounds for the conclusion. If the report includes an investment recommendation, then it is best practice for the professional explicitly to address the risks, along with any mitigating factors, so that the clients or prospective clients can make an informed decision.

The pertinence of the factors to be considered and communicated further depends, of course, upon the context. For example, an introductory discussion of the investment characteristics of an asset class, such as convertible bonds, will be broader and more general than an evaluation of the terms and pricing of a specific convertible issue. In the former case, the analyst will help the investor understand how convertibles are structured, how they respond to different equity and fixed income market conditions, how their valuation is related to the volatility of a particular stock as well as the creditworthiness of the issuer, what role they can play in an overall investment program, what tradeoffs and generic risks they represent, and how they are valued in the marketplace. In the latter case, the analyst will focus on security-specific valuation issues, considering among other things the prevailing and prospective equity and fixed income market conditions; the particular issue's bond characteristics, such as coupon and current yield; the price and the historical price variability of the related common stock; and the issuer's earnings outlook.

Accordingly, in deciding what topics to cover, investment professionals must not only review their own thought processes in reaching a conclusion but also think about the context and purpose of the communication. In the case of a one-on-one presentation or a memorandum written for a specific client or group of clients, investment professionals should consider the recipient's preparedness to understand the material. An investor who has not previously been exposed to convertibles may need to be given more background information about the asset class than someone who already grasps the opportunities, risks, and valuation techniques. When writing for a mass audience, it is not as easy to decide what "goes without saying," but the professional should take pains to be as clear as possible in communicating technical material.

Standard V(B.3) requires covered persons to distinguish between "facts" and "opinions" in the presentation of investment analysis and recommendations. For instance, it may be a fact that the general level of interest rates in a certain country is relatively low by post–World War II historical standards, but it is the analyst's opinion that resurgent inflation will cause rates to rise, or that the central bank will raise the short-term target rate by 25 basis points at its next meeting, or that the yield on five-year federal debt issues will increase by 50 basis points in the second half, or that residential mortgage refinancings will slow next year. The Standard requires investment professionals to differentiate facts and opinions in their communications, so that clients do not mistake a possibility for a certainty or an estimate for a guarantee.

Standard V(C), Record Retention, stipulates that covered persons must develop and maintain appropriate records to support their analysis, recommendations, actions, performance, and other investment-related communications with clients and prospective clients. The objective is to allow for subsequent review in the event that questions arise, for example, about the reasonability and adequacy of the research on which a recommendation or decision was based, or about the authorship of a report, or about the firm's investment results. Consulting firms and investment management organizations generally formulate record retention guidelines or policies for their staff, but whether or not individual members and candidates are subject to compliance audits, it remains their own professional responsibility to ensure that appropriate records are available for review.

13   STANDARD VI: CONFLICTS OF INTEREST

As we have seen, under the Code and Standards, covered persons must place the client's and their employer's interests before their own and exercise independent professional judgment. These mandates cannot be broken. Nonetheless, there are conflict-of-interest situations in which what is most beneficial for the client may or may not coincide with what is most advantageous to the investment professional. In other words, there may be incentives for the professional to make certain recommendations or decisions whether or not they are entirely suitable for the client. Even though the member or candidate scrupulously acts in the client's best interest, the very existence of a conflict may raise questions about the investment professional's independence and objectivity. Standard VI tacitly reaffirms the principle of the priority of client transactions and describes the disclosures required when there are conflicts of interest.

Standard VI(A) states that covered persons "must make *full and fair disclosure* of all matters that could *reasonably be expected to impair their independence and objectivity* or interfere with their respective duties to their employer, clients, and prospective clients." (Emphasis added.) For example, clients should be told if investment professionals own stock in a company they recommend. By giving clients information about situations or arrangements that might influence their reasoning, investment professionals alert them to the need for critical thinking. The clients are then well advised to judge for themselves whether there is a sound basis for the professionals' recommendations and they are indeed acting in the clients' best interest.

Take as an example the "bundled services" some financial services companies offer pension plan sponsors. The provider may conduct an asset allocation study and recommend an asset mix optimized on the basis of the provider's assumptions about asset class returns, volatilities, and correlations. The provider may additionally implement the recommended investment program by accepting the client's assets into commingled funds managed in accordance with the specified strategies. Although intended primarily to assist the sponsors of small to midsize pension plans lacking the expertise or the time to conduct manager searches, bundled services of the sort described here may have built-in conflicts of interest. For instance, the advisory fees for certain recommended strategies may be substantially greater than they are for others. If members or candidates are involved in the sale or management of bundled pension investment services, they are obligated by Standard VI(A) to ensure that the client or prospective client is fully aware that the fees for some alternatives are higher than for others.

The Standard goes on to specify that disclosures of conflicts of interest must be prominent and delivered in plain language, and they must "communicate the relevant information effectively." Ambiguous or excessively legalistic "disclosures" tucked away unnoticeably in a presentation would not suffice to satisfy the requirement.

It should be stressed that, whenever possible, conflicts of interest are to be avoided in the interest of independence and objectivity. Where conflicts exist, they must be fully and clearly disclosed, but disclosure is not a substitute for impartiality. The investment professional is in every case ethically obligated to make recommendations and decisions in the best interest of the client.

Standard VI(B), Priority of Transactions, states that investment transactions for clients and employers must have priority over investment transactions in which a covered person has a personal interest. Members and candidates cannot act on behalf of themselves or members of their household before clients and employers have been given a fair opportunity to act on a recommendation. If investment advisors have discretionary authority over a client's account, and the transaction is suitable, then the advisors cannot initiate the transaction for themselves before entering an order on behalf of the client. This requirement is consistent with a fundamental provision of the Code of Ethics, namely, that covered persons place the interests of clients and the interests of their employer above their own personal interests.

Standard VI(C), Referral Fees, specifically requires the disclosure of any compensation received by the member or candidate for recommending products or services. It additionally requires members and candidates to disclose if they have compensated others for recommending their own or their firms' products or services. It is not up to the client to ask about referral arrangements, and failure to inform them of compensation agreements might leave them with the misimpression that an endorsement was offered without inducement. Referral fees constitute the sort of arrangement that must be divulged under Standard VI(A) above, but they are of such importance and so frequently used that they warrant separate and explicit treatment. Indeed, not to disclose the existence, nature, and estimated value of referral fees is an abuse of the investor's trust.

judgment, and comply with applicable fiduciary duty. Covered persons must deal fairly and objectively with all clients. When in an advisory relationship, they must determine that an investment is suitable for the client, and when managing a portfolio to a specific mandate they must only make recommendations and take actions that are consistent with the stated objectives and constraints of the portfolio. When covered persons communicate investment performance information, they must make reasonable efforts to ensure that it is fair, accurate, and complete. They must keep information about current, former, and prospective clients confidential unless the information concerns illegal activities, disclosure is required by law, or the client provides permission to disclose the information.

► Standard IV, Duties to Employers, obligates covered persons to act for the benefit of their employer and not to deprive their employer of the advantage of their skills and abilities, divulge confidential information, or otherwise cause harm to their employer. They must not accept gifts, benefits, compensation, or consideration that competes with or might reasonably be expected to create a conflict of interest with their employer unless they obtain written consent from all parties involved. Supervisors must make reasonable efforts to detect and prevent violations of applicable laws, rules, regulations, and the Code and Standards by anyone subject to their supervision or authority.

► Standard V, Investment Analysis, Recommendations, and Actions, requires covered persons to exercise diligence, independence, and thoroughness and to have a reasonable and adequate basis for any investment analysis, recommendation, and action. Covered persons must disclose the basic format and general principles of the investment process and promptly disclose any material process changes; include the factors important to their analyses, recommendations, or actions in client communications; and distinguish between fact and opinion. Covered persons must develop and maintain appropriate records to support their investment analysis, recommendations, actions, and other investment-related communications with clients and prospective clients.

► Standard VI, Conflicts of Interest, requires covered persons to make full and fair disclosure, in plain language, of all matters that could reasonably be expected to impair their independence and objectivity or interfere with their respective duties to their employer, clients, and prospective clients. Investment transactions for clients and employers must have priority over transactions in which the covered person is the beneficial owner. Covered persons must disclose to their employer, clients, and prospective clients, as appropriate, any compensation, consideration, or benefit received by or paid to others for the recommendation of products or services (referral fees).

► Standard VII, Responsibilities as a CFA Institute Member or CFA Candidate, requires members and candidates not to engage in any conduct that compromises the reputation or integrity of CFA Institute or the CFA designation or the integrity, validity, or security of the CFA examinations. Members and candidates must not misrepresent or exaggerate the meaning or implications of membership in CFA Institute, holding the CFA designation, or candidacy in the CFA program.

APPENDIX 3A: CASE STUDIES

CASE STUDY 1: ARGENT CAPITAL MANAGEMENT

Case Facts

Françoise Vandezande, CFA, is a senior relationship manager in the New York office of Argent Capital Management, a French investment management firm. Her responsibilities include explaining the performance of separately managed global portfolios to institutional investors. One of her clients is the defined benefit pension plan sponsored by a U.S. subsidiary of Chimie Industrielle, a French manufacturer and distributor of specialty chemicals. The members of Chimie Industrielle's U.S. Investment Committee are highly sophisticated in the areas of international economics and finance, and Vandezande usually looks forward to interesting discussions at their quarterly meetings.

As the next quarterly meeting approached, however, she was worried. A performance attribution report prepared by Argent's performance analytics group showed that the Chimie Industrielle portfolio's disappointing results for the most recent quarter were due primarily to substantial losses incurred on foreign currency transactions. Moreover, Vandezande was aware that the client's investment policy statement imposed certain restrictions on active foreign currency management, and she suspected that Argent might have violated the constraints. She picked up her telephone to call Aidan McNamara, CFA, the portfolio manager for the Chimie Industrielle account.

Reputedly one of the leading managers of international mutual funds and separate accounts, Argent Capital Management is organized to capitalize on its strengths in economic forecasting. The global markets research team analyzes national economies and forecasts foreign exchange rates among major currencies, while the global industries group evaluates the relative attractiveness of industrial and commercial sectors in various regions of the world. Argent has always considered currency decisions to be distinct from asset allocation decisions.

After hearing the quarterly reports of the two research areas, the firm's investment council decides upon target weights both for industries within regions and for currency exposures. Although it is not always possible to find the requisite volume of fairly priced stocks in each category, Argent has generally been able to make this complex top-down investment decision process work by virtue of the firm's extensive cross-border network.

The two-day investment council meetings in Argent's headquarters are characterized by vigorous debate leading to a consensus view of near- and intermediate-term investment threats and opportunities across industries, regions, and currencies. The investment council accordingly defines tactical positions for the next quarter and communicates guidelines to the portfolio managers, securities analysts, and foreign exchange traders for execution. Guided by the target regional industry weights, the global securities analysis group recommends stock purchases and sales to the portfolio managers, and the foreign exchange desk enters forward and futures contracts to implement the currency strategy. The portfolio managers are responsible for monitoring positions for compliance with the clients' investment policies.

When Vandezande called him, McNamara sounded tense. "All the portfolios took a currency hit," the portfolio manager complained. "Global markets made a bad call on the Euro–yen exchange rate, but because they were so convinced they were right they maneuvered the Investment Council into approving a huge long position on the Euro and an equally short position on the yen. The markets moved against them." When Vandezande asked if these exposures were consistent with her client's investment policy statement, McNamara fell silent. "Off the top of my head, I don't know," he admitted. "I have a lot of portfolios to keep track of. I'll have to look into it."

Vandezande pulled Chimie Industrielle's investment policy statement from her filing cabinet. Three provisions leapt out at her:

1. Investment mandate: The international equity portfolio is benchmarked to the MSCI EAFE® Index.

5. The investment manager has explicit approval to manage currency risk but may not engage in currency speculation. The investment manager may enter currency forward and futures contracts to hedge currency risk back to U.S. dollars only up to 100% of the portfolio's underlying exposure.

9. The portfolio as a whole should be managed keeping in mind the original mandate under which the manager was hired. No extreme position should be taken which would alter the character of the portfolio that could produce results inconsistent with this mandate.

With Chimie Industrielle's U.S. Investment Committee meeting coming up in three days, Vandezande started to compose a high-priority e-mail message to the head of her department, the portfolio manager, the chief investment officer, and the director of compliance. The subject line read, "Foreign Exchange Losses in the Chimie Industrielle Portfolio."

Case Discussion

The portfolio manager appears to be unfamiliar with the client's mandate and constraints, and he has evidently violated the client's investment policies. His action is not in compliance with Standard III(C.1.b), which requires covered persons to "determine that an investment is suitable to the client's financial situation and consistent with the client's objectives, mandates, and constraints before making an investment recommendation or taking investment action."

In this case, Chimie Industrielle's written investment policy statement identifies the portfolio's investment mandate in terms of its benchmark, the MSCI EAFE® Index, and specifies that the advisor should not take any extreme position altering the character of the portfolio in such a way as to produce results inconsistent with the mandate. The benchmark does not hold short positions in currencies. In addition, the client's investment policy statement clearly states that the investment manager may not engage in currency speculation. By allowing Argent Capital Management's tactical currency management position to affect the risk profile of the Chimie Industrielle portfolio, the portfolio manager violated both these constraints.

Suggested Actions

Françoise Vandezande should:

► communicate to Chimie Industrielle a complete explanation of the events, including a review of the investment decision process and a statement of the Global Markets Research team's rationale in recommending atypical foreign exchange exposures; and

► explain how the firm will avoid similar situations in the future.

In order to improve internal controls, senior management should:

▶ modify the investment decision process to enable portfolio managers to exclude specific portfolios from firm-wide investment actions;

▶ re-educate the portfolio managers on the necessity of monitoring transactions for compliance with investment policy statements; and

▶ institute a policy of periodically auditing portfolios for compliance with client guidelines.

CASE STUDY 2: RIVER CITY PENSION FUND

Case Facts

Jack Aldred, CFA, was reviewing his notes in preparation for an Investment Commission meeting when his manager, River City treasurer, Barbara Castel, stepped into his office. "The meeting is in two hours," she said. "I want to know what you're planning to say about Northwest Capital."

Aldred is the chief investment officer of the River City Pension Fund, a mature defined benefit pension plan for municipal employees. He accepted this appointment six months ago after taking early retirement when his previous employer, an insurance company, was reorganized. While he worried that he was still a novice in navigating city politics, Aldred had already initiated significant improvements in the management of the city's pension assets. In particular, he recommended changes to the investment policy statement, designed more informative performance reports for the Investment Commission, and gained the commission's approval to engage in securities lending through the plan's custodian. Although he has only one person on his staff, Aldred sees further opportunities to improve the investment program. For example, he believes that the pension plan has more active managers than it needs, that their mandates overlap, and that the plan is consequently paying higher investment advisory fees than the investment program requires. His immediate problem, however, is deciding what to do about one of the pension plan's external managers in particular.

Northwest Capital Advisors has managed a small-cap value equity portfolio for the River City Pension Fund since the firm was founded eleven years ago. Under the leadership of the president and CEO, Roger Gray, a CFA charterholder, Northwest has emerged as one of the area's foremost small businesses. Among many other highly visible contributions to the community, Northwest donated financial expertise to a low-income housing program developed by the River City Interfaith Coalition, and the firm was credited with winning the Coalition a substantial grant from the state government. Northwest's employees also contributed large amounts in their own names to the election campaigns of local politicians with progressive policies, including the treasurer, as Aldred unintentionally discovered when he noticed some personal checks on her assistant's desk. Aldred was aware that the state legislature had enacted a law several years ago making it illegal for officers of firms doing business with municipalities to make campaign contributions to elected officials or candidates who might be in position to influence the selection of vendors.

Although Northwest Capital Advisors is well regarded in the community, in the last three years the firm's always mediocre investment performance has declined substantially. Aldred looked at the results as reported by the manager and the custodial bank's performance measurement group:

Standard III(C.2) reads, "When Members and Candidates are responsible for managing a portfolio to a specific mandate, strategy, or style, they must only make investment recommendations or take investment actions that are consistent with the stated objectives and constraints of the portfolio." If it is the case that Gray is introducing growth securities to a value portfolio, he is taking investment actions at variance with the portfolio's mandate in breach of the Standard.

Officers of Northwest Capital Advisors appear to be making illegal campaign contributions. If Gray himself is making such contributions, he is personally in violation of Standard I(A), which requires covered persons to understand and comply with all applicable laws, rules, and regulations. In any event, as president and CEO of the firm, he has supervisory responsibility under Standard IV(C) to make reasonable efforts to detect and prevent violations of applicable laws, rules, and regulations by those subject to his supervision or authority.

Suggested Actions

Roger Gray should:

▶ critically review the firm's pricing sources and practices to ensure that portfolio valuations are fair and accurate;

▶ re-examine portfolio holdings to ensure that they are consistent with the mandate to invest in small-cap value securities; and

▶ discontinue, and instruct his employees to discontinue, the practice of making illegal campaign contributions.

CASE STUDY 3: MACROECONOMIC ASSET MANAGEMENT

Case Facts

Alice Chapman, CFA, director of marketing for Macroeconomic Asset Management, was reading a letter from Arlington Verification Service, a verification firm, when she received an e-mail from Jack Storrs. Jack, who reports to Alice, heads the RFP unit for Macroeconomic Asset Management. Alice set aside the letter and opened the e-mail. The subject was "Leeds Request for Proposal (RFP)." She read:

> Alice:
>
> James River Consulting is conducting a manager search for Leeds Machine Tool Corporation. The deadline for responding to the RFP is the end of next week.
>
> I have two questions:
>
> 1. The RFP asks if our compliance with the GIPS standards has been verified. What is the status of the verification project?
> 2. The RFP asks for a GIPS-compliant performance presentation with year-to-date results through the most recent measurement period. Has the performance group released the third quarter returns?
>
> Thanks! Regards, Jack

Alice closed the e-mail and picked up the letter from Arlington Verification Service. The manager of the verification project had written:

> We regret to inform you that we cannot issue a verification report for Macroeconomic Asset Management. Our review of the firm's policies and processes and our examination of sample portfolios and composites revealed significant deficiencies in the following areas:
>
> ▶ missing or inadequate documentation (e.g., client agreements and composite definitions);
> ▶ actual, fee-paying, discretionary portfolios not included in at least one composite;
> ▶ inconsistent application of the firm's policies regarding asset valuations and the treatment of external cash flows, affecting the accuracy of reported composite returns; and
> ▶ missing or incorrect elements of performance presentations (e.g., certain composites did not include dispersion measures).
>
> The attached memorandum provides further details, along with our recommendations on how to correct the noncompliant conditions. . . .

Alice knew that James River Consulting was an influential organization and that Leeds Machine Tool Corporation would be a significant addition to Macroeconomic Asset Management's client list. She thought the consultants would accept the firm's not having been verified, but they would likely consider compliance with the GIPS standards a requirement for winning the mandate. She started to consider how Macroeconomic Asset Management could respond most advantageously to the RFP. Perhaps, she thought, they could gain time by continuing to claim compliance while challenging the verifier's conclusions. Alice picked up the telephone to call Terry Larson, CFA, the firm's director of performance measurement.

Case Discussion

Alice Chapman is subject to the CFA Institute Code of Ethics and Standards of Professional Conduct. The Code pertinently requires her to "act with integrity, competence, diligence, respect, and in an ethical manner with . . . prospective clients. . . ." The Standards prohibit covered persons from participating or assisting in any violation of applicable laws, rules, or regulations, including the Code and Standards themselves; prohibit misrepresentation; and obligate covered persons to "make reasonable efforts to ensure that [investment performance information] is fair, accurate, and complete."

Standard I(A) stipulates that covered persons "must understand and comply with all applicable laws, rules, and regulations (including CFA Institute's Code of Ethics and Standards of Professional Conduct) of any government, governmental agency, regulatory organization, licensing agency, or professional association governing professional activities. . . . Members and candidates must not knowingly participate or assist in and must dissociate from any violation of such laws, rules, or regulations." Standard I(C) prohibits covered persons from making "any statement that misrepresents facts relating to investment analysis, recommendations, actions, or other professional activities." It is Macroeconomic Asset Management as a firm that claims compliance with the GIPS standards, but Alice is responsible for communications with prospective clients, and she is in a position to determine if the claim of compliance is valid. It is unclear whether Alice has the authority to withdraw the claim of compliance, but it is certainly within her power to determine the facts, inform senior management of her conclusions, and recommend, if appropriate, that the claim be omitted from the firm's performance presentations. Arlington's refusal to issue a verification report constitutes strong evidence that Macroeconomic Asset Management is not justified in claiming to comply with the GIPS standards. If the verifier's findings are correct and Alice does not take appropriate action, she would appear to be in violation of Standard I(A) by knowingly helping the firm persist in making a false claim, and she herself would arguably be guilty of misrepresentation under Standard I(C).

Alice Chapman is not responsible for preparing performance presentations for Macroeconomic Asset Management; that assignment appears to fall to Terry Larson, CFA. However, she does communicate investment performance information to prospective clients. Moreover, she is aware of the seriousness of Arlington's allegations about "significant deficiencies" in the firm's performance-related policies and processes. Standard III(D) does not require firms to comply with the GIPS standards, but it does require covered persons to make "reasonable efforts" to ensure that performance information they communicate is "fair, accurate, and complete." Especially troubling in this regard are Arlington's assertions that not all actual, fee-paying, discretionary portfolios are included in at least one composite and that the accuracy of reported composite returns is questionable. Standard III(D) obliges Alice not to include performance data in the Leeds Machine Tool RFP without first attempting to ascertain whether it is a fair, accurate, and complete representation of Macroeconomic Asset Management's investment results for the strategy sought by the prospective client.

Suggested Actions

Alice Chapman should:

▶ determine whether Arlington Verification Service's conclusions about Macroeconomic Asset Management's performance policies and processes are justified;

▶ avoid making any statement that claims or implies that the firm complies with the GIPS standards unless and until the firm does in fact meet all the requirements for GIPS compliance; and

▶ make reasonable efforts to ensure that performance information provided by Macroeconomic Asset Management reflects the firm's investment results fairly, accurately, and completely.

CASE STUDY 4: BOB EHRLICH

Case Facts

"How was the luncheon, Bob?"

"Very interesting!"

"Good! When you get a chance, write a memorandum summarizing the discussion and circulate it to analytic group."

"I will. Probably not today, though—I have a deadline to meet for the McGregor Foundation."

Bob Ehrlich watched his supervisor go into a conference room, where a meeting was already in progress. Ehrlich, a performance analyst in the U.K. custodial division of a large international bank, had just returned from a luncheon sponsored by an investment consulting firm. A panel of speakers had discussed benchmark selection for fixed income portfolios, but Ehrlich found the informal talk at his table more stimulating.

One person seated at Ehrlich's table had been especially engaging. He introduced himself as Peter Neustadt and said that he had recently started his own firm to assist investment management boutiques in gathering assets. Neustadt seemed extremely interested in Ehrlich's work at the bank. Ehrlich was flattered by the attention, and he readily agreed with Neustadt's suggestion that they meet in a pub at the end of the day to continue their conversation.

"Bob," Neustadt confided, "I have many contacts in the money management business, and the future is promising, but right now I have a small firm without much technological support. I'm hoping that, with your analytical talent and your access to information, you might be willing to join me as a part-time consultant. The work would be light, and you might find the extra income very attractive. Over the long term, as my business grows, I may be able to offer you a full-time position with equity in the firm. What do you think?"

"Well," Ehrlich said, "I'd certainly like to hear more!"

Neustadt explained that he represented newly organized investment management firms—he called them "emerging firms"—in search of institutional investors. Neustadt's clients typically had portfolio management and trading experience but lacked marketing skills and sophisticated performance analytics. "I can put together a first-rate marketing presentation," Neustadt concluded, "but I need the performance data—benchmark returns, attributions, style analyses, economic commentaries—all the things that you, and your bank, do so well."

The two men talked about Ehrlich's family and his career path at the bank until it was time for Ehrlich to head home for dinner. He promised to think about Neustadt's offer and to call him the next day.

Case Discussion

Neustadt is proposing an inappropriate arrangement. Even if Ehrlich were to do the work on his own time, it is clear that Neustadt expects him to make use of his employer's facilities for personal benefit in violation of the Code and Standards. The Code requires covered persons to "place the integrity of the investment profession . . . and the interests of their employer above their own personal interests" and to "practice in a professional and ethical manner that will reflect credit on themselves and the profession." Under Standard I(D), Misconduct, covered persons "must not engage in any professional conduct involving dishonesty, fraud, or deceit or commit any act that reflects adversely on their integrity, good reputation, [or] trustworthiness. . . ." If Ehrlich were to make unauthorized use of the bank's performance measurement and related systems in service to Neustadt, he would be engaging in professional misconduct.

Especially pertinent are provisions of Standard IV, Duties to Employers. Standard IV(A) addresses Loyalty, and Standard IV(B) addresses Additional Compensation Arrangements. In addition, Standard VI(A), Disclosure of Conflicts, might apply in this case.

19. The most accurate statement about referral fees is that they must be disclosed:

   A. only to prospective clients.

   B. if the client asks about them.

   C. to employers, clients, and prospective clients.

20. Earning the CFA designation signifies:

   A. superior investment insight.

   B. completion of a rigorous program.

   C. a commitment to active portfolio management.

THE CONSULTANT

by Jules A. Huot, CFA

LEARNING OUTCOMES

The candidate should be able to:	Mastery
a. evaluate professional conduct and formulate an appropriate response to actions which violate the CFA Institute Code of Ethics and Standards of Professional Conduct;	☐
b. prepare appropriate policy and procedural changes needed to assure compliance with the Code of Ethics and Standards of Professional Conduct.	☐

CASE FACTS   1

Mark Vernley, CFA, is quite disturbed by Plains Pipeline Systems' recent allegation that he has, in essence, acted unethically—the first such accusation in Vernley's career. Although Vernley was exonerated of any allegation of wrongdoing by the authorities, he is worried that his personal reputation and integrity and those of his engineering consulting firm have been damaged. He has decided to make some changes in his personal portfolio and the procedures of the firm to prevent unethical conduct, breaches of the law, or the appearance of improprieties.

Mark Vernley

Vernley, a petroleum engineer with a doctorate in engineering and 30 years' business experience, began his career as a reservoir engineer with Deepwell Explorations. After 15 years with Deepwell, he joined a major brokerage firm as a securities analyst specializing in energy issues. During that time, he acquired his CFA charter and became a member of CFA Institute. Some eight years later, he set up his own consulting firm, Energetics, Inc., which currently employs 10 professional engineers. Energetics consults on a broad array of projects, including asset and project valuations.

Ethics Cases. Copyright © 1996, rev. 2005 by CFA Institute. Reprinted with permission.

During his years in the investment industry, Vernley invested actively in the stock market (with a concentration in energy stocks). When he worked for Deepwell Explorations, however, he had participated in the employee stock purchase plan and had exercised the stock options granted to him. As a result, a sizable portion of his wealth is now in the shares of Deepwell Explorations.

The market value and composition of his current portfolio is as follows:

Deepwell Explorations	$250,000
National Marketing and Refining	50,000
Integrated Energy Resources	45,000
Highridge Oil Pipeline	50,000
Interplains Gas Pipeline	75,000
Logline Well Service	35,000
Subtotal	$505,000
Shares in other industries	475,000
Total portfolio	$980,000

Vernley's practice during the past seven years has been quite profitable, and business is brisk. His peers generally consider him very successful. He has kept up his membership in CFA Institute and has taken an active part in energy industry affairs. He is a long-standing member of his local and national professional engineers society. He has served as president of the local engineers society for several terms and as a member of the society's professional standards committee on the national level. Although he has never written down the professional standards he expects of the company's employees, all of the engineers belong to the professional engineers society, and he has made clear in personal communications that he expects them to meet high standards in honesty, fairness, and avoiding conflicts of interest. Vernley himself is known for his professionalism, expertise, and integrity.

The Consulting Contract

Energetics recently won a contract, for which Vernley wrote the proposal, from Highridge Oil Pipeline to devise a plan to resolve conflicts with Highridge's clients. Highridge has a long history of disputes with the users of its pipeline— the shippers of oil—over the tolls charged. Highridge wants to recover increases in its operating costs; the shippers want regulations that reflect the market-driven, competitive conditions of the industry. They believe such regulations will force Highridge to increase efficiency in its operations. Both parties have engaged in expensive and acrimonious hearings before the regulatory agency. Vernley's plan for Highridge consists of an incentive-based method to set pipeline tolls, which would give Highridge a financial incentive to operate its pipeline more economically than at present. Under the plan, Highridge will share with the oil companies, including Deepwell Explorations and Integrated Energy Resources, any increase in earnings that results from reduced costs. The result should lower pipeline tolls, eliminate contentious rate hearings, and increase Highridge's profits.

After lengthy hearings, the regulatory agency ratified this plan. But Plains Pipeline Systems, a consistently more efficient and profitable carrier than

Highridge, filed an objection with the regulatory agency to the effect that Vernley's plan is flawed because he has a conflict of interest arising from his personal portfolio positions. At a subsequent hearing, the regulatory agency rejected Plains Pipeline Systems' objection and confirmed its prior decision.

Discuss the actions that Vernley could have taken to avoid any allegations of conflict of interest based on his holdings of energy company shares. Create a plan that will enable Vernley to shield his company from unethical acts that his employees might commit.

CASE DISCUSSION 2

In this case, a professional engineer has been charged with having a conflict of interest that prevented him from offering objective advice to his client. The engineer/owner has spent his entire career in the oil industry and enjoyed an excellent reputation and strong financial success. This allegation is the first of any kind made against him or his firm. It has been dismissed, and he is confident that all his employees are honest and that he can rely on them to act in an ethical and professional manner, something he took for granted until now. He is disturbed, however, about the effect of the allegations on his and his firm's reputation, and he wants to avoid any further allegations in the future.

Conflicts of Interest in a Personal Portfolio

Vernley can deal with conflicts of interest in two ways. The ideal is to avoid all conflicts of interest, real or perceived. If a conflict of interest cannot be avoided, however, then full disclosure must be made to the interested parties. Each approach entails various options.

Avoidance

Vernley can avoid any conflict between the interests of his clients and his personal investments if he refrains from investing in any energy-related securities. Because he already holds a portfolio heavily invested in such stock, the next logical step if he follows this course is divestiture. Selling his investments is a drastic option, however, that Vernley might find unreasonable. After all, he built up his portfolio gradually over the course of his long career when he could not foresee his current situation.

Another option is to establish a "blind trust," in which the account is fully discretionary and the trust beneficiary is not aware of the holdings until they are reported by the manager to the extent required by law, usually on a quarterly basis. To retain his current holdings, Vernley's investment policy might specify that his account hold a certain percentage of energy-related issues. Under this arrangement, Vernley would still know what his holdings are, however, if only after the fact. Although he would not know the exact nature of future transactions in his portfolio, he could reasonably anticipate their general direction (because of the account policies and guidelines). In any event, he could still be perceived as having a conflict, which would require that he disclose it to his clients.

An option that would keep Vernley at arm's length would be to make his oil and gas investments by way of a mutual fund specializing in energy-related issues, which would be managed by a third party over which Vernley would have no influence. In this way, he would share in a portfolio that is likely to be much more diversified than his current portfolio, thereby removing any question of the materiality of any one holding. He would also not take part in any investment decision making.

Disclosure

Whenever Vernley has a real or perceived conflict of interest because he holds shares whose prices may change if his clients adopt his recommendations, he must disclose such conflicts to his clients. Disclosure can take many forms, which depend on the circumstances. At a minimum, Vernley must disclose to clients of Energetics the existence and the nature of any conflict of interest surrounding a consulting assignment. Vernley must ensure that such disclosures are prominent, are delivered in plain language, and communicate the relevant information effectively. Then, it is up to the client to evaluate the materiality of Vernley's beneficial ownership of shares and whether the conflict of interest is significant enough to affect Vernley's ability to give advice or make recommendations that are unbiased and objective. If, in order to keep his personal matters private, Vernley decides to disclose conflicts to clients only when they are material, he is flirting with danger. Establishing what is material is difficult in any context because of the judgment required. Many people will perceive a conflict of interest no matter what the materiality.

Some of Energetics's consulting assignments may entail the preparation of a submission to the regulatory agency. In certain circumstances, Energetics would need to disclose in the submission a detailed list of Vernley's holdings. Because these documents are usually in the public domain, such declarations generally constitute public disclosure.

A Plan for Energetics

Nothing in this case suggests that any member of Energetics acted unethically. On the contrary, the description of Vernley's activities, the engineers' affiliations, and the overall reputation of Vernley and his firm lead to the conclusion that ethical values permeate the company, infusing the organization and its operating systems with a self-sustaining ethical culture. Energetics operates in an environment, however, in which the absence of a formal compliance program could expose it to costly liabilities in the event of a mishap. At a minimum, the perception of a potential conflict of interest could place the firm in an unfavorable light in the eyes of its clients.

Vernley needs to establish a comprehensive formal compliance system. The main objectives of the program will be to deter unethical or illegal acts and to provide an "affirmative defense" in the event of employee violations. The fear of being caught and of being punished are prominent enforcement characteristics of compliance systems.

For proper implementation, a compliance program must have a number of features: communication, education, and compliance procedures.

Communication

The company must inform employees of the standards to which they must conform and must deliver to employees copies of these standards—whether statutes, codes of conduct, or standards of practice. In this case, Vernley could use the CFA Institute Code of Ethics and Standards of Professional Conduct as the basis for a formal compliance manual.

Education

The company must educate employees about the main features of the adopted standards and some of their intricacies through workshops and training sessions. Attendance at these sessions should be compulsory, and the sessions should include case studies to illustrate practical applications of the standards.

Procedures for Compliance

Companies should have written documents that spell out their compliance procedures. A company can document several measures that are aids in managing its compliance program effectively, including:

▶ annual certification by employees that they have maintained familiarity with the standards and agree to abide by them;

▶ for the purpose of detecting conflicts of interest or insider trading, required reporting by employees, at least quarterly, of all securities transactions for their own personal accounts or those in which they have a beneficial interest;

▶ disclosing to management the existence and nature of any possible or actual compensation from sources other than the employer;

▶ certification by employees that they have not entered into an independent business activity in competition with their employer. The purpose of this measure is to protect the firm from, for example, misappropriation of trade secrets, misuse of confidential information, solicitation of customers prior to cessation of employment, or self-dealing; and

▶ employee memberships in organizations that maintain standards required for the practice of their professions—for example, continued affiliation by Energetics's engineers with the association of professional engineers.

Culture and Leadership

Finally, Vernley should continue instilling an ethical culture in Energetics by developing a corporate credo and moral system based on his and his colleagues' professional standards, self-interest, values, and ideals. The intention is for the system to become a social arrangement among interdependent peers that is grounded in responsible conduct and self-governance according to the chosen values. The essential characteristic of this approach is that the culture be based on the collective integrity of the organization, with its members sharing a set of guiding principles and agreeing to joint accountability.

This approach recommended for Vernley is leader driven. Leaders gain credibility when they develop and communicate their guiding values, integrate them in their operations, and imbue the company's decision-making processes with them.

PEARL INVESTMENT MANAGEMENT (A), (B), AND (C)
by Glen A. Holden, Jr., CFA

LEARNING OUTCOMES

The candidate should be able to:	Mastery
a. evaluate professional conduct and formulate an appropriate response to actions which violate the CFA Institute Code of Ethics and Standards of Professional Conduct;	☐
b. prepare appropriate policy and procedural changes needed to assure compliance with the Code of Ethics and Standards of Professional Conduct.	☐

PEARL INVESTMENT MANAGEMENT (A)

1

Case Facts

After obtaining an M.B.A. in finance, Peter Sherman is offered a position as an account manager with Pearl Investment Management, an investment counseling firm specializing in equity portfolio management for pension and profit-sharing funds, endowment funds, and high-net-worth individuals' accounts. Sherman begins work in the firm's back office, handling administrative tasks for his assigned accounts, settling transactions, balancing the accounts to bank records, and ensuring that client guidelines are followed.

Pearl is a large firm with a number of different departments, including account administration, research, and portfolio management. Having its own research staff allows Pearl to temper its reliance on brokerage firm research, to weigh its conclusions against the opinions of others, and to perform security analysis on companies that are not well followed for Pearl's proprietary use in client portfolio recommendations.

Many of the portfolio managers and analysts at Pearl are CFA charterholders, and as a result, the firm has adopted the CFA Institute Code of Ethics and Standards of Professional Conduct as part of its policy for internal compliance.

The firm policy manual also contains excerpts from laws and regulations that govern investment advisors such as Pearl (and its employees), including sections from the U.S. Securities Act of 1933, the U.S. Securities Exchange Act of 1934, the Investment Advisers Act of 1940, and the National Association of Securities Dealers manual. All employees must read and sign a statement when they join the firm that they have read Pearl's policies and must repeat this procedure at the beginning of each subsequent year as a reminder of their compliance responsibilities.

On Sherman's first day on the job, his department head gives him the policy manual as part of his orientation program, requests that he read it during the day before signing the compliance statement, and advises him that the firm's compliance department will answer any questions he may have. Sherman reads through the manual quickly and then signs the company's personnel policies statement.

After a few months, Sherman feels comfortable handling the administrative tasks related to the client accounts he manages at Pearl and ensuring that client investment guidelines are being followed. He enjoys the challenges of being the account manager for his (and Pearl's) clients, the close access to investment information and strategies, and the opportunity to invest his savings with greater insight and understanding than he had before this job. Previously, his personal investments had been in no-load mutual funds, but in his new position, he sees that he can achieve greater reward by building a portfolio of his own.

To further this goal, Sherman reads books about investments and portfolio strategy, as well as the company summaries generated by the firm's research department, and he follows the daily price changes of the firm's major holdings. He enjoys discussing his new-found knowledge with family and friends. To put his new knowledge to work in his own portfolio, Sherman decides to open an account with a national discount broker and purchase a few of the stocks that are Pearl's largest equity positions.

Identify violations or possible violations of the CFA Institute Code and Standards in this case; state what actions are required by Sherman and/or his supervisor to correct the potential violations, and make a short policy statement a firm could use to prevent the violations.

Case Discussion

This case illustrates how easily a young, unwary analyst can slip into questionable actions. The potential violations evident in this case relate to the responsibilities of supervisors, the obligation to obey all laws and regulations, the standards for trading for personal accounts, and the prohibition against conveying confidential client information.

Knowledge of the Law

Under the Code and Standards, the basis for Pearl's policy manual, Peter Sherman, his supervisor, and all employees at Pearl have certain fundamental responsibilities.

Governing Laws and Regulations Standard I(A), Knowledge of the Law, requires Sherman to know about the laws and regulations governing his behavior and that of the firm. Allusions in the case to Sherman's use of information gained through employment at Pearl indicate that Sherman is not aware of all the regulations governing his behavior. Sherman is in a junior position, however, and the responsibility for educating junior employees generally lies with their supervisors. In a large firm such as Pearl, the compliance department, in addition to the supervisor's training, should offer instruction and education in this critical area.

Legal and Ethical Violations   For supervisors, top managers, or any employees, to knowingly participate in or assist in a violation of the Code and Standards gives rise to a violation of Standard I(A). The requirement "knowingly" is important: Although members are presumed to know all applicable laws, rules, and regulations, they may not recognize violations if they are not aware of all the facts giving rise to the violations.

Actions Required   Sherman's supervisor should monitor the activities of Sherman for any violations of the securities laws, the Code and Standards, or other firm policies and procedures.

Policy Statement for a Firm   "Supervisors shall exercise reasonable supervision over those employees subject to their control and shall monitor all actions of employees in their charge to determine that the firm's policies are being followed and to prevent any violation by such persons of applicable statutes, regulations, or provisions of the Code of Ethics and Standards of Professional Conduct. Supervisors shall review the contents of the compliance manual with all direct charges when they are hired and answer any questions or concerns the employees may have."

Responsibilities of Supervisors

Under Standard IV(C), Responsibilities of Supervisors, those in a supervisory position must make reasonable efforts to detect and prevent violations of applicable laws, rules, regulations, and the Code and Standards by anyone subject to their supervision or authority. CFA Institute members who act in supervisory roles should understand what constitutes an adequate compliance system for the firm and make reasonable efforts to see that appropriate procedures are established, documented, and communicated to covered personnel and to the legal, compliance, and auditing departments. The facts that Pearl has a compliance manual as part of the employee handbook and that compliance is monitored by the compliance department do not release Sherman's department head from his supervisory duty. A supervisor must take steps to ensure that the compliance procedures are adequate and followed by the employees they supervise. Sherman's supervisor should have reviewed the contents of the compliance manual with Sherman when he was hired and answered any of Sherman's questions or concerns. The supervisor should have also monitored all Sherman's actions to ensure that he was following the firm's policies.

Trading in Client Securities for Personal Accounts

Sherman may be trading in securities that the portfolio managers are purchasing (or selling) for the firm's client accounts and, in doing so, may be violating Standard III(B), Fair Dealing and Standard VI(B), Priority of Transactions. (Members also must not engage in trading ahead of the dissemination of research awarded the CFA charter. Sherman was thrilled at the prospect of moving into research, and he accepted the transfer.

Champa came to Pearl when he decided to remain in the United States after completing a five-year U.S. tour of duty for a major international bank with which he had served for 20 years. His background in international banking has made him particularly well suited to be the research director at Pearl. Champa has seven analysts in his department—five senior analysts and two junior analysts. Sherman is one junior analyst, and the other is a Level III CFA candidate. Champa is anxious to lead the firm's research efforts into international securities and wants to begin with companies in the developing countries whose markets have experienced spectacular performance in recent years. He tells the analysts that Pearl must come up with research recommendations in emerging market equities quickly or the department will face criticism from senior management and the firm's clients. He also wants to be able to attract prospective clients by demonstrating the firm's expertise in this area.

Although Sherman is new to the department, Champa gives him difficult assignments because he believes Sherman's lack of preconceived notions about emerging market companies makes him an ideal analyst for this area. Sherman is to concentrate on Central and South America, areas where Champa believes he has special insight and can direct Sherman.

Sherman reads several brokerage reports on Latin American markets, spends time with Champa and other members of the research department discussing trends in these markets, and browses through the statistical section of Standard & Poor's *International Stock Guide*. For a briefing by someone with actual experience, Champa refers Sherman to one of his old banking contacts, Gonzalo Alves, who is well connected in Mexico and on the board of directors of a number of important Mexican corporations.

Sherman spends several hours speaking with Alves about the Mexican economy and the companies for which Alves serves as a director. Alves tells Sherman about the strategic direction of each company, some potential acquisition targets, and how changes in the Mexican economy will affect each company directly. Sherman now feels comfortable using this information in writing his research reports.

Champa asks Sherman to produce a research report on several Mexican telecommunications and cable companies. Because of the deadline Champa gives Sherman for the report, Sherman cannot develop the research easily on his own, so he plans to incorporate information from his reading of the brokerage firm reports, his conversation with Alves, and other sources. Sherman hastily finishes his two-page report, "Telecommunications Companies in Mexico," which includes excerpts from the brokerage reports, general trends and ratios from the S&P *International Stock Guide*, and paraphrased opinions from Alves. It concludes with an internal recommendation that stock in the Mexican telecommunications companies be bought for Pearl clients for which such stock is suitable. Sherman does not cite the brokerage reports as sources because they are so widely distributed in the investment community.

Pearl's upper managers applaud Champa and his staff for their quick response to the market demand for emerging market research, and the portfolio managers ask the research department for more recommendations. Jill Grant, however, the other junior research analyst, asks Sherman why his report did not include specific details about the Mexican economy or the historical exchange rate fluctuations between the Mexican peso and the U.S. dollar. She questions the comparability of Mexican securities with U.S. securities and notes that the diversification available from investing in global markets is achieved only if the correlation between the specific non-U.S. market and the U.S. market is low. Sherman's response, supported by Champa, is, "Our clients are sophisticated investors; they know these things already."

The case reveals several activities at Pearl that are or could be in violation of the CFA Institute Code of Ethics and Standards of Professional Conduct. Identify violations and possible violations; state what actions are required by Sherman or his supervisor to correct the potential violations, and make a short policy statement a firm could use to prevent the violations.

Case Discussion

The pressures to succeed that come from one's self and one's boss can lead to noncompliance in perfectly ordinary business activities. The violations or potential violations in this case relate to using proper care and independent judgment, use of insider information (particularly under international applications of the Code and Standards and the obligation of members to comply with governing laws and regulations), several aspects of research and research reports, and representation of services.

Proper Care and Independent Judgment

A requirement stipulated in the CFA Institute Code of Ethics is to use reasonable care and exercise independent professional judgment when conducting investment analysis. When Sherman succumbed to the time pressures exerted by Tomas Champa, he was thus violating a basic provision of the Code and Standard V(A), Diligence and Reasonable Basis.

Actions Required   Sherman must keep in mind the necessary steps in the research and portfolio decision-making process and resist attempts to rush his analysis.

Policy Statement for a Firm   "Analysts shall use proper care and exercise independent professional judgment in the preparation of research reports to ensure that reports are thorough, accurate, and include all relevant factors."

Use of Insider Information

Sherman must base any investment recommendations on his research alone, without incorporating material nonpublic information and without engaging in illegal or unethical actions. The situation in which Sherman found himself discussing a number of important corporations with Alves was compromising at best. Based on the local laws and customs with which they were most familiar, Champa and Alves may have found a candid discussion about the corporations where Alves served in a close relationship to be perfectly acceptable. In the course of conversation, however, Alves could have conveyed material nonpublic information to Sherman. If Sherman used such material nonpublic information in his report, which contained recommendations for investment actions, he violated Standard II(A), Material Nonpublic Information.

One of the more difficult aspects for members is reconciling their obligations under the Code and Standards with the different laws, rules, regulations, and customs of various countries. CFA charterholders, CFA candidates, and CFA Institute members are held to the highest standards. Therefore, regardless of is actively soliciting new and existing clients based on its "expertise" in the research and management of emerging market portfolios, however, then a violation of Standard I(C) has occurred.

The presentation of performance—that is, actual investment returns for its emerging market strategy—will be problematic for Pearl in the beginning. Pearl will not be able to report actual performance until it begins to manage portfolios made up of emerging market securities or portfolios that include some meaningful concentration of securities from emerging markets.

Actions Required   Pearl must not hold itself out as having experience or any "track record" in the management of emerging market portfolios until it actually manages assets in this area. It can suggest to clients, however, that the qualifications of the firm as demonstrated by its current efforts *might* produce returns that are comparable in a different environment because of the use of a similar methodology.

Policy Statement for a Firm   "Employees shall make only those statements, either verbally or in writing, about the firm and its qualifications that represent the firm properly and with the integrity it has tried to achieve. The firm shall not solicit clients, new or existing, for a new investment style without full disclosure of the firm's qualifications and expectations for both risk and potential return. Performance results for a new investment style will be in compliance with Standard III(D), Performance Presentation, as discussed in the CFA Institute *Standards of Practice Handbook.*"

ASSET MANAGER CODE OF PROFESSIONAL CONDUCT

LEARNING OUTCOMES

The candidate should be able to:	Mastery
a. summarize the ethical responsibilities required by the six components of the Asset Manager Code;	☐
b. interpret the Asset Manager Code in situations presenting issues of compliance, disclosure, or professional conduct;	☐
c. recommend practices and procedures designed to prevent violations of the Asset Manager Code.	☐

CFA Institute formed the CFA Centre for Financial Market Integrity (the "CFA Centre") to explicitly support the CFA Institute mission to lead the investment industry in setting the highest standards of ethics and professional conduct. Asset managers in particular hold a unique place of trust in the lives of millions of investors. Investment professionals and firms who undertake and perform their responsibilities with honesty and integrity are critical to maintaining investors' trust and confidence and upholding the client covenant of trust, loyalty, prudence, and care. CFA Institute and its members are committed to reinforcing those principles. To foster this culture of ethics and professionalism, the CFA Centre offers this voluntary code of conduct. It is designed to be broadly adopted within the industry as a template and guidepost for investors seeking managers that adhere to sound ethical practice.

The Asset Manager Code of Professional Conduct (the "Code") outlines the ethical and professional responsibilities of firms that manage assets on behalf of clients. Although the CFA Institute Code of Ethics and Standards of Professional

Conduct address individual conduct, this Code is meant to apply, on a global basis, to firms ("Managers") who manage client assets as separate accounts or pooled funds (including collective investment schemes, mutual funds, and fund of funds). In part, this document responds to requests from Managers to extend the scope of the Code and Standards to the firm level. Although many institutional asset managers, particularly those in well-regulated jurisdictions, may already have such a code in place, they should use this Code to evaluate their own code and ensure that all of the principles have been included. This Code has also been developed for use by asset managers, including hedge fund managers, who may not already have such a code in place.

Ethical leadership begins at the highest level of an organization. The Code should, therefore, be adopted by the Manager's board of directors, senior management, or similar oversight body. Such adoption sends a strong message regarding the importance of ethical behavior at the firm. Rather than creating rules that only apply to certain people or groups, this Code is intended to cover all employees of the firm. Although not every employee is actively involved in conduct covered in the Code, a code that is broadly applied reinforces the need for all employees to understand the ethical issues involved in the asset management business. By adopting and enforcing a code of conduct for their firm, Managers demonstrate their commitment to ethical behavior and the protection of investors' interests. In doing so, the Managers also protect and enhance the reputation of their firms.

The Code sets forth minimum ethical standards for providing asset management services for clients. It is meant to be general in nature and allow flexibility for asset managers of various sizes and structures to develop the particular policies and procedures necessary to implement the Code. The goal of this Code is to set forth a useful framework for all asset managers to provide services in a fair and professional manner and to fully disclose key elements of these services to clients, regardless of whether individual Managers are required to register or comply with applicable securities laws or regulations. Unregistered hedge fund managers in particular are encouraged to adopt the Code and implement its provisions to ensure fair dealing and integrity and to promote self-regulation in this dynamic sector.

We recognize that in the highly regulated and complex business of investment management, a code of ethics is not sufficient by itself. To be implemented effectively, the principles and standards embodied in the Code must be supported by appropriate compliance procedures. The specific compliance procedures that translate principle into practice will vary based on a variety of factors, including the specific business of the Manager, the type of clients, the size of the firm (both assets under management and number of employees), the regulatory regime with which the Manager must comply, as well as many other factors.

Managers must adhere to any applicable laws or regulations governing their activities. The provisions of this Code may need to be supplemented with additional provisions to meet the requirements of applicable security regulation in markets around the world. Inevitably, as with any globally oriented work of this kind, there will be some markets in which the Code closely reflects or is aligned with existing regulation or accepted best practice. In other markets, the Code will expand on the existing work of regulatory authorities. In still others, the Code will break new ground. Managers may also operate in different market structures, which may affect the manner in which the Code can be applied. Despite these differences, the Code nevertheless provides a universal set of principles and standards relevant to all asset managers.

Clients have a responsibility to be aware of, understand, and monitor how their assets are invested. But to fulfill this responsibility, clients must be able to count on full and fair disclosure from their Manager. Providing clients with a code of ethics that sets a framework for how the Manager conducts its business is an important step in developing the trust and confidence necessary for a successful investment management relationship.

GENERAL PRINCIPLES OF CONDUCT

Managers Have the Following Responsibilities to Their Clients:

1. Act in a professional and ethical manner at all times.
2. Act for the benefit of clients.
3. Act with independence and objectivity.
4. Act with skill, competence, and diligence.
5. Communicate with clients in a timely and accurate manner.
6. Uphold the rules governing capital markets.

ASSET MANAGER CODE OF PROFESSIONAL CONDUCT

A. Loyalty to Clients

Managers Must:

1. Place client interests before their own.
2. Preserve the confidentiality of information communicated by clients within the scope of the Manager-client relationship.
3. Refuse to participate in any business relationship or accept any gift that could reasonably be expected to affect their independence, objectivity, or loyalty to clients.

B. Investment Process and Actions

Managers Must:

1. Use reasonable care and prudent judgment when managing client assets.

2. Not engage in practices designed to distort prices or artificially inflate trading volume with the intent to mislead market participants.

3. Deal fairly and objectively with all clients when providing investment information, making investment recommendations, or taking investment action.

4. Have a reasonable and adequate basis for investment decisions.

5. When managing a portfolio or pooled fund according to a specific mandate, strategy, or style:
   a. only take investment actions that are consistent with the stated objectives and constraints of that portfolio or fund;
   b. provide adequate disclosures and information so investors can consider whether any proposed changes in the investment style or strategy meet their investment needs.

6. When managing separate accounts and before providing investment advice or taking investment action on behalf of the client:
   a. evaluate and understand the client's investment objectives, tolerance for risk, time horizon, liquidity needs, financial constraints, and any other unique circumstances (including tax considerations, legal or regulatory constraints, etc.), and any other relevant information that would affect investment policy.
   b. determine that an investment is suitable to a client's financial situation.

C. Trading

Managers Must:

1. Not act, or cause others to act, on material nonpublic information that could affect the value of a publicly traded investment.

2. Give priority to investments made on behalf of the client over those that benefit their own interests.

3. Use commissions generated from client trades only to pay for investment-related products or services that directly assist the Manager in its investment decision-making process and not in the management of the firm.

4. Maximize client portfolio value by seeking best execution for all client transactions.

5. Establish policies to ensure fair and equitable trade allocation among client accounts.

D. Compliance and Support

Managers Must:

1. Develop and maintain policies and procedures to ensure that their activities comply with the provisions of this Code and all applicable legal and regulatory requirements.

2. Appoint a compliance officer responsible for administering the policies and procedures and for investigating complaints regarding the conduct of the Manager or its personnel.

3. Ensure portfolio information provided to clients by the Manager is accurate and complete and arrange for independent third-party confirmation or review of such information.

4. Maintain records for an appropriate period of time in an easily accessible format.

5. Employ qualified staff and sufficient human and technological resources to thoroughly investigate, analyze, implement, and monitor investment decisions and actions.

6. Establish a business-continuity plan to address disaster recovery or periodic disruptions of the financial markets.

E. Performance and Valuation

Managers Must:

1. Present performance information that is fair, accurate, relevant, timely, and complete. Managers must not misrepresent the performance of individual portfolios or of their firm.

2. Use fair market prices to value client holdings and apply, in good faith, methods to determine the fair value of any securities for which no readily available, independent, third-party market quotation is available.

F. Disclosures

Managers Must:

1. Communicate with clients on an ongoing and timely basis.

2. Ensure that disclosures are prominent, truthful, accurate, complete, and understandable and are presented in a format that communicates the information effectively.

3. Include any material facts when making disclosures or providing information to clients regarding themselves, their personnel, investments, or the investment process.

4. Disclose the following:

    a. Conflicts of interests generated by any relationships with brokers or other entities, other client accounts, fee structures, or other matters.

    b. Regulatory or disciplinary action taken against the Manager or its personnel related to professional conduct.

    c. The investment process, including information regarding lock-up periods, strategies, risk factors, and use of derivatives and leverage.

    d. Management fees and other investment costs charged to investors, including what costs are included in the fees and the methodologies for determining fees and costs.

    e. The amount of any soft or bundled commissions, the goods and/or services received in return, and how those goods and/or services benefit the client.

f.   The performance of clients' investments on a regular and timely basis.

g.   Valuation methods used to make investment decisions and value client holdings.

h.   Shareholder voting policies.

i.   Trade allocation policies.

j.   Results of the review or audit of the fund or account.

k.   Significant personnel or organizational changes that have occurred at the Manager.

APPENDIX 6A—
RECOMMENDATIONS AND GUIDANCE

Adoption of the Code, by itself, is insufficient for a Manager to meet its ethical and regulatory responsibilities. Managers must adopt additional, detailed policies and procedures to effectively implement the Code. This appendix provides guidance explaining the Code and includes further recommendations and illustrative examples to assist Managers seeking to implement the Code. These examples are not meant to be exhaustive, and the policies and procedures needed to support the Code will be dependent on the particular circumstances of each firm and the legal and regulatory environment in which the firm operates.

This guidance highlights particular issues that Managers should consider when developing their internal policies and procedures to accompany the Code. The guidance is not intended to cover all issues or aspects of a Manager's operations that would have to be included in such policies and procedures in order to fully implement and support the Code.

A. Loyalty to Clients

Managers Must:

1. Place client interests before their own.

Client interests are paramount. Managers should institute policies and procedures to ensure that client interests supersede Manager interests in all aspects of the Manager–client relationship, including (but not limited to) investment selection, transactions, monitoring, and custody. Managers should take reasonable steps to avoid situations where the Manager's interests and client interests conflict and institute operational safeguards to protect client interests. Managers should implement compensation arrangements that align the financial interests of clients and Managers and avoid incentives that could result in Managers taking action in conflict with client interests.

2. Preserve the confidentiality of information communicated by clients within the scope of the Manager–client relationship.

As part of their ethical duties, Managers must hold information communicated to them by clients or other sources within the context of the Manager–client relationship strictly confidential, and they must take all reasonable measures to preserve this confidentiality. This duty applies when Managers obtain information on the basis of their confidential relationship with the client or their special ability to conduct a portion of a client's business or personal affairs. Managers should create a privacy policy that addresses how confidential client information will be collected, stored, protected, and used.

This duty to maintain confidentiality does not supersede a duty (and in some cases the legal requirement) to report suspected illegal activities involving client accounts to the appropriate authorities. Where appropriate, Managers should consider creating and implementing a written anti-money-laundering policy to prevent their firms from being used for money laundering or the financing of other illegal activities.

3. **Refuse to participate in any business relationship or accept any gift that could reasonably be expected to affect their independence, objectivity, or loyalty to clients.**

As part of holding clients' interests paramount, Managers must establish policies for accepting gifts or entertainment in a variety of contexts. In order to avoid the appearance of a conflict, Managers must refuse to accept gifts or entertainment from service providers, potential investment targets, or other business partners of more than a minimal value. Managers should define what the minimum value is and should consult local regulations, which may also establish limits.

Managers should establish a written policy limiting the acceptance of gifts and entertainment to items of minimal value. Managers should consider creating limits (e.g., amount per time period, per vendor) for accepting gifts and prohibit the acceptance of any cash gifts. Employees should be required to document and disclose to the Manager, through a supervisor, the firm's compliance office, or senior management, the acceptance of any gift or entertainment.

This provision is not meant to preclude Managers from maintaining multiple business relationships with a client as long as potential conflicts of interest are managed and disclosed.

B. Investment Process and Actions

Managers Must:

1. **Use reasonable care and prudent judgment when managing client assets.**

Managers must exhibit the care and prudence necessary to meet their obligations to clients. Prudence requires caution and discretion. The exercise of prudence requires acting with the care, skill, and diligence that a person acting in a like capacity and familiar with such matters would use under the same circumstances. In the context of managing a client's portfolio, prudence requires following the investment parameters set forth by the client and balancing risk and return. Using care in managing client assets requires Managers to act in a prudent and judicious manner in avoiding harm to clients.

2. **Not engage in practices designed to distort prices or artificially inflate trading volume with the intent to mislead market participants.**

Market manipulation is illegal in most jurisdictions and damages the interests of all investors by disrupting the efficient functioning of financial markets and causing deterioration in investor confidence.

Market manipulation includes practices that distort security prices or values or artificially inflate trading volumes with the intent to deceive persons or entities that rely on information in the market. Such practices can, for example,

The information contained in an IPS will allow Managers to assess whether a particular strategy or security is suitable for a client (in the context of the rest of the client's portfolio) and serve as the basis for establishing the client's strategic asset allocation. (Note: In some cases, the client will determine the strategic asset allocation; in other cases, that duty will be delegated to the Manager.) The IPS should also specify the Manager's role and responsibilities in managing the client's assets as well as schedules for review and evaluation. The Manager should also reach agreement with the client as to an appropriate benchmark or benchmarks by which the Manager's performance will be measured and any other details of the performance evaluation process (e.g., when performance measurement should begin).

b. Determine that an investment is suitable to a client's financial situation.

Managers must evaluate investment actions and strategies in light of each client's circumstances. Not all investments are suitable for every client, and Managers have a responsibility to ensure that only appropriate investments and investment strategies are included in a client's portfolio. Ideally, individual investments should be evaluated in the context of clients' total assets and liabilities, and may include client assets held outside of the Manager's account, to the extent that such information is made available to the Manager and is explicitly included in the context of the client's IPS.

C. Trading

Managers Must:

1. Not act, or cause others to act, on material nonpublic information that could affect the value of a publicly traded investment.

Trading on material nonpublic information, which is illegal in most jurisdictions, erodes confidence in capital markets, institutions, and investment professionals and promotes the perception that those with inside and special access can take unfair advantage of the general investing public. Although trading on such information may lead to short-term profitability, over time, individuals and the profession as a whole will suffer if investors avoid capital markets because they perceive them to be unfair, favoring the knowledgeable insider.

Different jurisdictions and regulatory regimes may define materiality differently, but in general, information is material if it is likely that a reasonable investor would consider it important and that it would be viewed as significantly altering the total mix of information available. Information is "nonpublic" until it has been widely disseminated to the marketplace (as opposed to a select group of investors).

Managers must adopt compliance procedures, such as establishing information barriers (e.g., fire walls), to prevent the disclosure and misuse of material nonpublic information. In many cases, pending trades or client or fund holdings may be considered material nonpublic information, and Managers must be sure to keep such information confidential. In addition, merger and acquisition information, prior to its public disclosure, is generally considered material nonpublic information. Managers should evaluate company-specific information that they may receive and determine whether it meets the definition of material nonpublic information.

This provision is not meant to prevent Managers from using the mosaic theory to combine pieces of material public and nonmaterial nonpublic information to draw conclusions that are actionable.

2. Give priority to investments made on behalf of the client over those that benefit their own interests.

Managers must not execute their own trades in the same security prior to client transactions. Investment activities that benefit the Manager must not adversely affect client interests. Managers must not engage in trading activities that work to the disadvantage of clients (e.g., front-running client trades).

In some investment arrangements, such as limited partnerships or pooled funds, Managers put their own capital at risk alongside that of their clients in order to align their interests with the interests of their clients. These arrangements are permissible only if clients are not disadvantaged.

Managers should develop policies and procedures to monitor and, where appropriate, limit the personal trading of their employees. In particular, Managers should require employees to receive approval prior to any personal investments in initial public offerings or private placements. Managers should develop policies and processes designed to ensure that client transactions take precedence over employee or firm transactions. One possible method would be to create a restricted list and/or watch list of securities that are owned in client accounts or may be bought or sold on behalf of clients in the near future and require employees to seek approval prior to trading in any of these securities. In addition, Managers could require employees to provide the compliance officer with copies of trade confirmations each quarter and annual statements of personal holdings.

3. Use commissions generated from client trades only to pay for investment-related products or services that directly assist the Manager in its investment decision-making process and not in the management of the firm.

Managers must recognize that commissions paid (and any benefits received in return for commissions paid) are the property of the client. Consequently, any benefits offered in return for commissions must benefit the Manager's clients.

To determine whether a benefit generated from client commissions is appropriate, Managers must determine whether it will directly assist in the Manager's investment decision-making process. The investment decision-making process can be considered the qualitative and quantitative process and the related tools used by the Manager in rendering investment advice to clients, including financial analysis, trading and risk analysis, securities selection, broker selection, asset allocation, and suitability analysis.

Some Managers have chosen to eliminate the use of soft commissions (also known as soft dollars) to avoid any conflicts of interest that may exist. Managers should disclose their policy on how benefits are evaluated and used for the client's benefit. If Managers choose to use a soft commission or bundled brokerage arrangement, they should disclose their use to clients. Managers should also consider complying with industry best practices regarding their use and reporting, such as the CFA Institute Soft Dollar Standards.

4. Maximize client portfolio value by seeking best execution for all client transactions.

When placing client trades, Managers have a duty to seek terms that secure best execution for and maximize the value of (i.e., ensure the best possible result overall) each client's portfolio. Managers must seek the most favorable terms for client trades given the particular circumstances for each trade (such as transaction size, market characteristics, liquidity of security, security type). Managers also must consider which brokers or venues provide best execution while considering, among other things, commission rates, timeliness of trade executions, and the ability to maintain anonymity, minimize incomplete trades, and minimize market impact. In cases where a client directs the Manager to place trades through a specific broker or through a particular type of broker, Managers should alert the client that by limiting the Manager's ability to select the broker, the client may not be receiving best execution, and the Manager should seek written acknowledgment of such from the client.

5. Establish policies to ensure fair and equitable trade allocation among client accounts.

When placing trades for client accounts, Managers must allocate trades fairly so that some client accounts are not routinely traded first or receive preferential treatment. Where possible, Managers should use block trades and allocate shares on a pro rata basis using an average price or some other method that ensures fair and equitable allocations. When allocating shares of an initial or secondary offering, Managers should strive to ensure that all clients for whom the security is suitable are given opportunities to participate. When Managers do not receive a large enough allocation to allow all eligible clients to participate fully in a particular offering, they must ensure that certain clients are not given preferential treatment and should establish a system to ensure that new issues are allocated fairly (e.g., pro rata). Managers' trade allocation policies should specifically address how initial public offerings and private placements will be handled.

D. Compliance and Support

Managers Must:

1. Develop and maintain policies and procedures to ensure that their activities comply with the provisions of this Code and all applicable legal and regulatory requirements.

Detailed, firm-wide compliance policies and procedures are critical tools to ensure that Managers meet their legal requirements when managing client assets. In addition, the fundamental principle-based ethical concepts embodied in the Code should be implemented by more specific policies and procedures.

Documented compliance procedures will assist Managers in fulfilling the responsibilities enumerated in the Code and will ensure that the standards expressed therein are adhered to in the day-to-day operation of their firms. Precise compliance programs, internal controls, and self-assessment tools that are appropriate for each Manager will differ based on various factors, including the size of the firm and the nature of its investment management business.

2. Appoint a compliance officer responsible for administering the policies and procedures and for investigating complaints regarding the conduct of the Manager or its personnel.

Effective compliance programs require Managers to appoint a compliance officer that is competent, knowledgeable, and credible and is empowered to carry out their duties. Depending on the size and complexity of the Manager's operations, some Managers may designate an existing employee to also serve as the compliance officer or hire a separate individual for that role; others may require an entire compliance department. Where possible, the compliance officer should be independent from the investment and operations personnel and should report directly to the CEO or board of directors. The compliance officer and senior management should regularly convey to all employees that adherence to compliance policies and procedures is crucial and that anyone who violates them will be held liable. Managers should consider requiring all employees to acknowledge that they have received a copy of the Code (as well as any subsequent material amendments), that they understand and agree to comply with it, and that they will report any suspected violations of the Code to the designated compliance officer. Compliance officers should take steps to implement appropriate employee training and conduct continuing self-evaluations of the Manager's compliance practices to assess the effectiveness of such procedures.

Among other things, the compliance officer should also be charged with reviewing firm and employee transactions to ensure the priority of client interests. Because personnel, regulations, business practices, and products constantly change, the role of the compliance officer (particularly the role of keeping the firm up to date on such matters) is that much more important.

The compliance officer should document and act expeditiously to address any compliance breaches and work with management to take appropriate disciplinary action.

3. Ensure portfolio information provided to clients by the Manager is accurate and complete and arrange for independent third-party confirmation or review of such information.

Managers have a responsibility to ensure that the information they provide to clients is accurate and complete. By receiving an independent third-party confirmation or review of that information, clients can have an additional level of confidence that the information is correct and can enhance the Manager's credibility. Such verification is also good business practice because it can serve as a risk management tool to help the Manager identify potential problems. The confirmation of portfolio information can take the form of an audit or review, as is the case with most pooled vehicles, or copies of account statements and trade confirmations from the custodian bank where the client assets are held.

4. Maintain records for an appropriate period of time in an easily accessible format.

Managers must retain records that substantiate their investment activities, the scope of their research, the basis for their conclusions, and the reasons for actions taken on behalf of their clients. Managers should also retain copies of other compliance-related records that support and substantiate the implementation of the Code and related policies and procedures, as well as records of any violations and resulting actions taken. Records can be maintained either in hard copy or electronic form. Regulators often impose requirements related to record retention. In the absence of such regulation, Managers must determine the appropriate minimum time frame for keeping firm records. Unless otherwise required by local law or regulation, Managers should keep records for at least six years.

5. Employ qualified staff and sufficient human and technological resources to thoroughly investigate, analyze, implement, and monitor investment decisions and actions.

In order to safeguard the Manager–client relationship, Managers need to allocate all the resources necessary to ensure that client interests are not compromised.

F. Disclosures

Managers Must:

1. Communicate with clients on an ongoing and timely basis.

Developing and maintaining clear, frequent, and thorough communication practices is critical to providing high-quality financial services to clients. Understanding the information communicated to them allows clients to know how Managers are acting on their behalf and gives clients the opportunity to make well-informed decisions regarding their investments. Managers must determine how best to establish lines of communication that fit their circumstances and that enable clients to evaluate their financial status.

2. Ensure that disclosures are truthful, accurate, complete, and understandable and are presented in a format that communicates the information effectively.

Managers must not misrepresent any aspect of their services or activities, including (but not limited to) their qualifications or credentials, the services they provide, their performance records or the records of their firm, and characteristics of the investments or strategies they employ. A misrepresentation is any untrue statement or omission of fact or any statement that is otherwise false or misleading. Managers must ensure that misrepresentation does not occur in oral representations, marketing (whether through mass media or printed brochures), electronic communications, or written materials (whether publicly disseminated or not).

To be effective, disclosures must be made in plain language and in a manner designed to effectively communicate the information to clients and prospective clients. Managers must determine how often, in what manner, or under what particular circumstances disclosures must be made.

3. Include any material facts when making disclosures or providing information to clients regarding themselves, their personnel, investments, or the investment process.

Clients must have full and complete information in order to judge the abilities of Managers and their actions in investing client assets. "Material" information is information that reasonable investors would want to know relative to whether or not they would choose to use or continue to use the Manager.

4. Disclose the following:

    a. **Conflicts of interest generated by any relationships with brokers or other entities, other client accounts, fee structures, or other matters.**

       Conflicts of interest often arise in the investment management profession and can take many forms. Best practice is to avoid such conflicts if possible. When Managers cannot reasonably avoid conflicts, they must carefully manage them and disclose them to clients. Disclosure of conflicts protects investors by providing them with the information they need to evaluate the objectivity of their Managers' investment advice or actions taken on their behalf, and by giving them the information to judge the circumstances, motives, or possible Manager bias for themselves. Examples of some of the types of activities that can constitute actual or potential conflicts of interest include soft or bundled commissions, referral and placement fees, trailing commissions, sales incentives, directed brokerage arrangements, allocation of investment opportunities among similar portfolios, personal or firm holdings in the same securities as clients, whether the Manager co-invests alongside clients, and the use of affiliated brokers.

b. Regulatory or disciplinary action taken against the Manager or its personnel related to professional conduct.

Past professional conduct records are an important factor in an investor's selection of a Manager. This record includes actions taken against a Manager by any regulator or other organization.

Managers must fully disclose any significant instances in which any employee or the firm has been found to have violated conduct standards or other standards reflecting on the integrity, ethics, or competence of the individuals or organization involved.

c. The investment process, including information regarding lock-up periods, strategies, risk factors, and use of derivatives and leverage.

Managers must disclose to clients and prospective clients the manner in which investment decisions are made and implemented. Such disclosures should address the overall investment strategy and should include a discussion of the specific risk factors inherent in such a strategy.

Understanding the basic characteristics of an investment is an important factor in judging the suitability of each investment on a stand-alone basis, but it is especially important in determining the effect each investment will have on the characteristics of the client's portfolio. Only by thoroughly understanding the nature of the investment product or service can a client determine whether changes to that product or service could materially affect his or her investment objectives.

d. Management fees and other investment costs charged to investors, including what costs are included in the fees and the methodologies for determining fees and costs.

Investors are entitled to full and fair disclosures of costs associated with the investment management services provided. These disclosures include information relating to any fees paid to their Managers on an ongoing basis as well as periodic costs that are known to their Managers and that will affect investors' overall investment expenses. At a minimum, Managers should provide clients with gross- and net-of-fees returns and disclose any unusual expenses.

A general statement that certain fees and other costs will be assessed to investors may not adequately convey the total amount of expenses that investors may incur as a result of investing. Therefore, Managers not only must use plain language in presenting this information, they also must clearly explain the methods for determining all fixed and contingent fees and costs that will be borne by investors and explain the transactions that will trigger the imposition of these expenses.

Managers should also retrospectively disclose to each client the actual fees and other costs charged to them, together with itemizations of such charges, when requested by clients. This disclosure should include the specific management fee, incentive fee, and the amount of commissions Managers paid on their clients' behalf during the period. In addition, Managers must disclose to prospective clients the average or expected expenses or fees clients are likely to incur.

e. **The amount of any soft or bundled commissions, the goods and/or services received in return, and how those goods and/or services benefit the client.**

Commissions belong to the client and should be used in their best interests. Any soft or bundled commissions should only be used to benefit the client. Clients deserve to know how their commissions are spent, what is received in return for them, and how those goods and/or services benefit them.

f. **The performance of clients' investments on a regular and timely basis.**

It is reasonable for clients to expect to receive regular performance reporting about their accounts. Without the necessary performance information, even for investment vehicles with lock-up periods, clients cannot evaluate their overall asset allocations (i.e., including assets not held or managed by their Managers) and determine whether rebalancing is necessary. Accordingly, unless otherwise specified by the client, Managers must provide regular, ongoing performance reporting. Managers should report to clients at least quarterly, and when possible, such reporting should be provided within 30 days after the end of the quarter.

g. **Valuation methods used to make investment decisions and value client holdings.**

Clients deserve to know if the assets in their portfolios are valued based on closing market values, third-party valuations, internal valuation models, or other methods. This type of disclosure allows clients to compare performance and determine whether different valuation sources and methods may explain differences in performance results. This disclosure should be made by asset class and must be meaningful (i.e., not general or boiler-plate) so that clients can understand how the securities are valued.

h. **Shareholder voting policies.**

As part of their fiduciary duties, Managers that exercise voting authority over client shares must vote them in an informed and responsible manner. This obligation includes the paramount duty to vote shares in the best interests of clients.

To fulfill their duties, Managers must adopt policies and procedures for the voting of shares and disclose those policies and procedures to clients. These policies and procedures should specify, among other things, guidelines for instituting regular reviews for new or controversial issues, mechanisms for reviewing unusual proposals, guidance in deciding whether additional actions are warranted when votes are against management, and systems to monitor any delegation of share-voting responsibilities to others. Managers also must disclose to clients how to obtain information on the manner in which their shares were voted.

i. **Trade allocation policies.**

By disclosing their trade allocation policy, Managers give their clients a clear understanding of how trades are allocated and provide realistic expectations of what priority they will receive in the investment allocation process. Managers must disclose to clients any changes in the trade allocation policy. By establishing and disclosing trade allocation policies that treat clients fairly, Managers foster an atmosphere of openness and trust with their clients.

j. Results of the review or audit of the fund or account.

If a Manager submits its funds or accounts for an annual review or audit (as is generally the case with pooled or mutual funds), it must disclose the results to clients. Such disclosure enables clients to hold Managers accountable and alerts them to any potential problems.

k. Significant personnel or organizational changes that have occurred at the Manager.

Clients should be made aware of significant changes that have occurred at the Manager in a timely manner. Such significant changes could include personnel turnover and merger and acquisition activities of the Manager.

3. Are the firm's disclosures regarding management fees consistent with the required and recommended standards of the Asset Manager Code?

   A. Yes.

   B. No, because they do not use plain language.

   C. No, because they do not include the average or expected expenses or fees clients are likely to incur.

4. Are the performance reporting procedures described by the fund's administrator consistent with the required disclosure standards of the Asset Manager Code?

   A. Yes.

   B. No, because the AMC requires firms to report performance to all clients on a monthly basis.

   C. No, because the AMC requires firms to provide performance on a monthly basis when requested by clients.

5. To comply with both the required and recommended standards of the Asset Manager Code, must Bornelli honor Rossi's telephone request regarding an itemization of fees?

   A. Yes.

   B. No, because the firm is not required to disclose the amount of incentive fee charged to an individual client.

   C. No, because unless the firm claims compliance with the Soft Dollar Standards, it is not required to disclose the amount of commissions paid on clients' behalf.

6. Are the policies of the alternative assets fund consistent with the required and recommended standards of the Asset Manager Code?

   A. Yes.

   B. No, the frequency of reporting is inconsistent with the AMC.

   C. No, the use of internal valuation models is inconsistent with the AMC.

APPENDIX

SOLUTIONS FOR READING 2

1. B is correct. This question involves Standard III(B)—Fair Dealing. Smith disseminated a change in the stock recommendation to his clients but then received a request contrary to that recommendation from a client who likely had not yet received the recommendation. Prior to executing the order, Smith should take additional steps to ensure that the customer has received the change of recommendation. Answer A is incorrect because the client placed the order prior to receiving the recommendation and, therefore, does not have the benefit of Smith's most recent recommendation. Answer C is incorrect because it would result in a delay in executing an order requested by the client. Answer D is also incorrect; simply because the client request is contrary to the firm's recommendation does not mean a member can override a direct request by a client. After Smith contacts the client to ensure that the client received the changed recommendation, if the client still wants to place a buy order for the shares, Smith is obligated to comply with the client's directive.

2. D is correct. This question involves Standard III(A)—Loyalty, Prudence, and Care and the specific topic of soft dollars or soft commissions. Answer D is the correct choice because client brokerage commissions may not be directed to pay for the investment manager's operating expenses. Answer B would be an incorrect choice because brokerage commissions may be directed to pay for securities research used in managing a client's portfolio. Answer C describes how members and candidates should determine how to use brokerage commissions: if the use is in the best interests of clients and is commensurate with the value of the services provided. Answer A describes a practice that is commonly referred to as "directed brokerage." Because brokerage is an asset of the client and is used to benefit the client, not the manager, such practice does not violate a duty of loyalty to the client. Members and candidates are obligated in all situations to disclose to clients their practices in the use of client brokerage commissions.

3. C is correct. This question involves Standard VI(A)—Disclosure of Conflicts. The question establishes a conflict of interest whereby an analyst, Jamison, is asked to write a research report on a company that is a client of Jamison's employer. In addition, two directors of the company are senior officers of Jamison's employer. Both facts are conflicts of interest and must be disclosed by Jamison in her research report. Answer D would be incorrect because an analyst is not prevented from writing a report because of the special relationship the analyst's employer has with the company so long as that relationship is disclosed. Whether or not Jamison expresses any opinions in the report is irrelevant to her duty to disclose a conflict of interest. Not expressing opinions does not relieve the analyst of the responsibility to disclose the special relationships between the two companies. Therefore, answer A is incorrect. Answer B is also incorrect; although an employer should not put pressure on an analyst to alter a report in any way and Jamison cannot change the report based on her employer's influence, the relationships between the two companies posing the conflict of interest must be disclosed.

4. C is correct. This question asks about compliance procedures relating to personal investments of members and candidates. The statement in answer C clearly conflicts with the recommended procedures in the

Handbook. Employers should compare personal transactions of employees with those of clients on a regular basis regardless of the existence of a requirement by a regulatory organization. Such comparisons ensure that employees' personal trades do not conflict with their duty to their clients, and the comparisons can be conducted in a confidential manner. The statement in answer A does not conflict with the procedures in the *Handbook.* Disclosure of such policies will give full information to clients regarding potential conflicts of interest on the part of those entrusted to manage their money. Answer B is incorrect because firms are encouraged to establish policies whereby employees clear personal holdings and transactions. Answer D describes the categories of securities that compliance procedures designed to monitor personal transactions should cover.

5. B is correct. This question relates to Standard III(A)—Loyalty, Prudence, and Care and Standard III(E)—Preservation of Confidentiality. In this case, the member manages funds of a private endowment. Members and candidates owe a fiduciary duty to their clients, who are in this case the trustees of the fund. Bronson cannot disclose confidential financial information to anyone without the permission of the fund, regardless of whether the disclosure may benefit the fund. Therefore, answer A is incorrect. Answer C is also incorrect because Bronson must notify the fund and obtain the fund's permission before publicizing the information. Answer D is incorrect because, even if the information is nonmaterial, the member cannot disclose the information because it is confidential. Only if Bronson receives permission from the trustees can he disclose the information to the alumnus.

6. C is correct. Under Standard IV(C)—Responsibilities of Supervisors, members and candidates may delegate supervisory duties to subordinates but such delegation does not relieve members or candidates of their supervisory responsibilities. As a result, answers B and D are incorrect. Moreover, whether or not Miller's subordinates are subject to the CFA Institute Code and Standards is irrelevant to her supervisory responsibilities. Therefore, answer A is incorrect.

7. D is correct. This question relates to Standard V(A)—Diligence and Reasonable Basis. Willier's action in changing the recommendation based on the opinion of another financial analyst is not an adequate basis for the recommendation. Answer A is thus incorrect. So is answer B because, although it is true that members and candidates must distinguish between facts and opinions in recommendations, the question does not illustrate a violation of that nature. Answer C is incorrect; whether or not a member or candidate has to seek approval from the firm of a change in a recommendation is a matter of policy set by the firm; the Standards do not require that members and candidates seek such approval. If the opinion overheard by Willier had sparked him to conduct additional research and investigation that justified a change of opinion, then a changed recommendation would be appropriate.

8. B is correct. This question relates to Standard I(B)—Independence and Objectivity. When asked to change a recommendation on a company stock to gain business for the firm, the head of the brokerage unit must refuse in order to maintain his independence and objectivity in making the recommendation. He must not yield to pressure by the firm's investment banking department. To avoid the appearance of a conflict of interest, the firm should discontinue issuing recommendations about the company. Answer A is incorrect; changing the recommendation in any manner that is

contrary to the analyst's opinion violates the duty to maintain independence and objectivity. Answer C is incorrect because merely assigning a new analyst to decide if the stock deserves a higher rating will not address the conflict of interest. Answer D would actually exacerbate the conflict of interest.

9. A is correct. Standard VII(B)—Reference to CFA Institute, the CFA Designation, and the CFA Program is the subject of this question. The reference on Albert's business card implies that there is a "CFA Level II" designation; Tye merely indicates in promotional material that he is participating in the CFA Program and has completed Levels I and II. Candidates may not imply that there is some sort of partial designation earned after passing a level of the CFA examination. Therefore, Albert has violated Standard VII(B). Candidates may communicate that they are participating in the CFA Program, however, and may state the levels that they have completed. Therefore, Tye has not violated Standard VII(B).

10. B is correct. This question relates to Standard V(B)—Communication with Clients and Prospective Clients. Scott has issued a research report stating that he expects the price of Walkton Industries stock to rise by $8 a share "because the dividend will increase" by $1.50 per share. He has made this statement knowing that the dividend will increase only if Congress enacts certain legislation, an uncertain prospect. By stating that the dividend will increase, Scott failed to separate fact from opinion. Therefore, B is correct. The information regarding passage of legislation is not material nonpublic information because it is conjecture, and it is not clear that the U.S. Representative gave Scott her opinion on the passage of the legislation in confidence. She could be offering this opinion to anyone who asks. Therefore, statement A is incorrect. It may be acceptable to base a recommendation, in part, on an expectation of future events, even though they may be uncertain. Therefore, answer C is incorrect. Answer D is incorrect because there is a violation of the Standards as indicated in answer B.

11. B is correct. This question, which relates to Standard III(B)—Fair Dealing tests the knowledge of the procedures that will assist members and candidates to treat clients fairly when making investment recommendations. The steps listed in A, C, and D will all help ensure the fair treatment of clients. Answer B, distributing recommendations to institutional clients before distributing them to individual accounts, discriminates among clients based on size and class of assets and is a violation of Standard III(B).

12. B is correct. This question deals with Standard II(A)—Material Nonpublic Information. The mosaic theory states that an analyst may use material public information or nonmaterial nonpublic information in creating a larger picture than shown by any individual piece of information and the conclusions the analyst reaches become material only after the pieces are assembled. Answers A, C, and D are accurate statements relating to the Code and Standards but do not describe the mosaic theory.

13. C is correct. This question involves Standard IV(B)—Additional Compensation Arrangements. The arrangement described in the question, whereby Jurgens would be compensated beyond that provided by her firm, based on the account's performance is not a violation of the Standards so long as Jurgens discloses the arrangement in writing to her employer and obtains permission from her employer prior to entering into the arrangement. Answer A is incorrect; although the private compensation

arrangement could conflict with the interests of other clients, members and candidates may enter into such agreements so long as they have disclosed the arrangements to their employer and obtained permission for the arrangement from their employer. Answer D is also incorrect; this potential conflict can be managed through disclosure. Answer B is incorrect because members and candidates are not required to receive permission from CFA Institute for such arrangements.

14. B is correct. This question relates to Standard III(A)—Loyalty, Prudence, and Care—specifically, a member or candidate's responsibility for voting proxies and the use of client brokerage. According to the facts stated in the question, Farnsworth did not violate Standard III(A). Although the company president asked Farnsworth to vote the shares of the Jones Corporation profit-sharing plan a certain way, Farnsworth investigated the issue and concluded, independently, the best way to vote. Therefore, even though his decision coincided with the wishes of the company president, Farnsworth is not in violation of his fiduciary responsibility to his clients. In this case, the participants and the beneficiaries of the profit-sharing plan are the clients, not the company's management. Had Farnsworth not investigated the issue or had he yielded to the president's wishes and voted for a slate of directors that he had determined was not in the best interest of the company, Farnsworth would have violated his fiduciary responsibility to the beneficiaries of the plan. In addition, because the brokerage firm provides the lowest commissions and best execution for securities transactions, Farnsworth has met his fiduciary duties to the client in using this brokerage firm. It does not matter that the brokerage firm also provides research information that is not useful for the account generating the commission, because Farnsworth is not paying extra money of the client's for that information.

15. A is correct. In this question, Brown is providing investment recommendations before making inquiries about the client's financial situation, investment experience, or investment objectives. Brown is thus violating Standard III(C)—Suitability. As for answer B, why the client changed investment firms might be useful information, but it is not the only information the member needs to provide suitable investment recommendations, and Brown is under no obligation to notify CFA Institute of any violation of the Code and Standards other than her own. Answers C and D provide examples of information members and candidates should discuss with their clients at the outset of the relationship, but these answers do not constitute a complete list of those factors. Answer A is the best answer.

16. B is correct. This question involves Standard I(C)—Misrepresentation. Statement I is a factual statement that discloses to clients and prospects accurate information about the terms of the investment instrument. Statement II, which guarantees a specific rate of return for a mutual fund, is an opinion stated as a fact and, therefore, violates Standard I(C). If Statement II were rephrased to include a qualifying statement, such as "in my opinion, investors may earn . . . ," it would not be in violation of the Standards.

17. D is correct. This question involves three Standards. Anderb, the portfolio manager, has been obtaining lower prices for her personal securities transactions than she gets for her clients, which is a breach of Standard III(A)—Loyalty, Prudence, and Care. In addition, she violated Standard I(D)—Misconduct, by failing to adhere to company policy and

hiding her personal transactions from her firm. Anderb's supervisor, Bates, violated Standard IV(C)—Responsibilities of Supervisors; although the company had requirements for reporting personal trading, Bates failed to adequately enforce those procedures. There is no indication that the company has a prohibition against employees using the same broker they use for their personal accounts that they also use for their client accounts. There is also no such prohibition in the Code and Standards. Therefore, statements A, B, and C are all consistent with the Standards and answer D is inconsistent with the Standards.

18. A is correct. This question relates to Standard I(A)—Knowledge of the Law—specifically, global application of the Code and Standards. Members and candidates who practice in multiple jurisdictions may be subject to various securities laws and regulations. If applicable law is more strict than the requirements of the Code and Standards, members and candidates must adhere to applicable law; otherwise, members and candidates must adhere to the Code and Standards. Therefore, answer A is correct. Answer B is incorrect because members and candidates must adhere to the higher standard set by the Code and Standards if local applicable law is less strict. Statement C is incorrect because when no applicable law exists, members and candidates are required to adhere to the Code and Standards, and the Code and Standards prohibit the use of material nonpublic information. Answer D is incorrect because members and candidates must always comply with applicable law.

19. B is correct. The best course of action under Standard I(B)—Independence and Objectivity is to avoid a conflict of interest whenever possible. Therefore, paying for all expenses is the correct answer. Answer C details a course of action in which the conflict would be disclosed, but the solution is not as appropriate as avoiding the conflict of interest. Answer A would not be the best course because it would not remove the appearance of a conflict of interest; even though the report would not be affected by the reimbursement of expenses, it could appear to be. Answer D is not appropriate because, by failing to take advantage of close inspection of the company, Ward would not be using all the information available in completing his report.

20. A is correct. Under Standard IV(A)—Duties to Employer: Loyalty, members and candidates may undertake independent practice that may result in compensation or other benefit in competition with their employer so long as they obtain consent from their employer. Answers B and C are consistent with Standard IV(A). Answer D is also consistent with the Standards because the Standards allow members and candidates to make arrangements or preparations to go into competitive business so long as those arrangements do not interfere with their duty to their current employer. Answer A is not consistent with the Standards because the Standards do not include a complete prohibition against undertaking independent practice.

21. D is correct. This question involves Standard VI(A)—Disclosure of Conflicts. Answers A, B, and C describe conflicts of interest for Smithers or her firm that would have to be disclosed. Answer A describes an employment relationship between the analyst and the company that is the subject of the recommendation. Answer B describes the beneficial interest of the analyst's employer in the company's stock, and answer C describes the analyst's own beneficial interest in the company stock. In answer D, the relationship between the analyst and the company through a relative is so tangential that it does not create a conflict of interest necessitating disclosure.

22. D is correct. This question relates to Standard I(C)—Misrepresentation. Although Michelieu's statement regarding the total return of his client's accounts on average may be technically true, it is misleading because the majority of the gain resulted from one client's large position taken against Michelieu's advice. Therefore, this statement misrepresents the investment performance the member is responsible for. He has not taken steps to present a fair, accurate, and complete presentation of performance. Answer C is thus incorrect. Answer B is incorrect because although Michelieu is not guaranteeing future results, his words are still a misrepresentation of his performance history. Answer A is incorrect because failing to disclose the risk preferences of clients does not make a statement misleading and is not a violation of the Standards in this context.

23. B is correct. The best policy to prevent violation of Standard II(A)—Material Nonpublic Information is the establishment of "fire walls" within a firm to prevent exchange of insider information. The physical and informational barrier of a fire wall between the investment-banking department and the brokerage operation prevents the investment-banking department from providing information to analysts on the brokerage side who may be writing recommendations regarding a company stock. Prohibiting recommendations of the stock of companies that are clients of the investment banking department is an alternative, but answer A states that this prohibition would be permanent, which is not the best answer. Once an offering is complete and the material nonpublic information obtained by the investment-banking department becomes public, resuming publishing recommendations on the stock is not a violation of the Code and Standards because the information of the investment-banking department no longer gives the brokerage operation an advantage in writing the report. Answer C is incorrect; whether or not a fiduciary duty is owed to clients does not override the prohibition against use of material nonpublic information. Answer D is incorrect because no exchange of information should be occurring between the investment-banking department and the brokerage operation, so monitoring of such exchanges is not an effective compliance procedure for preventing the use of material nonpublic information.

24. C is correct. Under Standard III(A)—Loyalty, Prudence, and Care, members and candidates who manage a company's pension funds owe a fiduciary duty to the participants and beneficiaries of the plan, not the management of the company or the company shareholders.

25. C is correct. Answers A and B give the two primary reasons listed in the *Standards of Practice Handbook* for disclosing referral fees to clients under Standard VI(C)—Disclosure of Referral Fees. Answer D describes the type of disclosure that must be made according to the guidance in the *Standards of Practice Handbook*. Answer C is inconsistent with Standard VI(C) because disclosure of referral fees, to be effective, should be made to prospective clients before entering into a formal client relationship.

26. B is correct. Standard IV(A) prohibits employees from soliciting the clients of employers prior to, but not subsequent to, their departure.

27. B is correct. The CFA Code and Standards apply to individual members and candidates of CFA Institute, but firms are encouraged to adopt the Code and Standards as part of their firm code of ethics. The CFA Institute Asset

Manager Code of Professional Conduct has been drafted specifically for firms.

28. C is correct. Standard IV(C) states that the member or candidate should decline in writing to accept supervisory responsibility until the firm adopts reasonable procedures to allow him to adequately exercise such responsibility.

29. A is correct. Standard III(D) states that both terminated and active accounts must be included as part of the performance history.

30. A is correct. By placing all clients in one of the two specialized portfolios it operates, Markoe Advisors is not giving adequate consideration to the individual needs, circumstances, and objectives of each client as required by the Standards. In addition, the Standards require that members and candidates disclose all actual and potential conflicts of interest, not just those that relate to current portfolio holdings.

31. A is correct. The Standards require that the supervisor promptly initiate an investigation to ascertain the extent of the violation and should take steps to ensure that violations will not be repeated by limiting or monitoring the employees' activities. The Standards also require that members and candidates obtain written permission from their employer before accepting any compensation or benefits from third parties that may create a conflict of interest.

32. A is correct. Jollie did not act on the material nonpublic information she possessed but waited until it became public. According to the *Standards of Practice Handbook*, "It is not necessary . . . to wait for the slowest methods of delivery."

33. A is correct. Jollie's transaction is a legitimate market order in a thinly-traded security, and Mahsud Financial's policy statement is consistent with CFA Institute Standards relating to the Integrity of Capital Markets.

34. B is correct. It is not a violation to accept compensation from an issuer in exchange for research but such arrangements must be disclosed prominently and in plain language.

35. B is correct. Receiving Dean's written permission does not absolve Jollie of her responsibility to provide attribution. Because Jollie uses the results of the research studies and does not use Dean's interpretation of the studies, it is appropriate to cite the original authors only.

36. B is correct. The first statement is incorrect and the second statement is correct. What is legal is not necessarily ethical. A weak barrier between the employer's research department and investment banking department is a potential source of conflicts.

37. B is correct. Statement 3 is incorrect. The disclosure of a conflict should be made—prominently and in plain language—regardless of whether the member views the conflict as material, so the client can determine the materiality of the conflict. Gifts (the $100 threshold is no longer applicable) from clients should be disclosed to the employer, which is responsible for determining whether the gift could affect the employee's independence and objectivity. Statement 4 is in compliance with CFA Institute Standards. The Mahsud Financial disclosure requirement exceeds, and therefore meets, CFA Institute Standards.

38. A is correct. Klein does not violate CFA Standards of Professional Conduct when recommending a PlusAccount to Vanderon. His actions comply with Standard III(A) Loyalty, Prudence, and Care; Standard III(C) Suitability; and Standard V(A) Diligence and Reasonable Basis. As required, Klein discloses the fee structure associated with the PlusAccount. Based on the fee structure and Vanderon's trading activity, the PlusAccount appears to be a suitable investment vehicle. By converting to PlusAccount status, Vanderon will incur an annual fee of $1,000 and eliminate approximately $1,800 in annual brokerage commissions. The potential savings of approximately $800 provides a reasonable basis for recommending PlusAccount status.

39. A is correct. Klein does not violate CFA Standards when recommending a PlusAccount to Brown. His actions comply with Standard III(A) Loyalty, Prudence, and Care; Standard III(C) Suitability; and Standard V(A) Diligence and Reasonable Basis. As required, he discloses the fee structure. Based on the fee structure and Brown's annual commissions, the PlusAccount appears to be a suitable investment vehicle. By converting to PlusAccount status, Brown will incur an annual fee of $5,750 and save approximately $6,400 in annual brokerage commissions. The potential savings of approximately $650 provides a reasonable basis for recommending PlusAccount status.

40. B is correct. Klein improperly references the CFA designation when he states "As a CFA charterholder, I am the best qualified to manage your investments." He is in violation of Standard VII(B), Reference to CFA Institute, the CFA Designation, and the CFA Program.

41. C is correct. Klein violates Standard VI(C) relating to Referral Fees because he fails to provide appropriate disclosure. The Standard states that members must disclose the nature of the consideration or benefit—for example, whether flat fee or percentage basis; one-time or continuing benefit; based on performance—together with the estimated dollar value. Although Klein acknowledges receipt of referral fees from the fund, he does not disclose an estimated dollar value or the nature of the consideration.

42. C is correct. In the months following Brown's change in financial status, Klein is least likely to violate Standard V(B) relating to communication with clients because he disclosed the basic format and other pertinent information regarding PlusAccounts and he distinguished between fact and opinions. During the time period, Klein does not make any new recommendations to Brown and thus is least likely to violate the Standard relating to Communication with Clients and Prospective Clients. During the period, Klein is in jeopardy of violating several other standards including those relating to Loyalty, Prudence, and Care; Suitability; and Diligence and Reasonable Basis. Because of the fee structure, PlusAccount status is not suitable for a client who trades infrequently. Klein neglects his duty of loyalty, prudence, and care by maintaining the PlusAccount Status for more than one year after Brown's change in trading activity. A diligent review of the account would indicate whether a client has a reasonable basis for maintaining PlusAccount status. Thus, Klein is most likely to violate Standards III(A), III(C), and V(A) during the period in question.

43. B is correct. Finnegan violates Standard IV(C), Responsibilities of Supervisors, by failing to ensure that compliance procedures are enforced. As she informed her staff, Harvest "must review each account on an annual basis to determine whether PlusAccount status remains appropriate." Had Brown's account been reviewed annually in accordance with compliance procedures, it would have been clear that the PlusAccount was no longer suitable for Brown. Delegating supervisory authority to another individual does not violate the Standards.

44. A is correct. Vinken does not violate any CFA Standards of Professional Conduct in his letter. In accordance with Standard III(D) Performance

Presentation, he presents fair, accurate, and complete information when he identifies actual and simulated performance results. Also in accordance with the Standard, he does not guarantee superior future investment returns. In accordance with Standard V(B) Communication with Clients and Prospective Clients, Vinken describes to his clients and prospective clients the process and logic of the new investment model. By providing the basic details of the model, Vinken provides his clients the basis for understanding the limitations or inherent risks of the investment strategy.

45. A is correct. The policies of both Khadri and Vinken are consistent with Standard V(C), Record Retention, which states that members and candidates must develop and maintain appropriate records to support their investment analyses, recommendation, actions, performance and other communications with clients and prospective clients. The records required to support recommendations and/or investment actions depend on the role of the member or candidate in the investment decision-making process. Records can be maintained either in hard copy or electronic form. Even though they use different methods, Khadri and Vinken each maintain the appropriate records and have adequate systems of record control.

46. B is correct. Khadri is in violation of Standard III(D). When claiming compliance with GIPS, firms must meet all the requirements. GIPS standards, while voluntary, only apply on a firm-wide basis. Neither a firm nor a fund can claim partial compliance with GIPS standards.

47. B is correct. Standard V(B), Communications with Clients and Prospective Clients, requires the member or candidate to separate and distinguish "facts from opinions" in the presentation of analyses and investment recommendations. Statement 1 in the newsletter states that "China's pegging of the yuan to the U.S. dollar *will* end within the next 12 months which *will* lead to the yuan increasing in value by more than 40%, supporting our over-weighting of Chinese-related stocks in the portfolio." Khadri does not clearly differentiate between opinion and fact. The statement about the future of oil pricing is not as questionable because Khadri uses the term "should" which helps clients understand that this is an opinion and not a certainty. Members may communicate opinions, estimates, and assumptions about future values and possible events but they must take care to differentiate fact from opinion.

48. C is correct. Khadri violates the Standard relating to Performance Presentation because he does not disclose whether the performance results are before or after fees. Standard III(D) requires that members make reasonable efforts to ensure that investment performance information is "fair, accurate, and complete." According to the guidance provided in the *Standards of Practice Handbook*, members should include disclosures that fully explain the performance results (for example, whether the performance is gross of fees, net of fees, or after tax).

49. C is correct. As Khadri provides the corrected information in her letter to the client, she is least likely to violate the Standard relating to performance presentation. She is more likely to violate the Standards relating to Misconduct and Misrepresentation because she knowingly misrepresents the cause of the error. Standard I(D) Misconduct requires that members not engage in any professional conduct involving dishonesty. Standard I(C) prohibits members from knowingly making any misrepresentation relating to investment actions and professional activities.

50. A is correct. Mark-ups and mark-downs in net trades are considered fees paid by clients. Standard III(B), Fair Dealing, requires that members treat all clients fairly in light of their investment objectives and circumstances. Treating institutional and retail investors differently is not a violation. According to the Standards, members can differentiate their services to clients but different levels of service must be disclosed and should not negatively affect clients. Omega has made the appropriate disclosures to its clients in compliance with legal and regulatory requirements as well as the Standards.

51. C is correct. Brown is in violation of Standard IV(C), Responsibilities of Supervisors, because he did not ensure that the final system complied with regulatory requirements. According to the Standard, Brown has a responsibility to make reasonable efforts to detect and prevent violations of applicable laws, rules, and regulations. Alerted to potential problems by the compliance department, he had a responsibility to ensure that the modifications corrected the potential problems without introducing new problems.

52. B is correct. Only the institutional trades comply with CFA Institute Standards. All the trades were processed on a net basis. Because the firm disclosed that institutional orders may be executed on a net basis, the institutional trades did not result in a violation. The firm disclosed to clients that in riskless principal trades, retail clients will receive the same execution price without mark-up. Executing the retail orders on a net basis with a $.01 mark-up resulted in a violation of Standards I(C) and III(B) relating to misrepresentation and fair dealing.

53. C is correct. Smith violated his duties to both clients and Omega by not protecting confidential information. By providing Garcia access to confidential information such as changes in recommendations and information regarding block trades, Smith provided Garcia the opportunity to front-run, which could cause harm to both Omega and its clients. Thus, Smith's actions violate his duty of loyalty, prudence, and care to his clients and his duty of loyalty to his employer, Standards III(A) and IV(A), respectively.

54. B is correct. Garcia violated the Standard of Professionalism by engaging in eavesdropping on confidential information including changes in analyst recommendations and pending block trades. According to Standard I(D) members must not engage in professional conduct involving dishonesty, deceit, or fraud or commit any act that reflects adversely on their professional reputation, integrity, or competence. Garcia engages in deceitful conduct in obtaining information from the squawk box. His actions reflect adversely on his professional reputation and integrity and thus violate Standard I(D). Garcia is not in violation of Standard II(A), Material Nonpublic Information, although he listens to the material nonpublic information on pending block trades. Possession of such material nonpublic information is not a violation of the Standard, which prohibits acting on the information.

55. C is correct. Garcia is in possession of material nonpublic information and acted on it in violation of Standard II(A). After the analyst's recommendation has been issued and/or distributed publicly, Garcia would be free to make the trade.

56. C is correct. According to Standard IV(B), members must not accept compensation that competes with their employers' interest unless they obtain written consent from all parties involved. Thus Riser must receive written, not verbal, consent from his employer before accepting the position on the subsidiary's board. According to the recommended procedures for compliance, Riser should make an immediate written report to his employer specifying the terms of the agreement; the nature of the compensation; the approximate amount of the compensation; and the duration of the agreement. The Standards do not require that members receive permission from clients before accepting board positions.

57. C is correct. Riser least likely violates Standard IV(B) Additional Compensation Arrangements when participating in the road shows. The Standard provides guidance regarding the acceptance and disclosure of compensation that might conflict with an employer's interests. Participating in the road shows and receiving compensation from the subsidiary do not appear to conflict with his employer's interests.

When participating in the road shows, Riser may violate Standards I(B) Independence and Objectivity and VI(A) Disclosure of Conflicts. The Standard relating to Independence and Objectivity requires that members use reasonable care and judgment to achieve and maintain independence and objectivity in their professional activities. Riser's role as board member could jeopardize his objectivity and create a conflict of interest. Standard VI(A) Disclosure of Conflicts requires that members make full and fair disclosure of all matters that could reasonably be expected to impair the independence and objectivity or interfere with respective duties to the clients, and prospective clients. Full disclosure allows clients to judge motives and possible biases for themselves. Riser does not appear to make adequate disclosure.

58. A is correct. No violation occurred. Riser's recommendation is based on his knowledge of Komm and the firm's "well-managed proprietary funds." He does not have a conflict when he makes the recommendation.

59. A is correct. No violation occurred. Riser is not required to resign his position with the subsidiary. Riser did not engage in any activities that would conflict with his employer's interest before his resignation became effective.

60. A is correct. Riser least likely violates Standard III(C) relating to suitability when purchasing shares for his own account. Riser may violate Standard II(A) Material Nonpublic Information and possibly Standard VI(B) Priority of Transactions when making the purchase. If, when trading for his own account, Riser knows that he will place a large block trade for Komm clients, he may be in possession of material nonpublic information. Standard VI(B) covers the activities of all members who have knowledge of pending transactions that may be made on behalf of their clients or employers. Riser has accepted the position of managing partner, has recommended the manager for the product, and knows, or should know, that he will purchase the product for at least some Komm clients once he begins work at Komm. His purchase ahead of Komm's clients might be front-running. Best practice would be to delay his private account purchase until after he purchases shares for clients.

61. C is correct. Standard VI(A) Disclosure of Conflicts requires that members and candidates make full and fair disclosure of all matters that could reasonably be expected to impair their independence and objectivity or interfere with respective duties to their clients, prospective clients, and their employer. Riser's holdings of the Japanese equity product and his position on the board of the subsidiary could impair his objectivity and must be disclosed to clients. He need not disclose his compensation from the subsidiary because it is not a referral fee.

SOLUTIONS FOR READING 3

1. A is correct.

2. C is correct.

3. B is correct.

4. C is correct.

5. C is correct.

6. C is correct.

7. B is correct.

8. C is correct.

9. B is correct.

10. A is correct.

11. C is correct.

12. B is correct.

13. A is correct.

14. B is correct.

15. C is correct.

16. C is correct.

17. B is correct.

18. B is correct.

19. C is correct.

20. B is correct.

SOLUTIONS FOR READING 6

1. **C is correct.** According to the recommendations of Section D(2) of the Asset Manager Code, where possible, the CCO should be independent from the investment and operations personnel and should report directly to the CEO or the board of directors.

2. **B is correct.** According to the guidance provided in Section D(6) of the Asset Manager Code, the level and complexity of business-continuity planning depends on the size, nature, and complexity of the organization involved. Bornelli is a large firm with hedge fund investments and it should have alternative plans for monitoring, analyzing, and trading investments if primary systems become unavailable.

3. **C is correct.** According to the recommendations and guidance of Section F(4d) of the Asset Manager Code, managers must disclose to prospective clients the average or expected expenses or fees clients are likely to incur, and to existing clients the actual fees and other costs charged to them.

4. **A is correct.** The performance reporting procedures described by the administrator are consistent with the Asset Manager Code (AMC) which requires disclosing the "performance of clients' investments on a regular and timely basis." The AMC recommends that "managers should report to clients at least quarterly, and when possible, such reporting should be provided within 30 days after the end of the quarter." The AMC also states that "at a minimum, Managers should provide clients with gross- and net-of-fees returns." Because quarterly reporting is the recommended minimum, managers may choose to provide more timely performance to clients.

5. **A is correct.** According to the recommendations of Section F(4d) of the Asset Manager Code, managers should disclose to each client the actual fees and other costs charged to them, together with itemizations of such charges, when requested by clients. The disclosure should include the specific management fee, incentive fee, and the amount of commissions paid on clients' behalf during the period.

6. **B is correct.** Clients must have regular performance information to evaluate their overall asset allocations and to determine whether rebalancing is necessary. This concept applies even to investment vehicles with lock-up periods. According to the Asset Manager Code, unless otherwise specified by the client, managers should report to clients at least quarterly, and when possible, within 30 days of the end of the period.

Absolute return objective A return objective that is independent of a reference or benchmark level of return.

Absolute-return vehicles Investments that have no direct benchmark portfolios.

Accounting risk The risk associated with accounting standards that vary from country to country or with any uncertainty about how certain transactions should be recorded.

Accreting swap A swap where the notional amount increases over the life of the swap.

Accumulated benefit obligation (ABO) The present value of pension benefits, assuming the pension plan terminated immediately such that it had to provide retirement income to all beneficiaries for their years of service up to that date.

Accumulated service Years of service of a pension plan participant as of a specified date.

Active investment approach An approach to portfolio construction in which portfolio composition responds to changes in the portfolio manager's expectations concerning asset returns.

Active management An approach to investing in which the portfolio manager seeks to outperform a given benchmark portfolio.

Active return The portfolio's return in excess of the return on the portfolio's benchmark.

Active risk A synonym for tracking risk.

Active/immunization combination A portfolio with two component portfolios: an immunized portfolio which provides an assured return over the planning horizon and a second portfolio that uses an active high-return/high-risk strategy.

Active/passive combination Allocation of the core component of a portfolio to a passive strategy and the balance to an active component.

Active-lives The portion of a pension fund's liabilities associated with active workers.

Actual extreme events A type of scenario analysis used in stress testing. It involves evaluating how a portfolio would have performed given movements in interest rates, exchange rates, stock prices, or commodity prices at magnitudes such as occurred during past extreme market events (e.g., the stock market crash of October 1987).

Ad valorem fees Fees that are calculated by multiplying a percentage by the value of assets managed; also called assets under management (AUM) fees.

Add-on interest A procedure for determining the interest on a bond or loan in which the interest is added onto the face value of a contract.

Adverse selection risk The risk associated with information asymmetry; in the context of trading, the risk of trading with a more informed trader.

Algorithmic trading Automated electronic trading subject to quantitative rules and user-specified benchmarks and constraints.

Allocation/selection interaction return A measure of the joint effect of weights assigned to both sectors and individual securities; the difference between the weight of the portfolio in a given sector and the portfolio's benchmark for that sector, times the difference between the portfolio's and the benchmark's returns in that sector, summed across all sectors.

Alpha Excess risk-adjusted return.

Alpha and beta separation An approach to portfolio construction that views investing to earn alpha and investing to establish systematic risk exposures as tasks that can and should be pursued separately.

Alpha research Research related to capturing excess risk-adjusted returns by a particular strategy; a way investment research is organized in some investment management firms.

Alternative investments Groups of investments with risk and return characteristics that differ markedly from those of traditional stock and bond investments.

American option An option that can be exercised on any day through the expiration day. Also referred to as *American-style exercise.*

Amortizing and **accreting swaps** A swap in which the notional principal changes according to a formula related to changes in the underlying.

Amortizing swap A swap where the notional amount declines over the life of the swap.

Anchoring trap The tendency of the mind to give disproportionate weight to the first information it receives on a topic.

Angel investor An accredited individual investing chiefly in seed and early-stage companies.

Appraisal data Valuation data based on appraised rather than market values.

Arbitrage The condition in a financial market in which equivalent assets or combinations of assets sell for two different prices, creating an opportunity to profit at no risk with no commitment of money. In a well-functioning financial market, few arbitrage opportunities are possible. Equivalent to the *law of one price.*

G-1

Arrears swap A type of interest rate swap in which the floating payment is set at the end of the period and the interest is paid at that same time.

Ask price (or ask, offer price, offer) The price at which a dealer will sell a specified quantity of a security.

Ask size The quantity associated with the ask price.

Asset allocation reviews A periodic review of the appropriateness of a portfolio's asset allocation.

Asset covariance matrix The covariance matrix for the asset classes or markets under consideration.

Asset swap A swap, typically involving a bond, in which fixed bond payments are swapped for payments based on a floating rate.

Asset/liability management The management of financial risks created by the interaction of assets and liabilities.

Asset/liability management approach In the context of determining a strategic asset allocation, an asset/liability management approach involves explicitly modeling liabilities and adopting the allocation of assets that is optimal in relationship to funding liabilities.

Asset-only approach In the context of determining a strategic asset allocation, an approach that focuses on the characteristics of the assets without explicitly modeling the liabilities.

Assurity of completion In the context of trading, confidence that trades will settle without problems under all market conditions.

Assurity of the contract In the context of trading, confidence that the parties to trades will be held to fulfilling their obligations.

Asynchronism A discrepancy in the dating of observations that occurs because stale (out-of-date) data may be used in the absence of current data.

At the money An option in which the underlying value equals the exercise price.

AUM fee A fee based on assets under management; an ad valorem fee.

Automated trading Any form of trading that is not manual, including trading based on algorithms.

Average effective spread A measure of the liquidity of a security's market. The mean effective spread (sometimes dollar weighted) over all transactions in the stock in the period under study.

Back office Administrative functions at an investment firm such as those pertaining to transaction processing, record keeping, and regulatory compliance.

Backtesting A method for gaining information about a model using past data. As used in reference to VAR, it is the process of comparing the number of violations of VAR thresholds over a time period with the figure implied by the user-selected probability level.

Back-to-back transaction A transaction where a dealer enters into offsetting transactions with different parties, effectively serving as a go-between.

Backwardation A condition in the futures markets in which the benefits of holding an asset exceed the costs, leaving the futures price less than the spot price.

Balance of payments An accounting of all cash flows between residents and nonresidents of a country.

Bancassurance The sale of insurance by banks.

Barbell portfolio A portfolio made up of short and long maturities relative to the investment horizon date and interim coupon payments.

Basis The difference between the cash price and the futures price.

Basis point value (BPV) Also called *present value of a basis point* or *price value of a basis point* (PVBP), the change in the bond price for a 1 basis point change in yield.

Basis risk The risk that the basis will change in an unpredictable way.

Basis swap A swap in which both parties pay a floating rate.

Bear spread An option strategy that involves selling a put with a lower exercise price and buying a put with a higher exercise price. It can also be executed with calls.

Behavioral finance An approach to finance based on the observation that psychological variables affect and often distort individuals' investment decision making.

Benchmark Something taken as a standard of comparison; a comparison portfolio; a collection of securities or risk factors and associated weights that represents the persistent and prominent investment characteristics of an asset category or manager's investment process.

Best efforts order A type of order that gives the trader's agent discretion to execute the order only when the agent judges market conditions to be favorable.

Beta A measure of the sensitivity of a given investment or portfolio to movements in the overall market.

Beta research Research related to systematic (market) risk and return; a way investment research is organized in some investment management firms.

Bid price (or bid) The price at which a dealer will buy a specified quantity of a security.

Bid size The quantity associated with the bid price.

Bid–ask spread The difference between the current bid price and the current ask price of a security.

Binary credit options Options that provide payoffs contingent on the occurrence of a specified negative credit event.

Binomial model A model for pricing options in which the underlying price can move to only one of two possible new prices.

Binomial tree A diagram representing price movements of the underlying in a binomial model.

Block order An order to sell or buy in a quantity that is large relative to the liquidity ordinarily available from dealers in the security or in other markets.

Bond option An option in which the underlying is a bond; primarily traded in over-the-counter markets.

Bond-yield-plus-risk-premium method An approach to estimating the required return on equity which specifies that required return as a bond yield plus a risk premium.

Bottom-up Focusing on company-specific fundamentals or factors such as revenues, earnings, cash flow, or new product development.

Box spread An option strategy that combines a bull spread and a bear spread having two different exercise prices, which produces a risk-free payoff of the difference in the exercise prices.

Broad market indexes An index that is intended to measure the performance of an entire asset class. For example, the S&P 500 Index, Wilshire 5000, and Russell 3000 indexes for U.S. common stocks.

Broker An agent of a trader in executing trades.

Brokered markets Markets in which transactions are largely effected through a search-brokerage mechanism away from public markets.

Brokers See *futures commission merchants.*

Bubbles Episodes in which asset market prices move to extremely high levels in relation to estimated intrinsic value.

Buffering With respect to style index construction, rules for maintaining the style assignment of a stock consistent with a previous assignment when the stock has not clearly moved to a new style.

Build-up approach Synonym for the risk premium approach.

Bull spread An option strategy that involves buying a call with a lower exercise price and selling a call with a higher exercise price. It can also be executed with puts.

Bullet portfolio A portfolio made up of maturities that are very close to the investment horizon.

Business cycle Fluctuations in GDP in relation to long-term trend growth, usually lasting 9–11 years.

Business risk The equity risk that comes from the nature of the firm's operating activities.

Butterfly spread An option strategy that combines two bull or bear spreads and has three exercise prices.

Buy side Investment management companies and other investors that use the services of brokerages.

Buy-side analysts Analysts employed by an investment manager or institutional investor.

Buy-side traders Professional traders that are employed by investment managers and institutional investors.

Calendar rebalancing Rebalancing a portfolio to target weights on a periodic basis; for example, monthly, quarterly, semiannually, or annually.

Calendar-and-percentage-of-portfolio rebalancing Monitoring a portfolio at regular frequencies, such as quarterly. Rebalancing decisions are then made based upon percentage-of-portfolio principles.

Call An option that gives the holder the right to buy an underlying asset from another party at a fixed price over a specific period of time.

Calmar ratio The compound annualized rate of return over a specified time period divided by the absolute value of maximum drawdown over the same time period.

Cap A combination of interest rate call options designed to hedge a borrower against rate increases on a floating-rate loan.

Cap rate With respect to options, the exercise interest rate for a cap.

Capital adequacy ratio A measure of the adequacy of capital in relation to assets.

Capital allocation line A graph line that describes the combinations of expected return and standard deviation of return available to an investor from combining an optimal portfolio of risky assets with a risk-free asset.

Capital flows forecasting approach An exchange rate forecasting approach that focuses on expected capital flows, particularly long-term flows such as equity investment and foreign direct investment.

Capital market expectations (CME) Expectations concerning the risk and return prospects of asset classes.

Caplet Each component call option in a cap.

Capped swap A swap in which the floating payments have an upper limit.

Carried interest A private equity fund manager's incentive fee; the share of the private equity fund's profits that the fund manager is due once the fund has returned the outside investors' capital.

Carry Another term for owning an asset, typically used to refer to commodities. (See also *Carry market*).

Carry market A situation where the forward price is such that the return on a cash-and-carry is the risk-free rate.

Cash balance plan A defined-benefit plan whose benefits are displayed in individual recordkeeping accounts.

Cash flow at risk A variation of VAR that measures the risk to a company's cash flow, instead of its market value; the minimum cash flow loss expected to be exceeded with a given probability over a specified time period.

Cash flow matching An asset/liability management approach that provides the future funding of a liability stream from the coupon and matured principal payments of the portfolio. A type of dedication strategy.

Cash price or **spot price** The price for immediate purchase of the underlying asset.

Cash settlement A procedure used in certain derivative transactions that specifies that the long and short parties engage in the equivalent cash value of a delivery transaction.

Cause-and-effect relationship A relationship in which the occurrence of one event brings about the occurrence of another event.

Cautious investors Investors who are generally averse to potential losses.

Cell-matching technique (stratified sampling) A portfolio construction technique used in indexing that divides the benchmark index into cells related to the risk factors affecting the index and samples from index securities belonging to those cells.

Centralized risk management or **companywide risk management** When a company has a single risk management group that monitors and controls all of the risk-taking activities of the organization. Centralization permits economies of scale and allows a company to use some of its risks to offset other risks. See also *enterprise risk management.*

Chain-linking A process for combining periodic returns to produce an overall time-weighted rate of return.

Cheapest to deliver A bond in which the amount received for delivering the bond is largest compared with the amount paid in the market for the bond.

Cherry-picking When a bankrupt company is allowed to enforce contracts that are favorable to it while walking away from contracts that are unfavorable to it.

Claw-back provision With respect to the compensation of private equity fund managers, a provision that specifies that money from the fund manager be returned to investors if, at the end of a fund's life, investors have not received back their capital contributions and contractual share of profits.

Clearinghouse An entity associated with a futures market that acts as middleman between the contracting parties and guarantees to each party the performance of the other.

Closed-book markets Markets in which a trader does not have real-time access to all quotes in a security.

Closeout netting In a bankruptcy, a process by which multiple obligations between two counterparties are consolidated into a single overall value owed by one of the counterparties to the other.

Coincident economic indicators Economic indicators that correlate with current economic activity; a set of economic variables whose values reach peaks and troughs at about the same time as the aggregate economy.

Collar An option strategy involving the purchase of a put and sale of a call in which the holder of an asset gains protection below a certain level, the exercise price of the put, and pays for it by giving up gains above a certain level, the exercise price of the call. Collars also can be used to provide protection against rising interest rates on a floating-rate loan by giving up gains from lower interest rates.

Collateral return (or collateral yield) The component of the return on a commodity futures contract that comes from the assumption that the full value of the underlying futures contract is invested to earn the risk-free interest rate.

Collateralized debt obligation A securitized pool of fixed-income assets.

Combination matching (or horizon matching) A cash flow matching technique; a portfolio is duration-matched with a set of liabilities with the added constraint that it also be cash-flow matched in the first few years, usually the first five years.

Commingled real estate funds (CREFs) Professionally managed vehicles for substantial commingled (i.e., pooled) investment in real estate properties.

Commitment period The period of time over which committed funds are advanced to a private equity fund.

Commodities Articles of commerce such as agricultural goods, metals, and petroleum; tangible assets that are typically relatively homogeneous in nature.

Commodity forward A contract in which the underlying asset is oil, a precious metal, or some other commodity.

Commodity futures Futures contracts in which the underlying is a traditional agricultural, metal, or petroleum product.

Commodity option An option in which the asset underlying the futures is a commodity, such as oil, gold, wheat, or soybeans.

Commodity spread Offsetting long and short positions in closely related commodities. (See also *Crack spread* and *Crush spread*.)

Commodity swap A swap in which the underlying is a commodity such as oil, gold, or an agricultural product.

Commodity trading advisors Registered advisors to managed futures funds.

Completeness fund A portfolio that, when added to active managers' positions, establishes an overall portfolio with approximately the same risk exposures as the investor's overall equity benchmark.

Confidence band With reference to a quality control chart for performance evaluation, a range in which the manager's value-added returns are anticipated to fall a specified percentage of the time.

Confidence interval An interval that has a given probability of containing the parameter it is intended to estimate.

Confirming evidence trap The bias that leads individuals to give greater weight to information that supports an existing or preferred point of view than to evidence that contradicts it.

Consistent growth A growth investment substyle that focuses on companies with consistent growth having a long history of unit-sales growth, superior profitability, and predictable earnings.

Constant maturity swap or **CMT swap** A swap in which the floating rate is the rate on a security known as a constant maturity treasury or CMT security.

Constant maturity treasury or **CMT** A hypothetical U.S. Treasury note with a constant maturity. A CMT exists for various years in the range of 2 to 10.

Constraints 1) Restricting conditions; 2) Relating to an investment policy statement, limitations on the investor's ability to take full or partial advantage of particular investments. Such constraints are either internal (such as a client's specific liquidity needs, time horizon, and unique circumstances) or external (such as tax issues and legal and regulatory requirements).

Contango A condition in the futures markets in which the costs of holding an asset exceed the benefits, leaving the futures price more than the spot price.

Contingent claims Derivatives in which the payoffs occur if a specific event occurs; generally referred to as options.

Contingent immunization A fixed-income strategy in which immunization serves as a fall-back strategy if the actively managed portfolio does not grow at a certain rate.

Continuous auction markets Auction markets where orders can be executed at any time during the trading day.

Continuous time Time thought of as advancing in extremely small increments.

Contrarian A value investment substyle focusing on stocks that have been beset by problems.

Convenience yield The nonmonetary return offered by an asset when the asset is in short supply, often associated with assets with seasonal production processes.

Conversion factor An adjustment used to facilitate delivery on bond futures contracts in which any of a number of bonds with different characteristics are eligible for delivery.

Convexity A measure of how interest rate sensitivity changes with a change in interest rates.

Convexity adjustment An estimate of the change in price that is not explained by duration.

Cooling degree day The greater of (i) 65 degrees Fahrenheit minus the average daily temperature, and (ii) zero.

Core-plus A fixed-income mandate that permits the portfolio manager to add instruments with relatively high return potential to core holdings of investment-grade debt.

Core-satellite A way of thinking about allocating money that seeks to define each investment's place in the portfolio in relation to specific investment goals or roles.

Core-satellite portfolio A portfolio in which certain investments (often indexed or semiactive) are viewed as the core and the balance are viewed as satellite investments fulfilling specific roles.

Corner portfolio Adjacent corner portfolios define a segment of the minimum-variance frontier within which portfolios hold identical assets and the rate of change of asset weights in moving from one portfolio to another is constant.

Corner portfolio theorem In a sign-constrained mean–variance optimization, the result that the asset weights of any minimum-variance portfolio are a positive linear combination of the corresponding weights in the two adjacent corner portfolios that bracket it in terms of expected return (or standard deviation of return).

Corporate governance   The system of internal controls and procedures used to define and protect the rights and responsibilities of various stakeholders.

Corporate venturing   Investments by companies in promising young companies in the same or a related industry.

Cost of carry   The costs of holding an asset.

Cost of carry model   A model for pricing futures contracts in which the futures price is determined by adding the cost of carry to the spot price.

Country beta   A measure of the sensitivity of a specified variable (e.g., yield) to a change in the comparable variable in another country.

Covariance   A measure of the extent to which the returns on two assets move together.

Coverage   Benchmark coverage is defined as the proportion of a portfolio's market value that is contained in the benchmark.

Covered call   An option strategy involving the holding of an asset and sale of a call on the asset.

Covered interest arbitrage   A transaction executed in the foreign exchange market in which a currency is purchased (sold) and a forward contract is sold (purchased) to lock in the exchange rate for future delivery of the currency. This transaction should earn the risk-free rate of the investor's home country.

Crack spread   The difference between the price of crude oil futures and that of equivalent amounts of heating oil and gasoline.

Credit default swap   A swap used to transfer credit risk to another party. A protection buyer pays the protection seller in return for the right to receive a payment from the seller in the event of a specified credit event.

Credit derivative   A contract in which one party has the right to claim a payment from another party in the event that a specific credit event occurs over the life of the contract.

Credit event   An event affecting the credit risk of a security or counterparty.

Credit forwards   A type of credit derivative with payoffs based on bond values or credit spreads.

Credit protection seller   With respect to a credit derivative, the party that accepts the credit risk of the underlying financial asset.

Credit risk or **default risk**   The risk of loss caused by a counterparty's or debtor's failure to make a timely payment or by the change in value of a financial instrument based on changes in default risk.

Credit spread forward   A forward contract used to transfer credit risk to another party; a forward contract on a yield spread.

Credit spread option   An option based on the yield spread between two securities that is used to transfer credit risk.

Credit spread risk   The risk that the spread between the rate for a risky bond and the rate for a default risk-free bond may vary after the purchase of the risky bond.

Credit swap   A type of swap transaction used as a credit derivative in which one party makes periodic payments to the other and receives the promise of a payoff if a third party defaults.

Credit VAR   A variation of VAR related to credit risk; it reflects the minimum loss due to credit exposure with a given probability during a period of time.

Credited rates   Rates of interest credited to a policyholder's reserve account.

Credit-linked notes   Fixed-income securities in which the holder of the security has the right to withhold payment of the full amount due at maturity if a credit event occurs.

Cross hedging   With respect to hedging bond investments using futures, hedging when the bond to be hedged is not identical to the bond underlying the futures contract. With respect to currency hedging, a hedging technique that uses two currencies other than the home currency.

Cross-default provision   A provision stipulating that if a borrower defaults on any outstanding credit obligations, the borrower is considered to be in default on all obligations.

Cross-product netting   Netting the market values of all contracts, not just derivatives, between parties.

Crush spread   The difference between the price of a quantity of soybeans and that of the soybean meal and oil that can be produced by those soybeans.

Currency forward   A forward contract in which the underlying is a foreign currency.

Currency option   An option that allows the holder to buy (if a call) or sell (if a put) an underlying currency at a fixed exercise rate, expressed as an exchange rate.

Currency return   The percentage change in the spot exchange rate stated in terms of home currency per unit of foreign currency

Currency risk   The risk associated with the uncertainty about the exchange rate at which proceeds in the foreign currency can be converted into the investor's home currency.

Currency swap A swap in which the parties make payments based on the difference in debt payments in different currencies.

Currency-hedged instruments Investment in nondomestic assets in which currency exposures are neutralized.

Current credit risk (or jump-to-default risk) The risk of credit-related events happening in the immediate future; it relates to the risk that a payment currently due will not be paid.

Cushion spread The difference between the minimum acceptable return and the higher possible immunized rate.

Custom security-based benchmark A custom benchmark created by weighting a manager's research universe using the manager's unique weighting approach.

Cyclical stocks The shares of companies whose earnings have above-average sensitivity to the business cycle.

Daily settlement See *marking to market*.

Data-mining bias Bias that results from repeatedly "drilling" or searching a dataset until some statistically significant pattern is found.

Day traders Traders that rapidly buy and sell stocks in the hope that the stocks will continue to rise or fall in value for the seconds or minutes they are prepared to hold a position. Day traders hold a position open somewhat longer than a scalper but closing all positions at the end of the day.

Dealer (or market maker) A business entity that is ready to buy an asset for inventory or sell an asset from inventory to provide the other side of an order.

Decentralized risk management A system that allows individual units within an organization to manage risk. Decentralization results in duplication of effort but has the advantage of having people closer to the risk be more directly involved in its management.

Decision price (also called arrival price or strike price) The prevailing price when the decision to trade is made.

Decision risk The risk of changing strategies at the point of maximum loss.

Dedication strategies Specialized fixed-income strategies designed to accommodate specific funding needs of the investor.

Deep in the money Options that are far in-the-money.

Deep out of the money Options that are far out-of-the-money.

Default risk The risk of loss if an issuer or counterparty does not fulfill its contractual obligations.

Default risk premium Compensation for the possibility that the issue of a debt instrument will fail to make a promised payment at the contracted time and in the contracted amount.

Default swap A contract in which the swap buyer pays a regular premium; in exchange, if a default in a specified bond occurs, the swap seller pays the buyer the loss due to the default.

Defaultable debt Debt with some meaningful amount of credit risk.

Deferred swap A swap with terms specified today, but for which swap payments begin at a later date than for an ordinary swap.

Defined-benefit plan A pension plan that specifies the plan sponsor's obligations in terms of the benefit to plan participants.

Defined-contribution plan A pension plan that specifies the sponsor's obligations in terms of contributions to the pension fund rather than benefits to plan participants.

Deflation A decrease in the general level of prices; an increase in the purchasing power of a unit of currency.

Delay costs (or slippage) Implicit trading costs that arise from the inability to complete desired trades immediately due to order size or market liquidity.

Delivery A process used in a deliverable forward contract in which the long pays the agreed-upon price to the short, which in turn delivers the underlying asset to the long.

Delivery option The feature of a futures contract giving the short the right to make decisions about what, when, and where to deliver.

Delta The relationship between the option price and the underlying price, which reflects the sensitivity of the price of the option to changes in the price of the underlying.

Delta hedge An option strategy in which a position in an asset is converted to a risk-free position with a position in a specific number of options. The number of options per unit of the underlying changes through time, and the position must be revised to maintain the hedge.

Delta-normal method A measure of VAR equivalent to the analytical method but that refers to the use of delta to estimate the option's price sensitivity.

Demand deposit A deposit that can be drawn upon without prior notice, such as a checking account.

Demutualizing The process of converting an insurance company from stock to mutual form.

Derivative A financial instrument that offers a return based on the return of some other underlying asset.

Derivatives dealers   The commercial and investment banks that make markets in derivatives. Also referred to as market makers.

Descriptive statistics   Methods for effectively summarizing data to describe important aspects of a dataset.

Deteriorating fundamentals sell discipline   A sell discipline involving ongoing review of holdings in which a share issue is sold or reduced if the portfolio manager believes that the company's business prospects will deteriorate.

Diff swap   A swap in which payments are based on the difference in floating interest rates on a given notional amount denominated in a single currency.

Differential returns   Returns that deviate from a manager's benchmark.

Diffusion index   An index that measures how many indicators are pointing up and how many are pointing down.

Diffusion index for stocks   An indicator of the number of stocks rising during a specified period of time relative to the number of stocks declining and not changing price.

Direct commodity investment   Commodity investment that involves cash market purchase of physical commodities or exposure to changes in spot market values via derivatives, such as futures.

Direct market access   Platforms sponsored by brokers that permit buy-side traders to directly access equities, fixed income, futures, and foreign exchange markets, clearing via the broker.

Direct quotation   Quotation in terms of domestic currency/foreign currency.

Discount interest   A procedure for determining the interest on a loan or bond in which the interest is deducted from the face value in advance.

Discounted cash flow (DCF) models   Valuation models that express the idea that an asset's value is the present value of its (expected) cash flows.

Discrete time   Time thought of as advancing in distinct finite increments.

Disintermediation   To withdraw funds from financial intermediaries for placement with other financial intermediaries offering a higher return or yield. Or, to withdraw funds from a financial intermediary for the purposes of direct investment, such as withdrawing from a mutual fund to make direct stock investments.

Distressed debt arbitrage   A distressed securities investment discipline that involves purchasing the traded bonds of bankrupt companies and selling the common equity short.

Distressed securities   Securities of companies that are in financial distress or near bankruptcy; the name given to various investment disciplines employing securities of companies in distress.

Diversification effect   In reference to VAR across several portfolios (for example, across an entire firm), this effect equals the difference between the sum of the individual VARs and total VAR.

Dividend recapitalization   A method by which a buyout fund can realize the value of a holding; involves the issuance of debt by the holding to finance a special dividend to owners.

Dollar duration   A measure of the change in portfolio value for a 100 bps change in market yields.

Downgrade risk   The risk that one of the major rating agencies will lower its rating for an issuer, based on its specified rating criteria.

Downside deviation   A measure of volatility using only rate of return data points below the investor's minimum acceptable return.

Downside risk   Risk of loss or negative return.

Due diligence   Investigation and analysis in support of an investment action or recommendation, such as the scrutiny of operations and management and the verification of material facts.

Duration   A measure of the approximate sensitivity of a security to a change in interest rates (i.e., a measure of interest rate risk).

Dynamic approach   With respect to strategic asset allocation, an approach that accounts for links between optimal decisions at different points in time.

Dynamic hedging   A strategy in which a position is hedged by making frequent adjustments to the quantity of the instrument used for hedging in relation to the instrument being hedged.

Earnings at risk (EAR)   A variation of VAR that reflects the risk of a company's earnings instead of its market value.

Earnings momentum   A growth investment substyle that focuses on companies with earnings momentum (high quarterly year-over-year earnings growth).

Econometrics   The application of quantitative modeling and analysis grounded in economic theory to the analysis of economic data.

Economic exposure   The risk associated with changes in the relative attractiveness of products and services offered for sale, arising out of the competitive effects of changes in exchange rates.

Economic indicators   Economic statistics provided by government and established private organizations that contain information on an economy's recent past activity or its current or future position in the business cycle.

Economic surplus The market value of assets minus the present value of liabilities.

Effective duration Duration adjusted to account for embedded options.

Effective spread Two times the distance between the actual execution price and the midpoint of the market quote at the time an order is entered; a measure of execution costs that captures the effects of price improvement and market impact.

Efficient frontier The graph of the set of portfolios that maximize expected return for their level of risk (standard deviation of return); the part of the minimum-variance frontier beginning with the global minimum-variance portfolio and continuing above it.

Electronic communications networks (ECNs) Computer-based auctions that operate continuously within the day using a specified set of rules to execute orders.

Emerging market debt The sovereign debt of nondeveloped countries.

Endogenous variable A variable whose values are determined within the system.

Endowments Long-term funds generally owned by operating non-profit institutions such as universities and colleges, museums, hospitals, and other organizations involved in charitable activities.

Enhanced derivatives products companies (or special purpose vehicles) A type of subsidiary separate from an entity's other activities and not liable for the parent's debts. They are often used by derivatives dealers to control exposure to ratings downgrades.

Enterprise risk management An overall assessment of a company's risk position. A centralized approach to risk management sometimes called firmwide risk management.

Equal probability rebalancing Rebalancing in which the manager specifies a corridor for each asset class as a common multiple of the standard deviation of the asset class's returns. Rebalancing to the target proportions occurs when any asset class weight moves outside its corridor.

Equal weighted In an equal-weighted index, each stock in the index is weighted equally.

Equitized Given equity market systematic risk exposure.

Equitizing cash A strategy used to replicate an index. It is also used to take a given amount of cash and turn it into an equity position while maintaining the liquidity provided by the cash.

Equity forward A contract calling for the purchase of an individual stock, a stock portfolio, or a stock index at a later date at an agreed-upon price.

Equity-indexed annuity A type of life annuity that provides a guarantee of a minimum fixed payment plus some participation in stock market gains, if any.

Equity options Options on individual stocks; also known as stock options.

Equity risk premium Compensation for the additional risk of equity compared with debt.

Equity swap A swap in which the rate is the return on a stock or stock index.

ESG risk The risk to a company's market valuation resulting from environmental, social, and governance factors.

Eurodollar A dollar deposited outside the United States.

European option An option that can be exercised only at expiration. Also referred to as *European-style exercise.*

Eurozone The region of countries using the euro as a currency.

Ex post alpha (or Jensen's alpha) The average return achieved in a portfolio in excess of what would have been predicted by CAPM given the portfolio's risk level; an after-the-fact measure of excess risk-adjusted return.

Excess currency return The expected currency return in excess of the forward premium or discount.

Exchange A regulated venue for the trading of investment instruments.

Exchange fund A fund into which several investors place their different share holdings in exchange for shares in the diversified fund itself.

Exchange for physicals (EFP) A permissible delivery procedure used by futures market participants, in which the long and short arrange a delivery procedure other than the normal procedures stipulated by the futures exchange.

Execution uncertainty Uncertainty pertaining to the timing of execution, or if execution will even occur at all.

Exercise or **exercising the option** The process of using an option to buy or sell the underlying.

Exercise rate or **strike rate** The fixed rate at which the holder of an interest rate option can buy or sell the underlying.

Exogenous shocks Events from outside the economic system that affect its course. These could be short-lived political events, changes in government policy, or natural disasters, for example.

Exogenous variable A variable whose values are determined outside the system.

Expiration date The date on which a derivative contract expires.

Explicit transaction costs The direct costs of trading such as broker commission costs, taxes, stamp duties, and fees paid to exchanges; costs for which the trader could be given a receipt.

Externality Those consequences of a transaction (or process) that do not fall on the parties to the transaction (or process).

Factor covariance matrix The covariance matrix of factors.

Factor push A simple stress test that involves pushing prices and risk factors of an underlying model in the most disadvantageous way to estimate the impact of factor extremes on the portfolio's value.

Factor sensitivities (also called factor betas or factor loadings) In a multifactor model, the responsiveness of the dependent variable to factor movements.

Factor-model-based benchmark A benchmark that is created by relating one or more systematic sources of returns (factors or exposures) to returns of the benchmark.

Fallen angels Debt that has crossed the threshold from investment grade to high yield.

Family offices Entities, typically organized and owned by a family for its benefit, that assume responsibility for services such as financial planning, estate planning, and asset management.

Federal funds rate The interest rate on overnight loans of reserves (deposits) between U.S. Federal Reserve System member banks.

Fee cap A limit on the total fee paid regardless of performance.

Fiduciary A person or entity standing in a special relation of trust and responsibility with respect to other parties.

Fiduciary call A combination of a European call and a risk-free bond that matures on the option expiration day and has a face value equal to the exercise price of the call.

Financial capital As used in the text, an individual investor's investable wealth; total wealth minus human capital. Consists of assets that can be traded such as cash, stocks, bonds, and real estate.

Financial equilibrium models Models describing relationships between expected return and risk in which supply and demand are in balance.

Financial futures Futures contracts in which the underlying is a stock, bond, or currency.

Financial risk Risks derived from events in the external financial markets, such as changes in equity prices, interest rates, or currency exchange rates.

Fiscal policy Government activity concerning taxation and governmental spending.

Fixed annuity A type of life annuity in which periodic payments are fixed in amount.

Fixed-income forward A forward contract in which the underlying is a bond.

Fixed-rate payer The party to an interest rate swap that is obligated to make periodic payments at a fixed rate.

Floating supply of shares (or free float) The number of shares outstanding that are actually available to investors.

Floating-rate loan A loan in which the interest rate is reset at least once after the starting date.

Floating-rate payer The party to an interest rate swap that is obligated to make periodic payments based on a benchmark floating rate.

Floor A combination of interest rate options designed to provide protection against interest rate decreases.

Floor broker An agent of the broker who, for certain exchanges, physically represents the trade on the exchange floor.

Floor traders or **locals** Market makers that buy and sell by quoting a bid and an ask price. They are the primary providers of liquidity to the market.

Floored swap A swap in which the floating payments have a lower limit.

Floorlet Each component put option in a floor.

Formal tools Established research methods amenable to precise definition and independent replication of results.

Forward contract An agreement between two parties in which one party, the buyer, agrees to buy from the other party, the seller, an underlying asset at a later date for a price established at the start of the contract.

Forward curve The set of forward or futures prices with different expiration dates on a given date for a given asset.

Forward discount (or forward premium) The forward rate less the spot rate, divided by the spot rate; called the forward discount if negative, and forward premium if positive.

Forward hedging Hedging that involves the use of a forward contract between the foreign asset's currency and the home currency.

Forward price or **forward rate** The fixed price or rate at which the transaction scheduled to occur at the expiration of a forward contract will take place. This price is agreed on at the initiation date of the contract.

Forward rate agreement (FRA)   A forward contract calling for one party to make a fixed interest payment and the other to make an interest payment at a rate to be determined at the contract expiration.

Forward strip   Another name for the *forward curve.*

Forward swap   A forward contract to enter into a swap.

Foundations   Typically, grant-making institutions funded by gifts and investment assets.

Fourth market   A term occasionally used for direct trading of securities between institutional investors; the fourth market would include trading on electronic crossing networks.

Front office   The revenue generating functions at an investment firm such as those pertaining to trading and sales.

Front-run   To trade ahead of the initiator, exploiting privileged information about the initiator's trading intentions.

Full replication   When every issue in an index is represented in the portfolio, and each portfolio position has approximately the same weight in the fund as in the index.

Fully funded plan   A pension plan in which the ratio of the value of plan assets to the present value of plan liabilities is 100 percent or greater.

Functional (or multifunctional) **duration**   The key rate duration.

Fund of funds   A fund that invests in a number of underlying funds.

Fundamental law of active management   The relation that the information ratio of a portfolio manager is approximately equal to the information coefficient multiplied by the square root of the investment discipline's breadth (the number of independent, active investment decisions made each year).

Funded status   The relationship between the value of a plan's assets and the present value of its liabilities.

Funding ratio   A measure of the relative size of pension assets compared to the present value of pension liabilities. Calculated by dividing the value of pension assets by the present value of pension liabilities. Also referred to as the funded ratio or funded status.

Funding risk   The risk that liabilities funding long asset positions cannot be rolled over at reasonable cost.

Futures commission merchants (FCMs)   Individuals or companies that execute futures transactions for other parties off the exchange.

Futures contract   An enforceable contract between a buyer (seller) and an established exchange or its clearinghouse in which the buyer (seller) agrees to take (make) delivery of something at a specified price at the end of a designated period of time.

Futures exchange   A legal corporate entity whose shareholders are its members. The members of the exchange have the privilege of executing transactions directly on the exchange.

Futures price   The price at which the parties to a futures contract agree to exchange the underlying.

Gain-to-loss ratio   The ratio of positive returns to negative returns over a specified period of time.

Gamma   A numerical measure of the sensitivity of delta to a change in the underlying's value.

Global custodian   An entity that effects trade settlement, safekeeping of assets, and the allocation of trades to individual custody accounts.

Global investable market   A practical proxy for the world market portfolio consisting of traditional and alternative asset classes with sufficient capacity to absorb meaningful investment.

Global minimum-variance portfolio   The portfolio on the minimum-variance frontier with smallest variance of return.

Gold standard currency system   A currency regime under which currency could be freely converted into gold at established rates.

Gordon (constant) **growth model**   A version of the dividend discount model for common share value that assumes a constant growth rate in dividends.

Government structural policies   Government policies that affect the limits of economic growth and incentives within the private sector.

Grinold–Kroner model   An expression for the expected return on a share as the sum of an expected income return, an expected nominal earnings growth return, and an expected repricing return.

Gross domestic product (GDP)   The total value of final goods and services produced in the economy during a year.

Growth in total factor productivity   A component of trend growth in GDP that results from increased efficiency in using capital inputs; also known as technical progress.

Growth investment style   With reference to equity investing, an investment style focused on investing in high-earnings-growth companies.

Guaranteed investment contract A debt instrument issued by insurers, usually in large denominations, that pays a guaranteed, generally fixed interest rate for a specified time period.

Heating degree day The greater of (i) the average daily temperature minus 65 degree Farenheit, and (ii) zero.

Hedge funds A historically loosely regulated, pooled investment vehicle that may implement various investment strategies.

Hedge ratio The relationship of the quantity of an asset being hedged to the quantity of the derivative used for hedging.

Hedged return The foreign asset return in local currency terms plus the forward discount (premium).

Hedging A general strategy usually thought of as reducing, if not eliminating, risk.

High yield A value investment substyle that focuses on stocks offering high dividend yield with prospects of maintaining or increasing the dividend.

High-water mark A specified net asset value level that a fund must exceed before performance fees are paid to the hedge fund manager.

High-yield investing A distressed securities investment discipline that involves investment in high-yield bonds perceived to be undervalued.

Historical method A method of estimating VAR that uses data from the returns of the portfolio over a recent past period and compiles this data in the form of a histogram.

Historical simulation method The application of historical price changes to the current portfolio.

Holdings-based style analysis An approach to style analysis that categorizes individual securities by their characteristics and aggregates results to reach a conclusion about the overall style of the portfolio at a given point in time.

Homogenization Creating a contract with standard and generally accepted terms, which makes it more acceptable to a broader group of participants.

Human capital The present value of expected future labor income.

Hybrid markets Combinations of market types, which offer elements of batch auction markets and continuous auction markets, as well as quote-driven markets.

Hypothetical events A type of scenario analysis used in stress testing that involves the evaluation of performance given events that have never happened in the markets or market outcomes to which we attach a small probability.

Illiquidity premium Compensation for the risk of loss relative to an investment's fair value if an investment needs to be converted to cash quickly.

Immunization An asset/liability management approach that structures investments in bonds to match (offset) liabilities' weighted-average duration; a type of dedication strategy.

Immunization target rate of return The assured rate of return of an immunized portfolio, equal to the total return of the portfolio assuming no change in the term structure.

Immunized time horizon The time horizon over which a portfolio's value is immunized; equal to the portfolio duration.

Implementation shortfall The difference between the money return on a notional or paper portfolio and the actual portfolio return.

Implementation shortfall strategy (or arrival price strategy) A strategy that attempts to minimize trading costs as measured by the implementation shortfall method.

Implicit transaction costs The indirect costs of trading including bid–ask spreads, the market price impacts of large trades, missed trade opportunity costs, and delay costs.

Implied repo rate The rate of return from a cash-and-carry transaction implied by the futures price relative to the spot price.

Implied volatility The volatility that option traders use to price an option, implied by the price of the option and a particular option-pricing model.

Implied yield A measure of the yield on the underlying bond of a futures contract implied by pricing it as though the underlying will be delivered at the futures expiration.

Incremental VAR A measure of the incremental effect of an asset on the VAR of a portfolio by measuring the difference between the portfolio's VAR while including a specified asset and the portfolio's VAR with that asset eliminated.

Index amortizing swap An interest rate swap in which the notional principal is indexed to the level of interest rates and declines with the level of interest rates according to a predefined schedule. This type of swap is frequently used to hedge securities that are prepaid as interest rates decline, such as mortgage-backed securities.

Index option An option in which the underlying is a stock index.

Indexing A common passive approach to investing that involves holding a portfolio of securities designed to replicate the returns on a specified index of securities.

Indirect commodity investment Commodity investment that involves the acquisition of indirect claims on commodities, such as equity in companies specializing in commodity production.

Individualist investors Investors who have a self-assured approach to investing and investment decision making.

Inferential statistics Methods for making estimates or forecasts about a larger group from a smaller group actually observed.

Inflation An increase in the general level of prices; a decrease in the purchasing power of a unit of currency.

Inflation hedge An asset whose returns are sufficient on average to preserve purchasing power during periods of inflation.

Inflation premium Compensation for expected inflation.

Information coefficient The correlation between forecast and actual returns.

Information ratio The mean excess return of the account over the benchmark (i.e., mean active return) relative to the variability of that excess return (i.e., tracking risk); a measure of risk-adjusted performance.

Information-motivated traders Traders that seek to trade on information that has limited value if not quickly acted upon.

Infrastructure funds Funds that make private investment in public infrastructure projects in return for rights to specified revenue streams over a contracted period.

Initial margin requirement The margin requirement on the first day of a transaction as well as on any day in which additional margin funds must be deposited.

Initial public offering The initial issuance of common stock registered for public trading by a formerly private corporation.

Input uncertainty Uncertainty concerning whether the inputs are correct.

Inside ask (or market ask) The lowest available ask price.

Inside bid (or market bid) The highest available bid price.

Inside bid–ask spread (also called market bid–ask spread, inside spread, or market spread) Market ask price minus market bid price.

Inside quote (or market quote) Combination of the highest available bid price with the lowest available ask price.

Institutional investors Corporations or other legal entities that ultimately serve as financial intermediaries between individuals and investment markets.

Interest rate call An option in which the holder has the right to make a known interest payment and receive an unknown interest payment.

Interest rate cap or **cap** A series of call options on an interest rate, with each option expiring at the date on which the floating loan rate will be reset, and with each option having the same exercise rate. A cap in general can have an underlying other than an interest rate.

Interest rate collar A combination of a long cap and a short floor, or a short cap and a long floor. A collar in general can have an underlying other than an interest rate.

Interest rate floor or **floor** A series of put options on an interest rate, with each option expiring at the date on which the floating loan rate will be reset, and with each option having the same exercise rate. A floor in general can have an underlying other than the interest rate.

Interest rate forward (See *forward rate agreement*)

Interest rate management effect With respect to fixed-income attribution analysis, a return component reflecting how well a manager predicts interest rate changes.

Interest rate option An option in which the underlying is an interest rate.

Interest rate parity A formula that expresses the equivalence or parity of spot and forward rates, after adjusting for differences in the interest rates.

Interest rate put An option in which the holder has the right to make an unknown interest payment and receive a known interest payment.

Interest rate risk Risk related to changes in the level of interest rates.

Interest rate swap A contract between two parties (counterparties) to exchange periodic interest payments based on a specified notional amount of principal.

Interest spread With respect to banks, the average yield on earning assets minus the average percent cost of interest-bearing liabilities.

Internal rate of return The growth rate that will link the ending value of the account to its beginning value plus all intermediate cash flows; money-weighted rate of return is a synonym.

In-the-money Options that, if exercised, would result in the value received being worth more than the payment required to exercise.

Intrinsic value or **exercise value** The value obtained if an option is exercised based on current conditions.

Inventory cycle   A cycle measured in terms of fluctuations in inventories, typically lasting 2–4 years.

Inverse floater   A floating-rate note or bond in which the coupon is adjusted to move opposite to a benchmark interest rate.

Investment objectives   Desired investment outcomes, chiefly pertaining to return and risk.

Investment policy statement (IPS)   A written document that sets out a client's return objectives and risk tolerance over a relevant time horizon, along with applicable constraints such as liquidity needs, tax considerations, regulatory requirements, and unique circumstances.

Investment skill   The ability to outperform an appropriate benchmark consistently over time.

Investment strategy   An investor's approach to investment analysis and security selection.

Investment style   A natural grouping of investment disciplines that has some predictive power in explaining the future dispersion in returns across portfolios.

Investment style indices   Indices that represent specific portions of an asset category. For example, subgroups within the U.S. common stock asset category such as large-capitalization growth stocks.

Investor's benchmark   The benchmark an investor uses to evaluate performance of a given portfolio or asset class.

J factor risk   The risk associated with a judge's track record in adjudicating bankruptcies and restructuring.

J-curve   The expected pattern of interim returns over the life of a successful venture capital fund in which early returns are negative as the portfolio of companies burns cash but later returns accelerate as companies are exited.

Key rate duration   A method of measuring the interest rate sensitivities of a fixed-income instrument or portfolio to shifts in key points along the yield curve.

Lagging economic indicators   Economic indicators that correlate with recent past economic activity; a set of economic variables whose values reach peaks and troughs after the aggregate economy.

Law of one price   The condition in a financial market in which two financial instruments or combinations of financial instruments can sell for only one price. Equivalent to the principle that no arbitrage opportunities are possible.

Leading economic indicators   A variable that varies with the business cycle but at a fairly consistent time interval before a turn in the business cycle; a set of economic variables whose values reach peaks and troughs in advance of the aggregate economy.

Legal and regulatory factors   External factors imposed by governmental, regulatory, or oversight authorities that constrain investment decision-making.

Legal/contract risk   The possibility of loss arising from the legal system's failure to enforce a contract in which an enterprise has a financial stake; for example, if a contract is voided through litigation.

Leverage-adjusted duration gap   A leverage-adjusted measure of the difference between the durations of assets and liabilities which measures a bank's overall interest rate exposure.

Leveraged floating-rate note or **leveraged floater**   A floating-rate note or bond in which the coupon is adjusted at a multiple of a benchmark interest rate.

Liability   As used in the text, a financial obligation.

Life annuity   An annuity that guarantees a monthly income to the annuitant for life.

Limit down   A limit move in the futures market in which the price at which a transaction would be made is at or below the lower limit.

Limit move   A condition in the futures markets in which the price at which a transaction would be made is at or beyond the price limits.

Limit order   An instruction to execute an order when the best price available is at least as good as the limit price specified in the order.

Limit up   A limit move in the futures market in which the price at which a transaction would be made is at or above the upper limit.

Linear programming   Optimization in which the objective function and constraints are linear.

Liquidity   The ability to trade without delay at relatively low cost and in relatively large quantities.

Liquidity event   An event giving rise to a need for cash.

Liquidity requirement   A need for cash in excess of new contributions (for pension plans and endowments, for example) or savings (for individuals) at a specified point in time.

Liquidity risk   Any risk of economic loss because of the need to sell relatively less liquid assets to meet liquidity requirements; the risk that a financial instrument cannot be purchased or sold without a significant concession in price because of the market's potential inability to efficiently accommodate the desired trading size.

Liquidity-motivated traders   Traders that are motivated to trade based upon reasons other than an information advantage. For example, to release cash proceeds to facilitate the purchase of another security, adjust market exposure, or fund cash needs.

Locked limit A condition in the futures markets in which a transaction cannot take place because the price would be beyond the limits.

Locked up Said of investments that cannot be traded at all for some time.

Lock-up period A minimum initial holding period for investments during which no part of the investment can be withdrawn.

Logical participation strategies Protocols for breaking up an order for execution over time. Typically used by institutional traders to participate in overall market volumes without being unduly visible.

London Interbank Offer Rate (LIBOR) The Eurodollar rate at which London banks lend dollars to other London banks; considered to be the best representative rate on a dollar borrowed by a private, high-quality borrower.

Long The buyer of a derivative contract. Also refers to the position of owning a derivative.

Longevity risk The risk of outliving one's financial resources.

Long-term equity anticipatory securities (LEAPS) Options originally created with expirations of several years.

Low P/E A value investment substyle that focuses on shares selling at low prices relative to current or normal earnings.

Lower bound The lowest possible value of an option.

M^2 A measure of what a portfolio would have returned if it had taken on the same total risk as the market index.

Macaulay duration The percentage change in price for a percentage change in yield. The term, named for one of the economists who first derived it, is used to distinguish the calculation from modified duration. See also *modified duration*.

Macro attribution Performance attribution analysis conducted on the fund sponsor level.

Macro expectations Expectations concerning classes of assets.

Maintenance margin requirement The margin requirement on any day other than the first day of a transaction.

Managed futures Pooled investment vehicles, frequently structured as limited partnerships, that invest in futures and options on futures and other instruments.

Manager continuation policies Policies adopted to guide the manager evaluations conducted by fund sponsors. The goal of manager continuation poli-

cies is to reduce the costs of manager turnover while systematically acting on indications of future poor performance.

Manager monitoring A formal, documented procedure that assists fund sponsors in consistently collecting information relevant to evaluating the state of their managers' operations; used to identify warning signs of adverse changes in existing managers' organizations.

Manager review A detailed examination of a manager that currently exists within a plan sponsor's program. The manager review closely resembles the manager selection process, in both the information considered and the comprehensiveness of the analysis. The staff should review all phases of the manager's operations, just as if the manager were being initially hired.

Mandate A set of instructions detailing the investment manager's task and how his performance will be evaluated.

Margin The amount of money that a trader deposits in a margin account. The term is derived from the stock market practice in which an investor borrows a portion of the money required to purchase a certain amount of stock. In futures markets, there is no borrowing so the margin is more of a down payment or performance bond.

Market bid The best available bid; highest price any buyer is currently willing to pay.

Market fragmentation A condition whereby a market contains no dominant group of sellers (or buyers) that are large enough to unduly influence the market.

Market impact (or price impact) The effect of the trade on transaction prices.

Market integration The degree to which there are no impediments or barriers to capital mobility across markets.

Market microstructure The market structures and processes that affect how the manager's interest in buying or selling an asset is translated into executed trades (represented by trade prices and volumes).

Market model A regression equation that specifies a linear relationship between the return on a security (or portfolio) and the return on a broad market index.

Market on open (close) order A market order to be executed at the opening (closing) of the market.

Market order An instruction to execute an order as soon as possible in the public markets at the best price available.

Market oriented With reference to equity investing, an intermediate grouping for investment disciplines that cannot be clearly categorized as value or growth.

Market resilience Condition where discrepancies between market prices and intrinsic values tend to be small and corrected quickly.

Market risk The risk associated with interest rates, exchange rates, and equity prices.

Market segmentation The degree to which there are some meaningful impediments to capital movement across markets.

Market timing Increasing or decreasing exposure to a market or asset class based on predictions of its performance; with reference to performance attribution, returns attributable to shorter-term tactical deviations from the strategic asset allocation.

Market-adjusted implementation shortfall The difference between the money return on a notional or paper portfolio and the actual portfolio return, adjusted using beta to remove the effect of the return on the market.

Market-not-held order A variation of the market order designed to give the agent greater discretion than a simple market order would allow. "Not held" means that the floor broker is not required to trade at any specific price or in any specific time interval.

Marking to market A procedure used primarily in futures markets in which the parties to a contract settle the amount owed daily. Also known as the *daily settlement*.

Mass affluent An industry term for a segment of the private wealth marketplace that is not sufficiently wealthy to command certain individualized services.

Matrix prices Prices determined by comparisons to other securities of similar credit risk and maturity; the result of matrix pricing.

Matrix pricing An approach for estimating the prices of thinly traded securities based on the prices of securities with similar attributions, such as similar credit rating, maturity, or economic sector.

Maturity premium Compensation for the increased sensitivity of the market value of debt to a change in market interest rates as maturity is extended.

Maturity variance A measure of how much a given immunized portfolio differs from the ideal immunized portfolio consisting of a single pure discount instrument with maturity equal to the time horizon.

Maximum loss optimization A stress test in which we would try to optimize mathematically the risk variable that would produce the maximum loss.

Mega-cap buy-out funds A class of buyout funds that take public companies private.

Methodical investors Investors who rely on "hard facts."

Micro attribution Performance attribution analysis carried out on the investment manager level.

Micro expectations Expectations concerning individual assets.

Middle-market buy-out funds A class of buyout funds that purchase private companies whose revenues and profits are too small to access capital from the public equity markets.

Midquote The halfway point between the market bid and ask prices.

Minimum-variance frontier The graph of the set of portfolios with smallest variances of return for their levels of expected return.

Missed trade opportunity costs Unrealized profit/loss arising from the failure to execute a trade in a timely manner.

Model risk The risk that a model is incorrect or misapplied; in investments, it often refers to valuation models.

Model uncertainty Uncertainty concerning whether a selected model is correct.

Modern portfolio theory (MPT) The analysis of rational portfolio choices based on the efficient use of risk.

Modified duration An adjustment of the duration for the level of the yield. Contrast with *Macaulay duration*.

Monetary policy Government activity concerning interest rates and the money supply.

Money markets Markets for fixed-income securities with maturities of one year or less.

Moneyness The relationship between the price of the underlying and an option's exercise price.

Money-weighted rate of return Same as the internal rate of return; the growth rate that will link the ending value of the account to its beginning value plus all intermediate cash flows.

Monitoring To systematically keep watch over investor circumstances (including wealth and constraints), market and economic changes, and the portfolio itself so that the client's current objectives and constraints continue to be satisfied.

Monte Carlo simulation method An approach to estimating VAR that produces random outcomes to examine what might happen if a particular risk is faced. This method is widely used in the sciences as well as in business to study a variety of problems.

Mortality risk The risk of loss of human capital in the event of premature death.

Multifactor model   A model that explains a variable in terms of the values of a set of factors.

Multifactor model technique   With respect to construction of an indexed portfolio, a technique that attempts to match the primary risk exposures of the indexed portfolio to those of the index.

Multiperiod Sharpe ratio   A Sharpe ratio based on the investment's multiperiod wealth in excess of the wealth generated by the risk-free investment.

Mutuals   With respect to insurance companies, companies that are owned by their policyholders, who share in the company's surplus earnings.

Natural liquidity   An extensive pool of investors who are aware of and have a potential interest in buying and/or selling a security.

Net interest margin   With respect to banks, net interest income (interest income minus interest expense) divided by average earning assets.

Net interest spread   With respect to the operations of insurers, the difference between interest earned and interest credited to policyholders.

Net worth   The difference between the market value of assets and liabilities.

Netting   When parties agree to exchange only the net amount owed from one party to the other.

Nominal default-free bonds   Conventional bonds that have no (or minimal) default risk.

Nominal gross domestic product (nominal GDP)   A money measure of the goods and services produced within a country's borders.

Nominal risk-free interest rate   The sum of the real risk-free interest rate and the inflation premium.

Nominal spread   The spread of a bond or portfolio above the yield of a Treasury of equal maturity.

Nondeliverable forwards (NDFs)   Cash-settled forward contracts, used predominately with respect to foreign exchange forwards.

Nonfinancial risk   Risks that arise from sources other than the external financial markets, such as changes in accounting rules, legal environment, or tax rates.

Nonparametric   Involving minimal probability-distribution assumptions.

Nonstationarity   A property of a data series that reflects more than one set of underlying statistical properties.

Normal backwardation   The condition in futures markets in which futures prices are lower than expected spot prices.

Normal contango   The condition in futures markets in which futures prices are higher than expected spot prices.

Normal portfolio   A portfolio with exposure to sources of systematic risk that are typical for a manager, using the manager's past portfolios as a guide.

Notional amount   The dollar amount used as a scale factor in calculating payments for a forward contract, futures contract, or swap.

Notional principal amount   The amount specified in a swap that forms the basis for calculating payment streams.

Objective function   A quantitative expression of the objective or goal of a process.

Off-market FRA   A contract in which the initial value is intentionally set at a value other than zero and therefore requires a cash payment at the start from one party to the other.

Offsetting   A transaction in exchange-listed derivative markets in which a party re-enters the market to close out a position.

Open market operations   The purchase or sale by a central bank of government securities, which are settled using reserves, to influence interest rates and the supply of credit by banks.

Open outcry auction market   Public auction where representatives of buyers and sellers meet at a specified location and place verbal bids and offers.

Operations risk or **operational risk**   The risk of loss from failures in a company's systems and procedures (for example, due to computer failures or human failures) or events completely outside of the control of organizations (which would include "acts of God" and terrorist actions).

Opportunistic participation strategies   Passive trading combined with the opportunistic seizing of liquidity.

Opportunity cost sell discipline   A sell discipline in which the investor is constantly looking at potential stocks to include in the portfolio and will replace an existing holding whenever a better opportunity presents itself.

Optimization   With respect to portfolio construction, a procedure for determining the best portfolios according to some criterion.

Optimizer   A heuristic, formula, algorithm, or program that uses risk, return, correlation, or other variables to determine the most appropriate asset allocation or asset mix for a portfolio.

Option   A financial instrument that gives one party the right, but not the obligation, to buy or sell an underlying asset from or to another party at a fixed price over a specific period of time. Also referred to as contingent claims.

Option price, option premium, or **premium**   The amount of money a buyer pays and seller receives to engage in an option transaction.

Option-adjusted spread (OAS) The current spread over the benchmark yield minus that component of the spread that is attributable to any embedded optionality in the instrument.

Options on futures (futures options) Options on a designated futures contract.

Options on physicals With respect to options, exchange-traded option contracts that have cash instruments rather than futures contracts on cash instruments as the underlying.

Order-driven markets Markets in which transaction prices are established by public limit orders to buy or sell a security at specified prices.

Ordinary life insurance (also whole life insurance) A type of life insurance policy that involves coverage for the whole of the insured's life.

Orphan equities investing A distressed securities investment discipline that involves investment in orphan equities that are perceived to be undervalued.

Orphan equity Investment in the newly issued equity of a company emerging from reorganization.

Out-of-the-money Options that, if exercised, would require the payment of more money than the value received and therefore would not be currently exercised.

Output gap The difference between the value of GDP estimated as if the economy were on its trend growth path (potential output) and the actual value of GDP.

Overall trade balance The sum of the current account (reflecting exports and imports) and the financial account (consisting of portfolio flows).

Overconfidence trap The tendency of individuals to overestimate the accuracy of their forecasts.

Overnight index swap (OIS) A swap in which the floating rate is the cumulative value of a single unit of currency invested at an overnight rate during the settlement period.

Pairs trade (or pairs arbitrage) A basic long–short trade in which an investor is long and short equal currency amounts of two common stocks in a single industry.

Panel method A method of capital market expectations setting that involves using the viewpoints of a panel of experts.

Partial correlation In multivariate problems, the correlation between two variables after controlling for the effects of the other variables in the system.

Partial fill Execution of a purchase or sale for fewer shares than was stipulated in the order.

Participate (do not initiate) **order** A variant of the market-not-held order. The broker is deliberately low-key and waits for and responds to the initiatives of more active traders.

Passive investment approach An approach to portfolio construction in which portfolio composition does not react to changes in capital market expectations; includes indexing and buy-and-hold investing.

Passive management A buy-and-hold approach to investing in which an investor does not make portfolio changes based upon short-term expectations of changing market or security performance.

Passive traders Traders that seek liquidity in their rebalancing transactions, but are much more concerned with the cost of trading.

Payer swaption A swaption that allows the holder to enter into a swap as the fixed-rate payer and floating-rate receiver.

Payment netting A means of settling payments in which the amount owed by the first party to the second is netted with the amount owed by the second party to the first; only the net difference is paid.

Payoff The value of an option at expiration.

Pension funds Funds consisting of assets set aside to support a promise of retirement income.

Pension surplus Pension assets at market value minus the present value of pension liabilities.

Percentage-of-portfolio rebalancing Rebalancing is triggered based on set thresholds stated as a percentage of the portfolio's value.

Percentage-of-volume strategy A logical participation strategy in which trading takes place in proportion to overall market volume (typically at a rate of 5–20 percent) until the order is completed.

Perfect markets Markets without any frictional costs.

Performance appraisal The evaluation of portfolio performance; a quantitative assessment of a manager's investment skill.

Performance attribution A comparison of an account's performance with that of a designated benchmark and the identification and quantification of sources of differential returns.

Performance evaluation The measurement and assessment of the outcomes of investment management decisions.

Performance guarantee A guarantee from the clearinghouse that if one party makes money on a transaction, the clearinghouse ensures it will be paid.

Performance measurement A component of performance evaluation; the relatively simple procedure of calculating an asset's or portfolio's rate of return.

Performance netting risk For entities that fund more than one strategy and have asymmetric incentive fee arrangements with the portfolio managers, the potential for loss in cases where the net performance of the group of managers generates insufficient fee revenue to fully cover contractual payout obligations to all portfolio managers with positive performance.

Performance-based fee Fees specified by a combination of a base fee plus an incentive fee for performance in excess of a benchmark's.

Periodic (or batch) **auction markets** Auction markets where multilateral trading occurs at a single price at a prespecified point in time.

Permanent income hypothesis The hypothesis that consumers' spending behavior is largely determined by their long-run income expectations.

Personality typing The determination of an investor's personality type.

Plain vanilla swap An interest rate swap in which one party pays a fixed rate and the other pays a floating rate, with both sets of payments in the same currency.

Plan sponsor An enterprise or organization—such as a business, labor union, municipal or state government, or not-for-profit organization—that sets up a pension plan.

Pledging requirement With respect to banks, a required collateral use of assets.

Point estimate A single-valued estimate of a quantity, as opposed to an estimate in terms of a range of values.

Policy portfolio A synonym of strategic asset allocation; the portfolio resulting from strategic asset allocation considered as a process.

Policyholder reserves With respect to an insurance company, an amount representing the estimated payments to policyholders, as determined by actuaries, based on the types and terms of the various insurance policies issued by the company.

Political risk (or geopolitical risk) The risk of war, government collapse, political instability, expropriation, confiscation, or adverse changes in taxation.

Portable Moveable. With reference to a pension plan, one in which a plan participant can move his or her share of plan assets to a new plan, subject to certain rules, vesting schedules, and possible tax penalties and payments.

Portable alpha A strategy involving the combining of multiple positions (e.g., long and short positions) so as to separate the alpha (unsystematic risk) from beta (systematic risk) in an investment.

Portfolio implementation decision The decision on how to execute the buy and sell orders of portfolio managers.

Portfolio management process An integrated set of steps undertaken in a consistent manner to create and maintain an appropriate portfolio (combination of assets) to meet clients' stated goals.

Portfolio optimization The combining of assets to efficiently achieve a set of return and risk objectives.

Portfolio segmentation The creation of subportfolios according to the product mix for individual segments or lines of business.

Portfolio selection/composition decision The decision in which the manager integrates investment strategies with capital market expectations to select the specific assets for the portfolio.

Portfolio trade (also known as program trade or basket trade) A trade in which a number of securities are traded as a single unit.

Position a trade To take the other side of a trade, acting as a principal with capital at risk.

Position trader A trader who typically holds positions open overnight.

Positive active position An active position for which the account's allocation to a security is greater than the corresponding weight of the same security in the benchmark.

Post-trade transparency Degree to which completed trades are quickly and accurately reported to the public.

Potential credit risk The risk associated with the possibility that a payment due at a later date will not be made.

Potential output The value of GDP if the economy were on its trend growth path.

Preferred return With respect to the compensation of private equity fund managers, a hurdle rate.

Pre-investing The strategy of using futures contracts to enter the market without an immediate outlay of cash.

Prepackaged bankruptcy A bankruptcy in which the debtor seeks agreement from creditors on the terms of a reorganization before the reorganization filing.

Prepaid swap A contract calling for payment today and delivery of the asset or commodity at multiple specified times in the future.

Present (price) value of a basis point (PVBP) The change in the bond price for a 1 basis point change in yield. Also called *basis point value* (BPV).

Present value distribution of cash flows A list showing what proportion of a portfolio's duration is attributable to each future cash flow.

Pretrade transparency Ability of individuals to quickly, easily, and inexpensively obtain accurate information about quotes and trades.

Price discovery Adjustment of transaction prices to balance supply and demand.

Price improvement Execution at a price that is better than the price quoted at the time of order placement.

Price limits Limits imposed by a futures exchange on the price change that can occur from one day to the next.

Price risk The risk of fluctuations in market price.

Price uncertainty Uncertainty about the price at which an order will execute.

Price weighted With respect to index construction, an index in which each security in the index is weighted according to its absolute share price.

Priced risk Risk for which investors demand compensation.

Primary risk factors With respect to valuation, the major influences on pricing.

Prime brokerage A suite of services that is often specified to include support in accounting and reporting, leveraged trade execution, financing, securities lending (related to short-selling activities), and start-up advice (for new entities).

Principal trade A trade with a broker in which the broker commits capital to facilitate the prompt execution of the trader's order to buy or sell.

Private equity Ownership interests in non-publicly-traded companies.

Private equity funds Pooled investment vehicles investing in generally highly illiquid assets; includes venture capital funds and buyout funds.

Private exchange A method for handling undiversified positions with built-in capital gains in which shares that are a component of an index are exchanged for shares of an index mutual fund in a privately arranged transaction with the fund.

Private placement memorandum A document used to raise venture capital financing when funds are raised through an agent.

Profit-sharing plans A defined-contribution plan in which contributions are based, at least in part, on the plan sponsor's profits.

Projected benefit obligation (PBO) A measure of a pension plan's liability that reflects accumulated service in the same manner as the ABO but also projects future variables, such as compensation increases.

Prospect theory The analysis of decision making under risk in terms of choices among prospects.

Protective put An option strategy in which a long position in an asset is combined with a long position in a put.

Proxy hedging Hedging that involves the use of a forward contract between the home currency and a currency that is highly correlated with the foreign asset's currency.

Prudence trap The tendency to temper forecasts so that they do not appear extreme; the tendency to be overly cautious in forecasting.

Psychological profiling The determination of an investor's psychological characteristics relevant to investing, such as his or her personality type.

Public good A good that is not divisible and not excludable (a consumer cannot be denied it).

Purchasing power parity The theory that movements in an exchange rate should offset any difference in the inflation rates between two countries.

Pure sector allocation return A component of attribution analysis that relates relative returns to the manager's sector-weighting decisions. Calculated as the difference between the allocation (weight) of the portfolio to a given sector and the portfolio's benchmark weight for that sector, multiplied by the difference between the sector benchmark's return and the overall portfolio's benchmark return, summed across all sectors.

Put An option that gives the holder the right to sell an underlying asset to another party at a fixed price over a specific period of time.

Put–call parity An equation expressing the equivalence (parity) of a portfolio of a call and a bond with a portfolio of a put and the underlying, which leads to the relationship between put and call prices.

Put–call–forward parity The relationship among puts, calls, and forward contracts.

Quality control charts A graphical means of presenting performance appraisal data; charts illustrating the performance of an actively managed account versus a selected benchmark.

Quality option (or swap option) With respect to Treasury futures, the option of which acceptable Treasury issue to deliver.

Quoted depth The number of shares available for purchase or sale at the quoted bid and ask prices.

Quote-driven markets (dealer markets) Markets that rely on dealers to establish firm prices at which securities can be bought and sold.

Rate duration A fixed-income instrument's or portfolio's sensitivity to a change in key maturity, holding constant all other points along the yield curve.

Ratio spread An option strategy in which a long position in a certain number of options is offset by a short position in a certain number of other options on the same underlying, resulting in a risk-free position.

Real estate Interests in land or structures attached to land.

Real estate investment trusts (REITs) Publicly traded equities representing pools of money invested in real estate properties and/or real estate debt.

Real option An option involving decisions related to tangible assets or processes.

Real risk-free interest rate The single-period interest rate for a completely risk-free security if no inflation were expected.

Rebalancing Adjusting the actual portfolio to the current strategic asset allocation because of price changes in portfolio holdings. Also: revisions to an investor's target asset class weights because of changes in the investor's investment objectives or constraints, or because of changes in capital market expectations; or to mean tactical asset allocation.

Rebalancing ratio A quantity involved in reestablishing the dollar duration of a portfolio to a desired level, equal to the original dollar duration divided by the new dollar duration.

Re-base With reference to index construction, to change the time period used as the base of the index.

Recallability trap The tendency of forecasts to be overly influenced by events that have left a strong impression on a person's memory.

Receiver swaption A swaption that allows the holder to enter into a swap as the fixed-rate receiver and floating-rate payer.

Recession A broad-based economic downturn, conventionally defined as two successive quarterly declines in GDP.

Reference entity An entity, such as a bond issuer, specified in a derivatives contract.

Regime A distinct governing set of relationships.

Regulatory risk The risk associated with the uncertainty of how a transaction will be regulated or with the potential for regulations to change.

Reinvestment risk The risk of reinvesting coupon income or principal at a rate less than the original coupon or purchase rate.

Relative economic strength forecasting approach An exchange rate forecasting approach that suggests that a strong pace of economic growth in a country creates attractive investment opportunities, increasing the demand for the country's currency and causing it to appreciate.

Relative return objective A return objective stated as a return relative to the portfolio benchmark's total return.

Relative strength indicators A price momentum indicator that involves comparing a stock's performance during a specific period either to its own past performance or to the performance of some group of stocks.

Remaindermen Beneficiaries of a trust; having a claim on the residue.

Replacement value The market value of a swap.

Repurchase agreement A contract involving the sale of securities such as Treasury instruments coupled with an agreement to repurchase the same securities at a later date.

Repurchase yield The negative of the expected percent change in number of shares outstanding, in the Grinold–Kroner model.

Required return (or return requirement) With reference to the investment policy statement, a return objective relating to the level of return that will be adequate to satisfy a need.

Resampled efficient frontier The set of resampled efficient portfolios.

Resampled efficient portfolio An efficient portfolio based on simulation.

Residue With respect to trusts, the funds remaining in a trust when the last income beneficiary dies.

Retired-lives The portion of a pension fund's liabilities associated with retired workers.

Return objective An investor objective that addresses the required or desired level of returns.

Returns-based benchmarks Benchmarks that are constructed using (1) a series of a manager's account returns and (2) the series of returns on several investment style indexes over the same period. These return series are then submitted to an allocation algorithm that solves for the combination of investment style indexes that most closely tracks the account's returns.

Returns-based style analysis An approach to style analysis that focuses on characteristics of the overall portfolio as revealed by a portfolio's realized returns.

Reverse optimization A technique for reverse engineering the expected returns implicit in a diversified market portfolio.

Rho The sensitivity of the option price to the risk-free rate.

Risk aversion The degree of an investor's inability and unwillingness to take risk.

Risk budget   The desired total quantity of risk; the result of risk budgeting.

Risk budgeting   The establishment of objectives for individuals, groups, or divisions of an organization that takes into account the allocation of an acceptable level of risk.

Risk exposure   A source of risk. Also, the state of being exposed or vulnerable to a risk.

Risk governance   The process of setting overall policies and standards in risk management.

Risk management   The process of identifying the level of risk an entity wants, measuring the level of risk the entity currently has, taking actions that bring the actual level of risk to the desired level of risk, and monitoring the new actual level of risk so that it continues to be aligned with the desired level of risk.

Risk objective   An investor objective that addresses risk.

Risk premium approach   An approach to forecasting the return of a risky asset that views its expected return as the sum of the risk-free rate of interest and one or more risk premiums.

Risk profile   A detailed tabulation of the index's risk exposures.

Risk tolerance   The capacity to accept risk; the level of risk an investor (or organization) is willing and able to bear.

Risk tolerance function   An assessment of an investor's tolerance to risk over various levels of portfolio outcomes.

Risk-neutral probabilities   Weights that are used to compute a binomial option price. They are the probabilities that would apply if a risk-neutral investor valued an option.

Risk-neutral valuation   The process by which options and other derivatives are priced by treating investors as though they were risk neutral.

Roll return (or roll yield)   The component of the return on a commodity futures contract that comes from rolling long futures positions forward through time.

Rolling return   The moving average of the holding-period returns for a specified period (e.g., a calendar year) that matches the investor's time horizon.

Sample estimator   A formula for assigning a unique value (a point estimate) to a population parameter.

Sandwich spread   An option strategy that is equivalent to a short butterfly spread.

Savings–investment imbalances forecasting approach   An exchange rate forecasting approach that explains currency movements in terms of the effects of domestic savings–investment imbalances on the exchange rate.

Scalper   A trader who offers to buy or sell futures contracts, holding the position for only a brief period of time. Scalpers attempt to profit by buying at the bid price and selling at the higher ask price.

Scenario analysis   A risk management technique involving the examination of the performance of a portfolio under specified situations. Closely related to *stress testing*.

Seats   Memberships in a derivatives exchange.

Secondary offering   An offering after the initial public offering of securities.

Sector/quality effect   In a fixed-income attribution analysis, a measure of a manager's ability to select the "right" issuing sector and quality group.

Security selection   Skill in selecting individual securities within an asset class.

Security selection effect   In a fixed-income attribution analysis, the residual of the security's total return after other effects are accounted for; a measure of the return due to ability in security selection.

Segmentation   With respect to the management of insurance company portfolios, the notional subdivision of the overall portfolio into sub-portfolios each of which is associated with a specified group of insurance contracts.

Sell side   Broker/dealers that sell securities and make recommendations for various customers, such as investment managers and institutional investors.

Sell-side analysts   Analysts employed by brokerages.

Semiactive management (also called enhanced indexing or risk-controlled active management)   A variant of active management. In a semiactive portfolio, the manager seeks to outperform a given benchmark with tightly controlled risk relative to the benchmark.

Semiactive, **risk-controlled active**, or **enhanced index approach**   An investment approach that seeks positive alpha while keeping tight control over risk relative to the portfolio's benchmark.

Semivariance   A measure of downside risk. The average of squared deviations that fall below the mean.

Settlement date or **payment date**   The designated date at which the parties to a trade must transact.

Settlement netting risk   The risk that a liquidator of a counterparty in default could challenge a netting arrangement so that profitable transactions are realized for the benefit of creditors.

Settlement period The time between settlement dates.

Settlement price The official price, designated by the clearinghouse, from which daily gains and losses will be determined and marked to market.

Settlement risk When settling a contract, the risk that one party could be in the process of paying the counterparty while the counterparty is declaring bankruptcy.

Sharpe ratio (or reward-to-variability) A measure of risk-adjusted performance that compares excess returns to the total risk of the account, where total risk is measured by the account's standard deviation of returns.

Short The seller of a derivative contract. Also refers to the position of being short a derivative.

Shortfall risk The risk that portfolio value will fall below some minimum acceptable level during a stated time horizon; the risk of not achieving a specified return target.

Shrinkage estimation Estimation that involves taking a weighted average of a historical estimate of a parameter and some other parameter estimate, where the weights reflect the analyst's relative belief in the estimates.

Shrinkage estimator The formula used in shrinkage estimation of a parameter.

Sign-constrained optimization An optimization that constrains asset class weights to be nonnegative and to sum to 1.

Single-payment loan A loan in which the borrower receives a sum of money at the start and pays back the entire amount with interest in a single payment at maturity.

Situational profiling The categorization of individual investors by stage of life or by economic circumstance.

Smart routing The use of algorithms to intelligently route an order to the most liquid venue.

Smoothing rule With respect to spending rates, a rule that averages asset values over a period of time in order to dampen the spending rate's response to asset value fluctuation.

Socially responsible investing (ethical investing) An approach to investing that integrates ethical values and societal concerns with investment decisions.

Soft dollars (also called soft dollar arrangements or soft commissions) The use of commissions to buy services other than execution services.

Sortino ratio A performance appraisal ratio that replaces standard deviation in the Sharpe ratio with downside deviation.

Sovereign risk A form of credit risk in which the borrower is the government of a sovereign nation.

Spontaneous investors Investors who constantly readjust their portfolio allocations and holdings.

Spot return (or price return) The component of the return on a commodity futures contract that comes from changes in the underlying spot prices via the cost-of-carry model.

Spread An option strategy involving the purchase of one option and sale of another option that is identical to the first in all respects except either exercise price or expiration.

Spread duration The sensitivity of a non-Treasury security's price to a widening or narrowing of the spread over Treasuries.

Spread risk Risk related to changes in the spread between Treasuries and non-Treasuries.

Stack and roll A hedging strategy in which an existing stack hedge with maturing futures contracts is replaced by a new stack hedge with longer dated futures contracts.

Stack hedge Hedging a stream of obligations by entering futures contracts with a *single* maturity, with the number of contracts selected so that changes in the *present value* of the future obligations are offset by changes in the value of this "stack" of futures contracts.

Stale price bias Bias that arises from using prices that are stale because of infrequent trading.

Standard deviation The positive square root of variance.

Stated return desire A stated desired level of returns.

Static approach With respect to strategic asset allocation, an approach that does not account for links between optimal decisions in future time periods.

Static spread (or zero-volatility spread) The constant spread above the Treasury spot curve that equates the calculated price of the security to the market price.

Stationary A series of data for which the parameters that describe a return-generating process are stable.

Status quo trap The tendency for forecasts to perpetuate recent observations—that is, to predict no change from the recent past.

Sterling ratio The compound annualized rate of return over a specified time period divided by the average yearly maximum drawdown over the same time period less an arbitrary 10 percent.

Stock companies With respect to insurance companies, companies that have issued common equity shares.

Stock index futures Futures contracts on a specified stock index.

Storage costs or **carrying costs**　The costs of holding an asset, generally a function of the physical characteristics of the underlying asset.

Straddle　An option strategy involving the purchase of a put and a call with the same exercise price. A straddle is based on the expectation of high volatility of the underlying.

Straight-through processing　Systems that simplify transaction processing through the minimization of manual and/or duplicative intervention in the process from trade placement to settlement.

Strangle　A variation of a straddle in which the put and call have different exercise prices.

Strap　An option strategy involving the purchase of two calls and one put.

Strategic asset allocation　1) The process of allocating money to IPS-permissible asset classes that integrates the investor's return objectives, risk tolerance, and investment constraints with long-run capital market expectations. 2) The result of the above process, also known as the policy portfolio.

Stratified sampling (representative sampling)　A sampling method that guarantees that subpopulations of interest are represented in the sample.

Stress testing　A risk management technique in which the risk manager examines the performance of the portfolio under market conditions involving high risk and usually high correlations across markets. Closely related to *scenario analysis*.

Strike spread　A spread used to determine the strike price for the payoff of a credit option.

Strip　An option strategy involving the purchase of two puts and one call.

Strip hedge　Hedging a stream of obligations by offsetting each individual obligation with a futures contract matching the maturity and quantity of the obligation.

Structural level of unemployment　The level of unemployment resulting from scarcity of a factor of production.

Structured note　A variation of a floating-rate note that has some type of unusual characteristic such as a leverage factor or in which the rate moves opposite to interest rates.

Style drift　Inconsistency in style.

Style index　A securities index intended to reflect the average returns to a given style.

Stylized scenario　A type of analysis often used in stress testing. It involves simulating the movement in at least one interest rate, exchange rate, stock price, or commodity price relevant to the portfolio.

Sunshine trades　Public display of a transaction (usually high-volume) in advance of the actual order.

Surplus　The difference between the value of assets and the present value of liabilities. With respect to an insurance company, the net difference between the total assets and total liabilities (equivalent to policyholders' surplus for a mutual insurance company and stockholders' equity for a stock company).

Surplus efficient frontier　The graph of the set of portfolios that maximize expected surplus for given levels of standard deviation of surplus.

Survey method　A method of capital market expectations setting that involves surveying experts.

Survivorship bias　Bias that arises in a data series when managers with poor track records exit the business and are dropped from the database whereas managers with good records remain; when a data series as of a given date reflects only entities that have survived to that date.

Swap　A contract calling for the exchange of payments over time. Often one payment is fixed in advance and the other is floating, based upon the realization of a price or interest rate.

Swap rate　The interest rate applicable to the pay-fixed-rate side of an interest rate swap.

Swap spread　The difference between the fixed rate on an interest rate swap and the rate on a Treasury note with equivalent maturity; it reflects the general level of credit risk in the market.

Swap tenor　The lifetime of a swap.

Swap term　Another name for *swap tenor*.

Swaption　An option to enter into a swap.

Symmetric cash flow matching　A cash flow matching technique that allows cash flows occurring both before and after the liability date to be used to meet a liability; allows for the short-term borrowing of funds to satisfy a liability prior to the liability due date.

Synthetic call　The combination of puts, the underlying, and risk-free bonds that replicates a call option.

Synthetic forward contract　The combination of the underlying, puts, calls, and risk-free bonds that replicates a forward contract.

Synthetic index fund　An index fund position created by combining risk-free bonds and futures on the desired index.

Synthetic put　The combination of calls, the underlying, and risk-free bonds that replicates a put option.

Tactical asset allocation　Asset allocation that involves making short-term adjustments to asset class weights based on short-term predictions of relative performance among asset classes.

Tactical rebalancing A variation of calendar rebalancing that specifies less frequent rebalancing when markets appear to be trending and more frequent rebalancing when they are characterized by reversals.

Tail value at risk (or conditional tail expectation) The VAR plus the expected loss in excess of VAR, when such excess loss occurs.

Target covariance matrix A component of shrinkage estimation; allows the analyst to model factors that are believed to influence the data over periods longer than observed in the historical sample.

Target semivariance The average squared deviation below a target value.

Target value The value that the portfolio manager seeks to ensure; the value that the life insurance company has guaranteed the policyholder.

Tax concerns Concerns related to an investor's tax position.

Tax efficiency The proportion of the expected pre-tax total return that will be retained after taxes.

Tax premium Compensation for the effect of taxes on the after-tax return of an asset.

Tax risk The uncertainty associated with tax laws.

Taylor rule A rule linking a central bank's target short-term interest rate to the rate of growth of the economy and inflation.

Tenor The original time to maturity on a swap.

Term life insurance A type of life insurance policy that provides coverage for a specified length of time and accumulates little or no cash values.

Termination date The date of the final payment on a swap; also, the swap's expiration date.

Theta The change in price of an option associated with a one-day reduction in its time to expiration; the rate at which an option's time value decays.

Tick The smallest possible price movement of a security.

Time deposit A deposit requiring advance notice prior to a withdrawal.

Time horizon The time period associated with an investment objective.

Time to expiration The time remaining in the life of a derivative, typically expressed in years.

Time value or **speculative value** The difference between the market price of the option and its intrinsic value, determined by the uncertainty of the underlying over the remaining life of the option.

Time value decay The loss in the value of an option resulting from movement of the option price toward its payoff value as the expiration day approaches.

Time-period bias Bias that occurs when results are time-period specific.

Time-series estimators Estimators that are based on lagged values of the variable being forecast; often consist of lagged values of other selected variables.

Time-weighted average price (TWAP) strategy A logical participation strategy that assumes a flat volume profile and trades in proportion to time.

Time-weighted rate of return The compound rate of growth over a stated evaluation period of one unit of money initially invested in the account.

Timing option With respect to certain futures contracts, the option that results from the ability of the short position to decide when in the delivery month actual delivery will take place.

Top-down Proceeding from the macroeconomy, to the economic sector level, to the industry level, to the firm level.

Total future liability With respect to defined-benefit pension plans, the present value of accumulated and projected future service benefits, including the effects of projected future compensation increases.

Total rate of return A measure of the increase in the investor's wealth due to both investment income (for example, dividends and interest) and capital gains (both realized and unrealized).

Total return The rate of return taking into account capital appreciation/depreciation and income. Often qualified as follows: **Nominal** returns are unadjusted for inflation; **real** returns are adjusted for inflation; **pretax** returns are returns before taxes; **post-tax** returns are returns after taxes are paid on investment income and realized capital gains.

Total return analysis Analysis of the expected effect of a trade on the portfolio's total return, given an interest rate forecast.

Total return swap A swap in which one party agrees to pay the total return on a security. Often used as a credit derivative, in which the underlying is a bond.

Tracking risk (also called tracking error, tracking error volatility, or active risk) The condition in which the performance of a portfolio does not match the performance of an index that serves as the portfolio's benchmark.

Trade blotter A device for entering and tracking trade executions and orders to trade.

Trade settlement Completion of a trade wherein purchased financial instruments are transferred to the buyer and the buyer transfers money to the seller.

Trading activity   In fixed-income attribution analysis, the effect of sales and purchases of bonds over a given period; the total portfolio return minus the other components determining the management effect in an attribution analysis.

Transaction exposure   The risk associated with a foreign exchange rate on a specific business transaction such as a purchase or sale.

Transcription errors   Errors in gathering and recording data.

Translation exposure   The risk associated with the conversion of foreign financial statements into domestic currency.

Transparency   Availability of timely and accurate market and trade information.

Treasury spot curve   The term structure of Treasury zero coupon bonds.

Treynor ratio (or reward-to-volatility)   A measure of risk-adjusted performance that relates an account's excess returns to the systematic risk assumed by the account.

Turnover   A measure of the rate of trading activity in a portfolio.

Twist   With respect to the yield curve, a movement in contrary directions of interest rates at two maturities; a nonparallel movement in the yield curve.

Type I error   With respect to manager selection, keeping (or hiring) managers with zero value-added. (Rejecting the null hypothesis when it is correct.)

Type II error   With respect to manager selection, firing (or not hiring) managers with positive value-added. (Not rejecting the null hypothesis when it is incorrect.)

Unconstrained optimization   Optimization that places no constraints on asset class weights except that they sum to 1. May produce negative asset weights, which implies borrowing or shorting of assets.

Underfunded plan   A pension plan in which the ratio of the value of plan assets to the present value of plan liabilities is less than 100 percent.

Underlying   An asset that trades in a market in which buyers and sellers meet, decide on a price, and the seller then delivers the asset to the buyer and receives payment. The underlying is the asset or other derivative on which a particular derivative is based. The market for the underlying is also referred to as the spot market.

Underwriting (profitability) **cycle**   A cycle affecting the profitability of insurance companies' underwriting operations.

Undisclosed limit order (reserve, hidden, or iceberg order)   A limit order that includes an instruction not to show more than some maximum quantity of the unfilled order to the public at any one time.

Unhedged return   A foreign asset return stated in terms of the investor's home currency.

Unique circumstances   Internal factors (other than a liquidity requirement, time horizon, or tax concern) that may constrain portfolio choices.

Universal life insurance   A type of life insurance policy that provides for premium flexibility, an adjustable face amount of death benefits, and current market interest rates on the savings element.

Unrelated business income   With respect to the U.S. tax code, income that is not substantially related to a foundation's charitable purposes.

Unstructured modeling   Modeling without a theory on the underlying structure.

Uptick rules   Trading rules that specify that a short sale must not be on a downtick relative to the last trade at a different price.

Urgency of the trade   The importance of certainty of execution.

Valuation   The process of determining the value of an asset or service.

Valuation reserve   With respect to insurance companies, an allowance, created by a charge against earnings, to provide for losses in the value of the assets.

Value   The amount for which one can sell something, or the amount one must pay to acquire something.

Value at risk (VAR)   A probability-based measure of loss potential for a company, a fund, a portfolio, a transaction, or a strategy over a specified period of time.

Value investment style   With reference to equity investing, an investment style focused on paying a relatively low share price in relation to earnings or assets per share.

Value weighted (or market-capitalization weighted)   With respect to index construction, an index in which each security in the index is weighted according to its market capitalization.

Value-motivated traders   Traders that act on value judgments based on careful, sometimes painstaking research. They trade only when the price moves into their value range.

Variable annuity   A life annuity in which the periodic payment varies depending on stock prices.

Variable life insurance (unit-linked life insurance)   A type of ordinary life insurance in which death benefits and cash values are linked to the investment performance of a policyholder-selected pool of investments held in a so-called separate account.

Variable prepaid forward A monetization strategy that involves the combination of a collar with a loan against the value of the underlying shares. When the loan comes due, shares are sold to pay off the loan and part of any appreciation is shared with the lender.

Variable universal life (or flexible-premium variable life) A type of life insurance policy that combines the flexibility of universal life with the investment choice flexibility of variable life.

Variance The expected value of squared deviations from the random variable's mean; often referred to as volatility.

Variation margin Additional margin that must be deposited in an amount sufficient to bring the balance up to the initial margin requirement.

Vega A measure of the sensitivity of an option's price to changes in the underlying's volatility.

Venture capital The equity financing of new or growing private companies.

Venture capital firms Firms representing dedicated pools of capital for providing equity or equity-linked financing to privately held companies.

Venture capital fund A pooled investment vehicle for venture capital investing.

Venture capital trusts An exchange-traded, closed-end vehicle for venture capital investing.

Venture capitalists Specialists who seek to identify companies that have good business opportunities but need financial, managerial, and strategic support.

Vested With respect to pension benefits or assets, said of an unconditional ownership interest.

Vintage year With reference to a private equity fund, the year it closed.

Vintage year effects The effects on returns shared by private equity funds closed in the same year.

Volatility Represented by the Greek letter sigma (σ), the standard deviation of price outcomes associated with an underlying asset.

Volatility clustering The tendency for large (small) swings in prices to be followed by large (small) swings of random direction.

Volume-weighted average price (VWAP) The average price at which a security is traded during the day, where each trade price is weighted by the fraction of the day's volume associated with the trade.

Volume-weighted average price strategy A logical participation strategy that involves breaking up an order over time according to a prespecified volume profile.

Wealth relative The ending value of one unit of money invested at specified rates of return.

Weather derivative A derivative contract with a payment based on a weather-related measurement, such as heating or cooling degree days.

Wild card option A provision allowing a short futures contract holder to delay delivery of the underlying.

Within-sector selection return In attribution analysis, a measure of the impact of a manager's security selection decisions relative to the holdings of the sector benchmark.

Worst-case scenario analysis A stress test in which we examine the worst case that we actually expect to occur.

Yield beta A measure of the sensitivity of a bond's yield to a general measure of bond yields in the market that is used to refine the hedge ratio.

Yield curve The relationship between yield and time to maturity.

Yield curve risk Risk related to changes in the shape of the yield curve.

Yield spread The difference between the yield on a bond and the yield on a default-free security, usually a government note, of the same maturity. The yield spread is primarily determined by the market's perception of the credit risk on the bond.

Yield to worst The yield on a callable bond that assumes a bond is called at the earliest opportunity.

Zero-cost collar A transaction in which a position in the underlying is protected by buying a put and selling a call with the premium from the sale of the call offsetting the premium from the purchase of the put. It can also be used to protect a floating-rate borrower against interest rate increases with the premium on a long cap offsetting the premium on a short floor.

Zero-premium collar A hedging strategy involving the simultaneous purchase of puts and sale of call options on a stock. The puts are struck below and the calls are struck above the underlying's market price.